A GRAMMAR
OF THE
TELOOGOO LANGUAGE

A GRAMMAR
OF THE
TELOOGOO LANGUAGE,

**COMMONLY TERMED THE GENTOO,
PECULIAR TO THE HINDOOS INHABITING THE NORTH EASTERN PROVINCES
OF THE
INDIAN PENINSULA.**

BY A. D. CAMPBELL

OF THE
HONORABLE EAST INDIA COMPANY'S CIVIL SERVICE
ON THE
MADRAS ESTABLISHMENT,
MEMBER OF THE BOARD OF SUPERINTENDENCE
FOR THE
COLLEGE OF FORT ST. GEORGE.

THIRD EDITION

GYAN

Published by

Gyan Publishing House
5, Ansari Road
Daryaganj, New Delhi-110002
Phone: 011-47034999, 9811692060
E-mail: books@gyanbooks.com

Distribution Network
gyanbooks.com
India, USA, Canada, UK, Australia, France

ISBN : 978-81-212-4383-4 (PB)
First Published, 1849

2nd Impression 2020

Printed at: Gyan Press, Delhi.

A Grammar of Teloogoo Languag
Author: A. D. Campbell

A

GRAMMAR

OF THE

TELOOGOO LANGUAGE,

COMMONLY TERMED THE GENTOO,

PECULIAR TO THE HINDOOS INHABITING THE NORTH EASTERN PROVINCES

OF THE

INDIAN PENINSULA.

By A. D. CAMPBELL,

OF THE

HONORABLE EAST INDIA COMPANY'S CIVIL SERVICE

ON THE

MADRAS ESTABLISHMENT,

MEMBER OF THE BOARD OF SUPERINTENDENCE

FOR THE

COLLEGE OF FORT St. GEORGE.

THIRD EDITION.

MADRAS:

PRINTED AT THE HINDU PRESS.

1849.

ADVERTISEMENT.

Since the establishment of the College of Fort William by Marquis Wellesley, the labors of many distinguished individuals have added much valuable information to the knowledge before possessed of oriental literature, and afforded many facilities to the attainment of an improved acquaintance with the several dialects peculiar to the provinces immediately subject to the Supreme Government. A similar Institution (on a modified and less extensive scale) has more recently been established at Fort St. George, and may be expected, in course of time, to produce the same favorable results as regards the languages of the South of India; respecting which very little has as yet appeared before the public through the medium of the press, though the languages themselves had, even before the establishment of the College, been cultivated with considerable success by many individuals.

For the establishment of the College of Fort St. George, and for the encouragement afforded in many other respects to the advancement of the literature of Southern India, the Public are in a great degree indebted to Sir George Barlow; and the following is one of several works which owe their rise to this source.

The Author, having been nominated to a seat at the Board of Superintendence for the College, had frequent opportunities of observing the disadvantage under which the Teloogoo Students laboured, from the want of a work on the elements of that language. An attempt to remove this impediment was a duty which the author's situation in some degree imposed; and actuated by this motive, as well as by a desire to rescue the Teloogoo from the undeserved neglect in which its great difficulty had involved it, and to extend among his countrymen the knowledge of a language spoken by a large portion of the native subjects of the British Government in the South of India, he proceeded to arrange the notes, on the native grammars of the language, which he had taken to assist his own studies, in the form which they have assumed in the following pages.

The manuscript, thus prepared, was submitted to the Government of Fort St. George, whose approbation it having been so fortunate as to obtain, the copy right was purchased on the public account, and the Right Honorable the Governor in Council was pleased to direct that the work should be printed at the College Press, whence it now issues to the Public.

Every first attempt to illustrate the principles of a foreign language is attended by peculiar difficulties; but to do justice to a language so highly cultivated as the Teloogoo required advantages to which the author makes no pretension: nevertheless he hopes that in essential respects, the work will not be found deficient. He does not expect that it will remove all the difficulties which have hitherto opposed the acquisition of the Teloogoo: if, by enabling the European Student to overcome the chief obstacles in his way, it lightens his labour, and facilitates his access to that eminence which all should endeavour to attain who seek distinction in the public service, the author's utmost wishes will be accomplished: at some future period, perhaps, the track which he has opened may be followed by others possessing more ability and leisure than himself, who, correcting those errors into which he has fallen, may give to the world improved works, on one of the most useful and polished languages of India.

TO HIS EXCELLENCY

THE RIGHT HONORABLE FRANCIS RAWDON HASTINGS,

EARL OF MOIRA, K. G.

GOVERNOR GENERAL AND COMMANDER IN CHIEF IN INDIA.

&c. &c. &c.

MY LORD,

In dedicating to your Lordship the following elementary work, in elucidation of the principles of one of the most ancient, useful, and elegant languages of India, permit me, most respectfully, to express my grateful acknowledgements for the honor which it derives, from being permitted to appear under the sanction of so illustrious a name.

Public utility, the chief object of this work, constitutes also its chief claim to the patronage of a Statesman whose liberal and enlightened mind deems nothing beneath its notice which may be calculated, however remotely, to promote the interests of the Great Empire intrusted to his care. If, by diffusing among the civil and military servants on the Coast a more extended knowledge of the language of Telingana, and an improved acquaintance with the character, customs, and manners, of the fine race of men who inhabit that country, the work here presented to your Lordship should contribute in any degree to the convenience of individuals, to the service of the Government. or to the security and happiness of its subjects, I shall have the satisfaction to reflect that, however imperfect its execution, it will not have proved altogether unworthy of the distinguished patronage with which it has been honored.

I have the honor to be,

My Lord,

with the greatest respect,

your Lordship's obliged and

very obedient humble servant

A. D. CAMPBELL

INTRODUCTION.

The language of which a Grammar is now offered to the Public is commonly, but improperly, termed by Europeans the Gentoo. It is the Andhra of Sanscrit authors, and, in the country where it is spoken, is known by the name of the Trilinga, Telinga, Teloogoo, or Tenoogoo.

This language is the vernacular dialect of the Hindoos, inhabiting that part of the Indian Peninsula, which, extending from the Dutch settlement of Pulicat on the Coast of Coromandel, inland to the vicinity of Bangalore, stretches northwards, along the coast as far as Chicacole, and in the interior to the sources of the Tapti; bounded on the east by the Bay of Bengal, and on the west by an irregular line, passing through the western districts belonging to the Soubahdar of the Deccan, and cutting off the most eastern provinces of the new state of Mysore:—a tract including the five Northern Circars of Ganjam, Vizagapatam, Rajahmundry, Masulipatam, and Guntoor; the greater portion of the Nizam's extensive territories; the districts of Cuddapah and Bellari ceded by him to the British; the eastern provinces of Mysore; and the northern portion of the Carnatick: nor is this language unknown in the more Southern parts of India, for the descendants of those Teloogoo families which were deputed by the Kings of Vidianagara to controul their southern conquests, or which occasionally emigrated from Telingana to avoid famine or oppression, are scattered all over the Dravida and Carnataca provinces; and ever retaining the language of their forefathers, have diffused a knowledge of it throughout the Peninsula. †

† Among numerous authorities which may be quoted in support of the concluding part of this statement, I subjoin the following passages from the Travels of Dr. Francis Buchanan, a work containing much statistical information, regarding the provinces in the interior of the Peninsula— "Every where in Karnata the palanquin-bearers are of Telinga descent, and in their own families "speak the language of their original country"—"The Woddás or Woddaru are a tribe of Te-"linga origin, and in their families retain that language; although they are scattered all over

A tradition current in Telingana, and noticed by many of it's best native * Authors, states the original name of this language, as well as that of the country in which it is spoken, to have been *Tri-lingum,* or in pure Teloogoo *Modaga-lingum ;* † namely the language or country of the three lingums : a name derived from the three lingums, or mystic symbols of the divinity, in the form of which Shiva, the destructive and re-producing power in the Indian Trinity, is reported to have descended upon the mountains of Shri Shuelum or Purvatum, Caleswarum, and Bheemeswarum or Dracharamum, where he is supposed still to hold his awful abode, and is worshipped under the respective names of Mullecarjoona, Calanadha, and Bheemeswara.

These three lingums are said to have marked the chief boundaries of the country known in modern times by the name of Telingana. The first, that of Shri Shuelum,

---

" the countries where the Tamil and Karnataca tongues are prevalent"—Speaking of a cast known by the name of Baydaru, he observes—" Those in the North-eastern parts of the Mysore Rajah's " dominions are of Telinga descent, and retain that language—They seem to be the true Sûdra " cultivators and military of Telingana, and to have been introduced in great numbers into the " southern countries of the Peninsula, when these became subject to Andray or Telingana princes."

* See the Preface of Maumidi Vencayab, a learned native inhabitant of Masulipatam, to his Teloogoo Dictionary, the copy right of which has been purchased by the Madras Government ; and the original authorities therein referred to. Among others, the Adhurvana Vyacurnum, as given in the Andhra Cowmudi, from which the following is a quotation. శ్రీశైలభీమకాళేశ
మహేంద్రగిరిసంయుతం। ప్రాకారంతుమహత్కృత్వా త్రీణిద్వారాణిచాకరోత్।
త్రిలోచనోమహేశస్తు త్రిశూలంచకరేవహన్। త్రిలింగరూపీన్యవసత్ త్రి
ద్వారేషుగణైర్వృతః। ఆంధ్రవిష్ణుస్సురయుతోదనుజేననిశంభునా। యుద్ధ్వా
త్రయోదశయుగాన్ హత్వాతంరాక్షసోత్తమం। అవసత్తత్ర ఋషిభిర్యుతో
గోదావరీతటే। తత్కాలప్రభృతిక్షేత్రం త్రిలింగమితివిశ్రుతం॥

He (alluding to Andhra Vishtnoo the son of Soochundra hereafter mentioned) *having built an immense wall, connecting Shri Shuelum, Bheemeswaram, and Caleswaram, with the Mahendra hills, formed in it three gates, in which the three eyed Ishwara, bearing the trident in his hand, and attended by a host of divinities, resided in the form of three lingums. Andhra-Vishtnoo, assisted by angels, having fought with the great giant Nishumboo, for thirteen yoogs, killed him in battle, and took up his residence with the sages on the banks of the Godâvery, since which time, this country has been named Trilingum.* Then follows the passage given in the last Teloogoo quotation in the notes to this introduction.

† *Tri* in Sanscrit, and *Moodoo* in the inferior, or *Modo* or *Modoga* in the superior dialect of the pure Teloogoo, all mean *three.*

still celebrated in the Deccan, is particularly described in the extract from Captain Colin Mc'Kenzie's journal inserted in the 5th volume of the Asiatic Researches, of which a part is subjoined in a note below. * It is romantically situated in an unfrequented spot, surrounded by an almost impenetrable forest, among the wild mountains through which the impetuous current of the Kistna forces it's passage from the high table land to the plains, and forms the termination of that chain of hills, which, from the vicinity of the great temple at Tripetty, winds to the north in irregular and separate ranges. In Arrowsmith's Map of 1804, it is placed near the Nalmul hills in Canoul (Kurnool) under the name of Parrawottum, upon the Kistna, just before that river takes a sudden but short direction to the north. It is the second of the twelve Jyotee lingums mentioned as peculiarly holy, in the 38th Adhyaye of the Sheev Pooran ; and, in the Brahmanda Pooran, it is also mentioned as the eighth of the second class of mountains. In the year 1677, we find Sevajee, the celebrated founder of the Mahratta Empire, performing penance at this shrine † ; and, on the annual recurrence of the Shivaratree, or the night sacred to Shiva, immense crowds of people still flock thither from all parts of Hindoostan. ‡

---

* " On entering the south gate," says Captain Mc'Kenzie, we descended by steps through a " small door to the inner court, where the temple are. In the center was the Pagoda of Mallecarjee, " the principal deity worshipped here. It is square, and the roof is terminated by a pyramid of steps, " the whole walls and roof on the outside are covered with brass plates, which have been guilt, but " the gilding is worn off. From hence I was conducted to the smaller and more ancient temple of " Mallecarjee, where he is adored in the figure of a rude stone, which I could just distinguish, " thro' the dark vista of the front buildings, on pillars. Behind this building, an immense fig tree " covers with it's shade the devotees and attendants, who repose on seats placed round it's trunk, " and carpeted ; among these was one Byragy who had devoted himself to a perpetual residence " here, his sole subsistence was the milk of a cow which I saw him driving before him. an orange " colored rag was tied round his loins, and his naked body was besmeared with ashes." " It ap- " pears that the GOD Mallecarjee is no other than the Lingum to which such reverence is paid by " certain casts of Gentoos." Captain McKenzie adds a curious account of the manner in which the lingum was shewn to him, by means of a mirror reflecting the rays of the sun upon it, and describes it as " a small oblong roundish white stone, " with dark rings, fixed in a silver case."

† see Wilkes' South of India.

‡ The present Nabob of Kurnool, a tributary of the East India Company, in whose territory this Pagoda is situated, collects on this occasion a considerable revenue from the pilgrims ; to secure which, he deputes an officer with a certain number of Sepoys : but, with that intolerant bigotry, which more or less influences all who profess the faith of Mahomed, he has resisted every application from the Hindoos to be permitted to repair this very ancient temple, which is now fast falling to decay.

The second lingum at Caleswarum, visited occasionally by a great concourse of pilgrims, is situated on the spot where Arrowsmith places Callysair Ghaut on the Godavary, and is the same that is described by Captain Blunt, in the seventh volume of the Asiatic Researches, under the name of a Pagoda sacred to Cali, standing on the very boundary of Telingana, where the Baun Gunga joins the Godavary. †

I have not yet succeeded in establishing to my satisfaction the site of the third lingum, worshipped under the name of Bheemeswara, which I am inclined to believe is the same as Bheema Shenker, the sixth of the twelve Jyotce lingums, enumerated in the Sheev Pooran, and there stated to be situated in the Deccan. The best informed natives give a very vague account of the site of this temple, some asserting it to be in the Northern Circars, where it is known by the name of Dracharamum, others in the western Ghauts, or, as they describe it, "towards Poona"—A Temple of this name is cursorily mentioned by Dr. Francis Buchanan as standing in the immense chain of hills which runs along the western side of the Peninsula; and, as this is near the southwest junction of the Mahratta, Mysore, and Telingana territories, it is perhaps the third lingum *—Be this as it may, the situations of the two other lingums sufficiently evince the correctness of the tradition which describes them as the boundaries of the country termed *Tri-lingum*, subsequently known to the Mahommedan conquerors of the Deccan under the modified name of Telingana; for the

† "I might now" says Captain Blunt "be said to have entered upon those parts of India known "by the name of Telingana—The inhabitants of which are called Telingahs and speak a language "peculiar to themselves—This dialect appears to bear a strong resemblance to what in the Circars "is called Gentoos—After the heat of the day, and length of the march, our situation close to the "river had a very refreshing and pleasing effect—I was highly delighted with the romantic view "which the confluence of the Godavery and Baun Gunga rivers now presented—I could see quite "up to the fort Suruncha, and an opening beyond it likewise shewed the junction of the Inderwotty "river with the latter—The blue mountains and distant forests which terminated the prospect rendered the whole a very sublime and interesting scene—There is a small Pagoda sacred to the Hindoo "Goddess Cali, situated on the north east bank of the river, at the confluence, which imparts it's "name to this passage over the Gunga Godavery, called Calesair Ghaut, and annually draws a "great concourse of pilgrims, who from ideas of purification come to wash in the waters of the "confluent streams."

* "Dr. Buchanan's travels Vol. III Chapter XVI Page 134—"At Sheraly is a river called Sheraly-tari-which comes from a temple on the Ghauts that is termed Bhimesara"—N. B. Sheraly "is placed by Arrowsmith to the South of Onore on the Coast of Canara, under the name of "Serowly"—in the latitude of which the boundaries of the three countries abovementioned meet.

northern and southern limits of Telingana proper, as exhibited in our best maps, will be found to coincide very nearly with the sites of these two temples.

In further confirmation of this tradition, it may be noticed that Ptolemy mentions "*Triglyphon vel Trilingum regia*" † but places it beyond the Ganges; and that Pliny, alluding to the same region, under it's purer name of Modogalingum ‡ makes it an island in the Ganges—"*Insula in gange estmagnæ amplitudinis, gentem continens unam, Modogalingum nomine.*"

Inaccuracies respecting situation are not uncommon in the writings of the ancients relative to Indian geography, and those which have just been mentioned, with some other similar inconsistencies, may perhaps be reconciled, by supposing that under the name of the Ganges, either the Ganges proper, or the Godavery, may occasionally be understood. In the Peninsula, each of these rivers is known by the name of the *Gunga,* and they are looked upon as sister streams. ** The Godavery is here considered the elder of the two, perhaps from it's being the first known to the inhabitants of these regions; and the Ganges proper is deemed the more holy, apparently from the present religion of India, having originated, or been more early established, on its banks. The ancient books* of the Hindoos, indeed, bear testimony that, even in the most remote times, these two rivers have occasionally been considered as one; for, in more than one place

† He adds, *in hac galli gallinacei barbati esse dicuntur, et corvi et psittaci albi-* శ్రీకాకుళము. the Sicacollum of Arrowsmith, which stands in the Masulipatam district, a little above the mouth of the Krishna, is the Sanscrit name for a peculiar red or whitish crow.

‡ It has been already stated that *Tri* and *Modoga* are synonimous terms.

** So intimate is the connexion between these two rivers, that those who carry the sacred water of the Ganges to the south of India, when they arrive on the banks of the Godavery, invariably replace the water of the Ganges, evaporated on the journey, by water taken from it's sister stream the Godavery. The whole is notwithstanding considered to be the pure water of the Ganges, and this ceremony is never omitted. If it were, it is believed, and perhaps with reason, that the water would disappear before it could reach Rameswarum.

* In the Vayu Puran the course of the Ganges is thus described "The Ganges flows through "the Gand,harvas, Cinnaras, Yacshas, Racshasas, Vidyad,haras. (Uragas or large snakes; these "are tribes of demons good and bad in the hills) Cálapagramacas, Paradas, Svigánas, Svasas, Ceratas, "Pulindas, Curavas, in Curu about Tanehsar, Sam-Bharatas, Panchalas, C'asi or Benares, Matsyas, "Magadhas (or south Behar) Brahmottaras, Angas, Bangas, *Calingas.*" &c. Asiatic researches Vol. 8th. Essay on the sacred isles in the west.

in the Poorans, the Ganges proper is described as passing through Calinga, a country which we know to be the region watered by the Godavery*. So far, therefore, as regards the course of the Ganges through Calinga, described in these ancient books, it must be the Godavery to which they allude.

From the adjective *Trilinga*, by a general grammatical rule ‡ is derived *Tilinga*,† or as it is more generally written *Telinga*—From Tilinga also, by corruption, the Native Grammarians derive the words *Tenoogoo* and *Teloogoo* which is the name now generally given to the language in the country where it is spoken.—The little resemblance between *Tenoogo* or *Teloogoo*, and *Telinga*, may induce an English reader to question this derivation: but, as I have remarked in a subsequent part of this work, great deference is due by a foreigner to the testimony of Native Authors; and when it is considered that many words have passed into Teloogoo through the medium of the Pracrit, or other corrupted dialects of the Sanscrit, and have been naturalized in it for ages, the little connexion now to be traced between some original words, and their corruptions, ought not alone to invalidate the established etymologies of successive Grammarians.—It may not be irrelevant, however, to observe, that Teloogoo may possibly be derived from the adjective *Tellu*. ** *fair*, *white*, an appellation which might with much propriety be applied to the people of Telingana, compared with the neighbouring nations;

In the Brahmanda Pooran, also, the course of the Ganges is thus described. " The southern branch " goes to Gadhamandana from hill to hill, from stone to stone; it encircles the forest of Gadhamandana or Deva-nandana, whence it is called Alacananda, it goes to the Northern lake, called Manasa, " thence to the king of mountains with three summits, thence to the Mountains of *Calinga*." Asiatic " Researches Vol. 8th. Essay on the sacred isles in the west.

* Asiatic Researches Vol. III article 3d.

‡ The reader is requested to refer to the conclusion of the second Chapter of the grammar.

† Tilinga is mentioned in the Brahmanda Puran as an inland Country, situated between Casicosala or Benares, and Magadha. Vol. 8th. of the Asiatic Researches. Essay on the sacred isles in the west.

** The participle అగు (the same as అయిన) may be added to each of these words, used adjectively, which thus became తెల్లగు *Tellugoo* and తేనగు *Tenugoo* respectively. These derivations, however, are not free from objection, for they are not in strict conformity to the grammatical rules for Sundhi.

and that *Tenoogoo* may be translated *sweet*, from *Tene, honey*, a denomination by no means inapplicable to a language that has often been termed *the Italian of the East.*

The Country known by the name of Modogalingum or Trilingum appears to have been subdivided, at a very early period, into the *Calinga* and *Andhra* provinces. Calinga* stretched northwards along the coast, from the Godavery towards the Ganges; including those regions which are situated in the vicinity of the second lingum at Caleswarum, from which it probably took it's name *Calingum***—The nation is mentioned by Pliny as " *Calingæ proximi mari*" and " *Gentes gangaridum Calingarum*" and the people and language of Telingana are still known to the inhabitants of the Eastern islands by no other name than Caling or Keling.‡ Andhra, whence the first ancient dynasty of Hindoo Emperors appear to have derived their name,*** seems to have been an inland subdivision to the south of the Godavery, greater in extent than Calinga. Pliny, after specifying the names of several Indian nations, alludes to the Andhræ as a superior people " *Validior deinde gens Andhræ* " *plurimis vicis* XXX *oppidis, quæ muris turribusque muniuntur; regi præbet peditum* " *C. M. equitum M. M. elephantos M.*"—and Andhra, which is the name given to the Teloogoo by all Sanscrit Grammarians who have written respecting it, continues to be the current appellation of the language in many parts of the Country.

The most ancient Teloogoo Grammarian of whom mention is made in the native books is the sage Kunva, who is said to have been the first that composed a treatise

---

* It has been already noticed that Telinga is mentioned in the Brahmunda Pooran, as situated between Casi-cosala and Magadha, that is between Benares and Bahar proper-Calinga is mentioned in the same Pooran, as situated between Cosala and Banga; in other words, between Benares and Bengal proper-8th Vol: of the Asiatic Researches.—Essay on the sacred isles of the west—This proves the two to have been at least contiguous, but the one is generally understood to have been a subdivision of the other.—

** *Caleswarum* is one of the names of the God Shiva, *Calingum* is the same name for the same deity, only under a different form, namely the form of the mystic lingum.

‡ Marsdens Malay Grammar.—

*** See article VII Vol: 2d of the Asiatic Researches.

on the principles of the language. It † is stated that he executed this work by command of a king of Andhra, named Andhra royoodoo, son ‡ of Soochundra who reigned at Siccacollum on the banks of the Krishna. On the death of Soochundra, Andhraroyoodoo quitted the capital of Siccacollum, and established his residence on the banks of the Godavery—possibly at Rajahmundry, which we afterwards find mentioned as the capital of the Kings of the Chalookia race. Many fabulous accounts of the feats of this prince are current in Telingana, and such has been the veneration of the people for his virtues, that they have deified him as an incarnation of the God Vishtnoo, in which character he is still worshipped at the ancient capital of Siccacollum § near Masulipatam.

The works of Kunva, of Audharvan Achary, and of several other ancient Grammarians, are not now to be found. All the treatises on Teloogoo grammar, at present extant, consist of Sanscrit commentaries, on a series of concise apothegms written in Sanscrit by a Bramin named Nannapa, or Nunniah Bhutt. The text of Nunniah Bhutt, as explained by his best commentators, has been my principal guide in the work which I now offer to the Public; but as the illustrations, comparisons, and arrangement of these Authors are borrowed exclusively from the language in which they compose, and from a system of grammar the most artificial perhaps ever invented by human ingenuity, I have adhered

---

† కణ్వస్తుయదాహ । ఆంధ్రవిష్ణోరనుజ్ఞాకృతస్య మద్వ్యాకరణస్యద్రోహీ గురుద్రోహీతి ॥

Kunva said " He who speaks irreverently of my Grammar, composed by the command of Andhra Vishtnoo, shall be considered as guilty of irreverence to his Priest." Andhra Cowmudi.

‡ ఆంధ్రనాథో మహావిష్ణుర్నిశుంభదనుజాపహః । పురాస్వాయంభువమనోః కాలేకలియుగేహరిః । కాకులేరాజవర్యస్యసుచంద్రస్యతనూభవః । అభవత్సర్వదేవైశ్చవేష్టితోలోకపూజితః ॥

Hari The King of Andhra, the great Vishtnoo, the destroyer of the giant Nishumbhoo, formerly, in the Caliyoog of the grand period called Swayumbhoova, was born as the son of the chief of kings Soochundra, ruling at Cacolum. Andhra Cowmudi. Then follows the passage quoted in the first note.

§ In Teloogoo, the name of this place, and of Chicacole in the Ganjam District, are the same; but the two must not be confounded.

to them in these respects, so far only as they are calculated to assist an English Student. I have often been obliged to deviate from them, and, in imitation of my guides, to accommodate my illustrations &c. &c. to the grammar of the language in which I write.

Nunniah Bhutt, the author of the apothegms above mentioned, undertook also the herculean labor of translating the voluminous Mahabarut from Sanscrit into Teloogoo verse; and although he did not live to finish this work, which was subsequently completed by Tickuna Somiazooloo, he succeeded in immortalizing his memory in this part of India, by rendering this book the great standard of Teloogoo poetry. We learn from the introduction to * the Teloogoo Mahabbharut that

* The following is an extract from the passage here alluded to సీ॥ నిజమహీమండలప్రజఁ బ్రీతిఁ బెంచుచుఁ బరమండలంబుల ధరణిపతుల । నదిమి కప్పంబులు ముదముతోఁ గొంచును బలిమి నియ్యని భూమివలయపతుల । నుక్కణంగింపుచు దిక్కులందనయాజ్ఞ వెలిఁగించుచును విప్రకులము నెల్ల । ఁబ్రోచుచు శరణన్నఁ గాఁచుచు భీతులనగ్రజన్ములకు ననుగ్రహమున । నారూఢతరమహాగ్రహారంబు లిచ్చుచు । దేవభోగములు మహావిభూతి । దనరఁ జేయుచు నిట్లు మనుమార్గుఁడగు విష్ణు । వర్ధనుండు వంశవర్ధనుండు ॥ వచనము ॥ అఖిలజలధి వేలావలయిత వసుమతీవనితావిభూషణంబైన వేఁగి దేశంబునకు నాయకరత్నంబునుంబోని రాజమహేంద్రపురంబునందు మహేంద్రమహిమతోఁ బరమానందంబున ననవరతంబు మహారాజ్యసుఖంబు ననుభవింపుచుండి సకలభువనలక్ష్మీనివాసంబైన రమ్యహర్మ్యతలంబున మంత్రిపురోహిత సేనాపతి దౌవారిక మహాప్రధాన దండనాయక సామంత విలాసినీపరివృతుండై యపారశబ్దశాస్త్రపారగులయిన వైయాకరణులును । భారతరామాయణానేకపురాణప్రవీణులయిన పౌరాణికులును । మృదుమధురభావభాసురసరసవచనరచనావిశారదులయిన మహాకవులును । వివిధవితర్కసాగరవిగాహితసమస్తప్రౌఢశాస్త్రగరిష్ఠులయిన తార్కికులును । నాదిగాఁగల విద్వజ్జనంబులు పరివేష్టించి కొలిచియుండ । విద్యావిలాసుండును సుఖోపవిష్టుండును నై యిష్టకథావినోదంబులందగిలి యొక్కనాఁడు ॥ సీ ॥ తనకులబ్రాహ్మణు ననురక్తు నవిరళజపహోమతత్పరు విపులశబ్ద । శాసను సంహితాభ్యాసు బ్రహ్మాండాదినానాపురాణవిజ్ఞాననిరతు । ఁబా

Nunniah Bhutt was cotemporary with the King Vishtnoo Vurdhana, ** of the Shiva sect and Chalookia race, who reigned at Rajahmundry on the banks of the Godavery. Colonel Wilkes, § in his Historical Sketches of the South of India, makes the Chalookia race more ancient than the Cadumba kings of Bunawassi, whose dynasty is stated to have been subverted in the second century of the christian æra. If this be admitted, the works of Nunnia Bhutt may boast of great antiquity.

త్రు నాపస్తంబసూత్రు ముద్గలగోత్రజాతు సద్వినుతావదాతచరితు । లోకజ్ఞ
నుభయభాషాకావ్యరచనాభిశోభినిజప్రతిభాభియోగ్యు । నిత్యసత్యవచనమ
త్యమరాధిపా । చార్యు సుజను నన్నపార్యుఁ జూచి । పరమధర్మవిదుఁడు వరచ
ళుక్యాన్వయా । భరణుఁడిట్టులనియెఁ గరుణతోడ ॥

Affectionately protecting the inhabitants of his Empire—receiving, with satisfaction, the tribute of foreign Sovereigns, whose kingdoms had been subdued by him, and humbling the pride of those princes who haughtily withheld payment—illuminating the corners of the world with his commands—protecting the whole race of Bramins—shielding the timid who solicited shelter—compassionately bestowing the most excellent and extensive Agraharams on the first born men (Bramins)—enlightening vast wealth by celestial enjoyment—and thus following the precepts of Menu, lived Vishtnoo Vurdhana, the increaser of his race. He, the ornament of the Chalookia family, constantly enjoying the glory of his vast empire—residing, with excessive delight, and with the splendour of the great Indra, in his capital of Rajahmahendra, which is the chief gem of the Vegu Empire, the great ornament of the goddess of the Earth, (encompassed by the waters of all the oceans)—attended, in his superb palace, which is the seat of glory of the whole world, by Ministers, Priests, Generals, Chamberlains, Counsellors, Magistrates, neighbouring princes, and beautiful damsels—and surrounded by Grammarians, skilled in the boundless doctrines of articulate sounds, Historians, acquainted with the Bharata, Rámayanum, and all the Poorans, Great Poets, celebrated for clothing the most pleasing and gentle images in the sweetest verse, famous Philosophers, skilled in all the sublime sciences, and diving into the ocean of abstruse reasoning, and many other learned men—amusing himself with study—deeply interested in agreeable history, and experienced in the rules of justice—sitting, with delight, thus affectionately addressed the venerable and virtuous Nannapa, the Brahmin and affectionate adherent of his family, incessantly devoted to sacrifice and meditation, auther of a copious grammar, skilled in the Sumhetas, fully versed in various Poorans, such as the Bramhanda &c. a meritorious man, the follower of the aphorisms of Apastamba, born in the gotram of Mudgola, commended by virtuous men, pure in his actions, experienced in worldly affairs, in wisdom like Broohusputee, celebrated for composing poetry in both languages, famed for genius, a speaker of truth which is everlasting.
The king then proceeds to request that he will translate the Mahabharut.

** This prince must not be confounded with another Vishtnoo Vurdhana, who reigned in the eleventh century of our era, but who was neither of the Chalookia race, nor of the Shiva sect; he was a Tilinga king of the Bellal dynasty, and was converted from the jain religion to the sect of Vishtnoo, by the famous Rama Anuj Achary, the head of the Shri Vaishnavas or Ayengars, one of the three great sects into which the Hindoos of the Peninsula are now divided.

§ Page 12 of Vol. 1st.

Although the Teloogoo would thus appear to have been a cultivated language at a very early period, it is hardly to be expected, among the different political and religious convulsions which have so often violently agitated the Deccan, that many of the productions of so remote an age should have reached these times. Accordingly, with the exception of the abovementioned works of Nunniah Bhutt, and some books composed towards the close of the twelfth century, during the reign of Pertaub Roodroo, one of the last kings of the Bellal dynasty, which succeeded that of Cadumba, we find that nearly all the Teloogoo works now current in the country were written after the dissolution of the ancient government of Telingana, and the establishment of the more modern empire of Vidianagara.

On the capture of Warunkul, † The capital of the Bellal Kings of Telingana, by the Pattans, A. D. 1323, certain officers of these ancient princes are stated to have emigrated to the southern provinces, where they founded the celebrated city of Vidianagara or Vizianagara, the Bijanagur of Arrowsmith, and established a new dynasty of twenty princes* known by the name of *Raya or Royaloo*, who gradually extended their sway all over the South of India, and reigned from the commencement of the fourteenth to the close of the sixteenth century. Of these kings, the most celebrated was Krishna Royaloo, a prince who reigned during the earlier part of the sixteenth century. He is highly renowned in Telingana for his piety in repairing the numerous temples in the Carnatick,

† This word is pure Teloogoo ఒరుకల్లు, and signifies *a single stone, a solid rock*, or perhaps ఒరకల్లు *a touch stone.*

* ' I am indebted to the friendship of that able and distinguished officer Colonel McKenzie C. B. of the Madras Engineers, now Surveyor General of India, for the following translation of an extract from the Gutpurtee Manuscript in his valuable and extensive collection, containing, in the form of a prophecy, a chronological account of these kings. Numerous inscriptions, and grants of land, in the possesion of Colonel McKenzie confirm the correctness of this account.

A. S.	AD.			Y.	M.	D.
1258	1336	1	In the Saleevahan Sakum 1258, in the year Daatoo, on the 2d of Vysakum month, on the new moon, *Hurryhur Raya* will commence his reign at Anagoondy........ The whole of his reign will be........	14	"	"
1272	1350	2	After him, his brother *Booka Royaloo* will succeed in that kingdom and will reign........	29	8	"

* and for the great personal bravery he displayed in the course of his extensive conquests in the Peninsula, but Chiefly for his munificent encouragement of Teloogoo literature.

A. S.	A. D.		Y	M.	D
1301	1379	3 Next *Hurrykur Royaloo the second* will rule....................................	22	"	"
1323	1401	4 After him *Veejaya Booka Royaloo* will rule....................................	17	"	"
1340	1418	5 Upon his death *Palla Booka Royaloo* will rule....................................	16	"	"
1356	1434	6 After which *Gunda Dava Royaloo* will rule....................................	20	"	"
1376	1454	7 After him *Raja Saker Royaloo* will rule....................................	"	9	"
1376	1455	8 After that *Veejoyooloo* will rule....................................	"	10	"
1378	1456	9 *Proudha* or *Pratapa Dava Royaloo* will rule....................................	21	"	"
1399	1477	10 After him *Veera Royaloo* will rule....................................	4	"	"
1403	1481	11 After him *Mallicar Royaloo* will govern....................................	6	"	"
1409	1487	12 *Ramachundra Royaloo* will next rule.	1	"	"
1410	1488	13 *Veeroopacha Royaloo* will govern....................................	2	"	"
1412	1490	14 *Narusinga Royaloo* will rule....................................	5	"	"
1417	1495	15 After him *Narasa Royaloo* will rule (including 5 years in the name	13	"	"
1426	1504	16 of) His son *Veera Narsimha Royaloo* from the Cycle year Raktachee A. S. 1426....................................			
1430	1509	17 The second son of *Narasa Royaloo*, named *Krishna Royaloo* will rule. from the Cycle year Sookla of the Visaka month,....................................	21	"	"
1452	1530	18 From the Cycle year Veecrooty *Achoota Dava Royaloo* will reign	12	"	"
1464	1542	19 From thence *Salica Timma Rauze* From the beginning of the Cycle year Soobacroot in the Jasta month, *Rama Royaloo* will rule 22 years in the name of....................................	22	"	"
1486	1564	20 *Sadasevoo Royaloo* and keeping him in his possession. The Kingdom of Veejeyanagur will then end with *Rama Royaloo*....................................			
1451	1569	The country will be in great confusion then for....................................	5	"	"
1451	1569	21 In the Cycle year Pramodoota *Teroomal Royaloo* will establish himself as King, at Penoogonda, and will rule....................................	"	11	"
1494	1572	22 His son *Sree Runga Royaloo* will then reign from the Cycle year Angeerasa of the 10th of Vysakam....................................	14	"	"
5507 "	1585	23 After which, from the Cycle Paardeva of the 10th of Maugum of the full moon *Vencataputty Royaloo* will rule....................................	28	8	15
		After him, of the Kings of the Chundra race none will remain ; and foreign kings will rule the land, deriving, their authority from no legal right			
1536	1614	24 First *Chicka Royaloo* will rule....................................	"	4	"
1552	1630	25 After him *Rama Rauze* changing his true name, to that of *Ramadava Rayel* for....................................	15	5	"
		After this, the Country will be in great disorder for some time, and prodigies and portentous omens will appear between the year Bahoodanya and Nundana....................................	15	"	"

(Here the Account terminates in a prophetical annunciation of a Deliverer of the Hindoo Race.) From circumstances, observes Colonel McKenzie, we may infer that this account was written A. D. 1630.

* By an inscription on the great tower erected over the grand entrance into the famous Shiva temple at Conjeveram, which is supposed to be the highest building of the kind in India, we find that it boasts of this prince as it's founder.

A great number of books, composed during the reign of Krishna Royaloo, are still to be found in the libraries of the present Polygars, of whom many in the Northern Districts, as far as Nellore, and several in the South, are descended from the former officers of the Vidianagara government: but the intolerant zeal of the Mahommedans, whose irruptions into the South of India terminated in the overthrow of the Vidianagara Empire, has left of the more ancient Teloogoo works little else remaining than the name. §

The works still extant, however, are sufficiently numerous and various to evince the great degree of refinement to which the Teloogoo has attained. Few languages will be found more copious, more nervous, or more regular in construction, and it may boast, in a peculiar manner, of great elegance of expression, and melody of sound. Under the fostering auspices of the British Government, it is confidently hoped that the Teloogoo may recover that place which it once held among the languages of the East, and that the liberal policy of the Legislature † may be successful in renewing, among the Natives of Telingana, that spirit of literature and science, which formerly so happily prevailed among them, and still so much endears to their remembrance the days of the most enlightened of their Hindoo Rulers.

Nearly the whole body of Teloogoo literature consists of Poetry, written in what may be termed the superior dialect of the language; but so different is this from the inferior or colloquial dialect, in common use among all classes of the

§ Having heard that a number of poems, engraved on some thousand sheets of copper, had been preserved by the pious care of a family of Bramins in the temple on the sacred hill at Tripetty, I deputed a Native for the purpose of examining them; but, with the exception of a treatise on Grammar, of which a copy was taken, the whole collection was found to contain nothing but voluminous hymns in praise of the deity.

† The following is an extract from the act of the British Parliament to which I allude. "And "be it further enacted, that it shall be lawful for the Governor General in Council to direct, "that out of any surplus which may remain of the rents revenues and profits, arising from the "said Territorial acquisitions, after defraying the expenses of the Military, Civil, and Com"mercial Establishments, and paying the Interest of the Debt, in manner herein-after provided, "a sum of not less than one Lack of Rupees in each year shall be set apart and applied to the "revival and improvement of literature, and the encouragement of the learned Natives of India, "and for the introduction and promotion of a knowledge of the science among the Inhabitants of "the British Territories in India.

people, that even to the learned, the use of commentaries is indispensable for the correct understanding of many of their best works. This peculiarity of two dialects is common to the Teloogoo, with the Tamil and the Karnataca. In the course of this work, I propose to give all the rules for the superior dialect, as being that from which the other is derived, but I shall carefully notice the peculiarities of the common dialect. The reader will bear in mind that in conversation and official business, the inferior is used to the entire exclusion of the superior dialect, and that in all books or studied compositions, a contrary rule obtains.

Such as have acquired a knowledge of the Teloogoo language merely with a view to colloquial intercourse with the people, or to the transaction of official business, and have confined their studies exclusively to the inferior dialect, may accuse me of entering on an unprofitable and unnecessary task, in treating of the other, which, in their estimation, may be deemed altogether foreign to the Teloogoo. An attentive examination of the two may possibly lead to a very different conclusion: at all events, as this work is intended as much to enable the student to understand the rules which regulate the classical compositions of the Natives, as to teach him to speak or write the common Teloogoo, I have deemed it my duty to follow the Native Grammarians by tracing the language to it's original source in the superior dialect—at the same time, I have not neglected it's more useful branches in the inferior dialect, which, as being vulgar, Native authors have considered beneath the notice of the learned.

The Teloogoo is spoken with the greatest purity in the Northern Circars, and with much of it's native simplicity by the Ratsawars, Velmawars, and other superior classes in those districts. More conversant with arms, however, than with books, the Ratsawars * and Velmawars are in general ignorant of the princi-

* The affecting tale of the Zemindar of Boobily, related by Orme, is one of many that might be quoted, in elucidation of the nice sense of honor, and romantic bravery, inherent in this fine race of men. Our want of sufficient attention to their habits and customs, rather than any callous disregard for their prejudices, has occasionally driven others of this tribe to similar acts of self destruction, which are much to be deprecated, and which, indelibly imprinted on the minds of the people, materially affect the popularity of our Government.

ples of their own tongue. Indeed the three inferior classes of Telingana, unlike their neighbours of the Tamil Nation, seem to have abandoned the culture of their language, with every other branch of literature and science, to the sacred tribe. The Vussoochuritru is the only Teloogoo work of note not composed by a Bramin. But, with the manners and habits of their ancestors, the Velmawars, Comtees, and Soodra casts, descended from the aborigines of the country, retain a great deal of the original language of Telingana, and are more sparing in the use of Sanscrit words than the Bramins.

It has been very generally asserted, and indeed believed, that the Teloogoo has it's origin in the language of the Vedums, and many of the most eminent oriental scholars have given their authority in support of this opinion. It is not without much deference, therefore, that I venture publicly to state my inquiries to have led me to contrary conclusion; but I do so with the less hesitation, as I find myself supported by the concurrent evidence of all Native Authors who have ever written on the subject of the Teloogoo language.

On this, and on several other material points connected with the structure of the Teloogoo, I regret that my sentiments should be entirely at variance with those of so celebrated an orientalist as Dr. Carey, one of the learned Professors in the College of Fort William, to whom the Public are indebted for a very copious Grammar of the Sanscrit language, and for a series of works on the elements of the spoken dialects of India. In the preface to a Telinga Grammar, which issued from the press after the present work had been completed and submitted to Government, Dr. Carey writes as follows, "The languages of the South of India "*i. e.* the Telinga, Karnata, Tamil, Malayala, and Cingalese, while they have "the same origin with those of the North" (viz. the Sanscrit) differ greatly from "them in other respects: and especially in having a large proportion of words the "origin of which is unascertained; or, as he afterwards terms them, words current "in the country, దేశ్యము, of which the derivation is uncertain."

While I coincide in opinion with Dr. Carey, that, "among these five languages, "the Telinga appears to be the most polished, and though confessedly a very "difficult language, it must be numbered with those which are the most worthy "of cultivation, it's variety of inflection being such as to give it a capacity of "expressing ideas with a high degree of facility, justness, and elegance"; with deference, I submit that he has given an erroneous view of the structure and derivation of the Teloogoo. In common with every other tongue now spoken in India, modern Teloogoo abounds with Sanscrit words, perhaps it has a greater proportion of them than any of the other southern dialects; nevertheless there is reason to believe that the origin of the two languages is altogether distinct.

With the exception of a few letters peculiar to Sanscrit words, and evidently taken from the Nagree alphabet, the round and flowing characters of the Teloogoo bear no resemblance to the square Devanagree: and even if the Teloogoo alphabet were found to be derived from the Nagree, it would only prove that the people of Telingana had borrowed the invention of a more civilized nation. The origin of their language might still be as different from that of their alphabet, as the origin of our present Roman characters, from that of our Saxon words.

It has already been mentioned that all the Native Teloogoo Grammars are written by Bramins, in the Sanscrit tongue; and that their arrangement of the alphabet, their illustrations, and their comparisons, are necessarily borrowed from the language in which they write. This circumstance might justify the supposition that the Bramins were the first who cultivated the Teloogoo, and brought it under fixed rules: but it cannot be urged in proof of any radical connexion between the Teloogoo and the Sanscrit.

It has also been noticed that, in speaking the Teloogoo, the Soodras use very few Sanscrit words: among the superior classes of Vysyas, and pretenders to the Rajah cast, Sanscrit terms are used only in proportion to their greater intimacy with the Bramins, and their books; and, when we find even such Sanscrit words as these classes do adopt, pronounced by them in so improper and rude a manner as to be a common jest to the Bramins, who, at the same time, never question their pronunciation of pure Teloogoo words, I think we may fairly infer it to be probable at least that these Sanscrit terms were originally foreign to the language spoken by the great body of the people.

Some Native Grammarians * maintain that, before the King Andhraroyadoo † established his residence on the banks of the Godavery, the only Teloogoo words were those peculiar to what is emphatically termed the *pure* Teloogoo, now generally named *the language of the land,* which they consider coeval with the people, or as they express it "created by the God Brimha." The followers of this prince, say they, for the first time began to adopt Sanscrit terms with Teloogoo terminations, and by degrees corruptions from the Sanscrit crept into the language, from the ignorance of the people respecting the proper pronunciation of the original words. This would imply that the nation still retain some faint remembrance of those times, in which their language existed independent of the Sanscrit; and it is certain that every Teloogoo Grammarian, from the days of Nunnia Bhutt to the present period, considers the two languages as derived from sources entirely distinct; for each commences his work by classing the words of the language under four separate heads, which they distinguish by the respective names of దేశ్యము *language of the land,* తత్సమము *Sanscrit derivatives,* తద్భవము *Sanscrit corruptions,* and గ్రామ్యము *provincial terms.* To these, latter authors have

---

* See the Adhurvana Vyacurnum, as given in the Audhra Cowmudi. తత్రత్యాస్తత్సమాలాపాస్తత్రాలీనా హరేర్భటాః । కాలేనమహతా సర్వంతత్సమం స్వల్పబుద్ధిభిః । అస్ఫుటోచ్చార్యమాణం సత్తద్భవంచేతిసమ్మతం । వికర్షణాద్వ్యత్యయాద్భ్యాంచపాదార్ధోక్తివిశేషతః । తద్భవా ఇతికథ్యన్తే కాలేనమహతాసమాః । బ్రహ్మణానిర్మితావాచః పూర్వమాంధ్రేశితుర్హరేః । అచ్చా ఇతిచకథ్యన్తే సుప్తిఙ్ధాతు సమన్వితాః ॥ *The adherents of And,hra Vishtnoo* (before mentioned) *who then resided on the banks of the Godavery spoke Tutsama words,* (Sanscrit derivatives). *In the course of time, these words, not being properly articulated by the unlearned, by the change or obliteration of letters, or by being contracted, a fourth, or a half, became Tudb havas,* (Sanscrit corruptions.) *Those words consisting of nouns, verbals, and verbs, created by the God Brimha, before the time of Hari, the Lord of And,hra, are called Uch,ha,* (pure.)

† This is the prince who is now worshipped as a divinity at Siccacollum on the river Krishna, and who was the patron of Kunva, the first Teloogoo Grammarian.

added అన్యదేశ్యము *foreign words* or those from other lands.

As this arrangement is essential to a proper illustration of the structure of the Teloogoo language, it will be adhered to in the following work. Of the different classes of words specified above, the tree first only are mentioned in the Telinga Grammar by Dr. Carey; the first is there stated to comprize "words current in the country of which the derivaton is uncertain", a "large proportion" of which are allowed to be included in the language; the second is stated to contain "pure Sungskrita words;" and the third "words derived from the Sungskrita, "but written and pronounced differently."

The words included in the first class, which I have denominated *the language of the land,* are not only a "large proportion" of words, but the most numerous in the language, and the model by which those included in the other classes are modified and altered, from the diffrent languages to which they originally belong. Why the origin of this class of terms is supposed to be unascertained has not been stated; nor can I conceive how so erroneous a conclusion could have been adopted; for the name given to them by all Sanscrit Grammarians, by the whole body of the people, and by Dr. Carey himself, at once points out their derivation. This name is దేశ్యము, a noun used either as a substantive or an adjective, in the former sense denoting *a country or land,* in the latter, in which it is here used, implying *that which belongs to the country or land*; it marks the words in question, not as merely "current in the country," but as the growth and produce of the land; it would be difficult to define more precisely the origin of any words, and to this class must we look for the pure Teloogoo—for the true *language of the land.*

The second class of words I have termed *Sanscrit derivatives,* and I prefer this denomination to that of "pure Sungskrita words" given to it by Dr. Carey; for although the words included in it contain the crude forms of pure Sanscrit words, they cannot appear in Teloogoo in their original shape, but invariably assume terminations or undergo changes *peculiar to the pure Teloogoo, or language of the land.*

The third class of words which is generally mentioned by Dr. Carey as "derived from the Sungskrita," I have named *Sanscrit Corruptions*; it consists of words which have passed into Teloogoo, either directly from the Sanscrit, or through the medium of some of it's corrupted dialects, such as the Pracrit, and which, in order to be assimilated to the *language of the land,* have undergone radical alterations, by the elision, insertion, addition, or subtraction of letters. these changes have been sometimes carried so far, that it is difficult to trace any connexion between the adulterated word and it's original in Sanscrit.

In the course of this work, it will be obvious to the Sanscrit scholar that the declension of the noun, by particles or words added to it—the use of a plural pronoun (మనము) applicable to the first and second persons conjointly—the conjugation of the affirmative verb—the existence of a negative aorist, a negative imperative and other negative forms in the verb—the union of the neuter and feminine genders in the singular, and of the masculine and feminine genders in the plural, of the pronouns and verbs—and the whole body of the syntax, are entirely unconnected with the Sanscrit; while the Tamil and Karnataca scholar will at once recognize their radical connexion with each of these languages. The reader will find all words denoting the different parts of the human frame, the various sorts of food or utensils in common use among the Natives, the several parts of their dress, the compartments of their dwellings, the degrees of affinity and consanguinity peculiar to them, in short all terms expressive of primitive ideas or of things necessarily named in the earlier stages of society, to belong to the pure Teloogoo or *language of the land**. It is true, (so mixed have the two languages now become) that *Sanscrit derivatives or corruptions* may, without impropriety, be occasionally used to denote some of these. This, however, is not common, the great body of Sanscrit words admitted into the language consists of abstract terms, and of words connected with science, religion, or law

* The reader is requested to refer to the irregular దేశ్యము nouns.

as is the case, in a great degree, with the Greek and Latin words incorporated with our own tongue: but even such Sanscrit words as are thus introduced into Telogoo are not allowed to retain their original forms, they undergo changes, and assume terminations and inflections unknown to the Sanscrit, and, except as foreign quotations, are never admitted into Teloogoo until they appear in the dress peculiar *to the language of the land.*

This brief notice of the structure of the Teloogoo seemed necessary, in order to explain the principles on which the following chapters are founded: the further consideration of the subject I leave to others, as the prolonged discussion of it is foreign to a work of this nature. I am inclined, however, to believe that the Teloogoo will be found to have it's origin in a source different from the Sanscrit, a source common perhaps to the Teloogoo, with the superior dialects of the Tamil and Karnatca. But the introduction of Sanscrit words into this language must have taken place at so remote a period, as to be now almost beyond the reach of inquiry. With the religion of the Bramins, the people of Tilingana could not fail to adopt much of the language of that extraordinary tribe; their constant intercourse with each other for a long series of years has necessarily confirmed this intermixture of language, and it must be admitted that the Teloogoo has been as much improved by adopting an indefinite number of words from the Sanscrit, as our own tongue has been ameliorated by borrowing from the more refined languages of Greece and Rome.

Having concluded the few introductory remarks which I had to offer to the reader in explanation of the plan of my work, I avail myself of this occasion to make my public acknowledgments for the assistance with which I have been favoured in the course of it's progress.

To my friend Mr. Stokes of the civil service on this establishment, who did me the favour to peruse the manuscript before it was submitted to the Government, I owe many valuable suggestions; and I am under particular obligations to my colleagues in the Board of Superintendence for a most laborious and critical examination of the whole work. Mr. Ellis and Archdeacon Mousley are in a special manner entitled to my thanks; for their criticisms enabled me to correct many imperfections that had otherwise escaped my notice.

In examining the principles inculcated by the best native grammarians, I was assisted by my Teloogoo instructor Woodiagherry Vencatanarrain Ayah, a young bramin of superior intelligence and remarkable acquirements, who, by his own merits alone, subsequently rose to the situation of Head English master at the College of Fort St. George, and lately to the more honorable office of Interpreter to the Supreme Court of judicature at the Presidency. He generally sat by me while I wrote the notes from which this Grammar has been compiled, and I may therefore be said to have availed myself of his aid and advice throughout the work.

I have only further to add that on all intricate points of grammar I have invariably consulted the learned Pundit Putabhi Rama Sastry Head Sanscrit and Teloogoo master at the College, and where I found the native grammarians at variance, have been regulated chiefly by his opinions, in attempting to reconcile their differences, or in selecting that authority to which the preference has been given.

NOTE TO THE INTRODUCTION.

In support of what I have ventured to advance, in the preceding introduction, on the subject of the structure and derivation of the Teloogoo *language, it is peculiarly gratifying to me to be allowed to quote the high authority of my friend Mr. Francis W. Ellis, at the head of the Board of Superintendence for the College of Fort St. George, as contained in the following observations with which he has favoured me. The knowledge which this Gentleman possesses of the various spoken dialects of the Peninsula, added to his acquirements as a Sanscrit scholar, peculiarly qualify him to pronounce a judgment on this subject.*

The real affiliation of the Telugu language appears not to have been known to any writer, by whom the subject has been noticed. Dr. Carey in the preface to his Sanscrit Grammar says—"The Hindoostanee and *the* Tamil, with the languages of Gujarat and *Malayala, are evidently derived from the Sanscrit, but the two former are greatly mixed with foreign words.* The Bengalee, Orissa, Maratta, *Kurnata, and* Telinga languages *are almost wholly composed of Sanscrit words."* In the preface to a Grammar of the Telugu lately published by him he, also, says—"The languages of India are principally derived from the Sanscrit": &c. "The structure of most of the languages in the middle and north of India, is generally the same, the chief difference in them lies in the termination of the nouns and verbs, and in those deviations from Sanscrit orthography which custom has gradually established in the countries where they are spoken. The languages of the south of India, i. e. *The Telinga, Karnatic, Tamil, Malayala,* and Cingalese, *while they have the same origin with those of the north,* differ greatly from them in other respects: and especially in having a large proportion of words, the origin of which is unascertained."—To this testimony Dr. Wilkins adds the weight of his authority, when he says in the preface to his Grammar of the Sanscrit—"*the Tamil, the Telugu, the Carnatic, the Malabar,* together with that" (the idiom) "of the Marratta states and of Gujarat so abound with Sanscrit, that *scarcely a sentence can be expressed in either of them without it's assistance.*"—Mr. Colebrooke, also, in his dissertation on the Sanscrit and Pracrit languages in the 7th Volume of the Asiatick Researches, though he has not given so decided an opinion, yet, by including these under the general term Pracrit, appropriate only to dialects of Sanscrit derivation and construction, and by the tendency of his remarks, appears to favor the received notion of their origin; he states indeed in express terms that the *Tamil* (which word he writes Támla, deducing it from Támraparnà the Sanscrit name of the river of Tirunelvéli) is written in a character which is greatly corrupted from tho present Dévanágari, and that both the "*Carnata*" and "*Telingana*" characters are from the same source. In arrangement the two latter, which are nearly the same, certainly follow the Nágari, but in the form of the letters, mode of combination, and other particulars, there is no resemblance; and the T*amil is totally different,* rejecting all aspirates, and having many sounds which cannot be expressed by any alphabet in which the Sanscrit is written.

It is the intent of the following observations to shew that the statements contained in the preceding quotations are not correct; that neither the Tamil, the Telugu, nor any of their cognate dialects are derivations from the Sanscrit; that the latter, however it may contribute to their polish, is not necessary for their existence; and that they form a distinct family of languages, with which the Sanscrit has, in latter times especially, intermixed, but with which it has no radical connexion.

The members, constituting the family of languages, which may be appropriately called the dialects of Southern India, are the high and low Tamil; the Telugu, grammatical, and vulgar; Carnátaca or Cannadi, ancient and modern; Malayálma or Malayálam, which, after Paulinus a St. Bartholomæo may be divided into Sanscrit (Grandonico-Malabarica) and common Malayálam, though the former differs from the latter only in introducing Sanscrit terms and forms in unrestrained profusion; and the Tuluva, the native speech of that part of the country to which in our maps the name of Canara is confined.

Besides these, there are a few other local dialects of the same derivation, such as the Codugu, a variation of the Tuluva spoken in the district of that name called by us Coorg; the Cingalese, Mahàrástra and the Oddiya, also, though not of the same stock, borrow many of their words and idioms from these tongues. A certain intercommunication of language may indeed, always be expected from neighbouring nations, however dissimilar in origin, but it is extraordinary that the uncivilized races of the north of India should in this respect bear any resemblance to the Hindus of the south; it is, nevertheless, the fact, that, if not of the same radical derivation, the language of the mountaineers of Rájmahàl abounds in terms common to the Tamil and Telugu.

The Telugu, to which attention is here more specially directed, is formed from it's own roots, which, in general, have no connexion with the Sanscrit, nor with those of any other language, the cognate dialects of Southern India, the Tamil, Cannadi &c. excepted, with which, allowing for the occasional variation of consimilar sounds, they generally agree; the actual difference in the three dialects here mentioned is in fact to be found only in the affixes used in the formation of words from the roots; the roots themselves are not similar merely, but the same.

The roots of the Telugu Language, like those of the Sanscrit, are mostly the themes of verbs, but they may often be used in the crude form, or with a single affix, as nouns or adjectives, and many of them are used only in the latter acceptation; thus గుద్దు, as a noun, signifies *a blow with the fist* and is the root of the verb గుద్దడము *to strike with the fist;* thus also, నడు *nadu,* with the affix క *ca,* నడక *Nadaca,* signifies, as a noun, *a step, progress, conduct, manner,* and is the root of the verb నడవడము *nadavadamu to walk.* In this use of the roots, all the dialects differ; the root that is used as a noun only in Tamil and Telugu may serve as the theme of a verb in Cannadi, and *vice versâ:* thus in Tamil the term அக்கறை, *accarei* is used as a noun in such impersonals sentences as எனக்கக்கறையில்லை *yenac' accareiyillei, it is not a* want *to me—I do not require it;* in Cannadi అక్కఱెయు *accariy* is the root of the verb అక్కఱెయుడు *accariyudu to be desired—to be endeared to.* It frequently happens, also, that a term occurs which cannot be referred to any root of the tongue to which it belongs, though it is readily traced to a radical in one of the cognate dialects; thus in the compound అగపడడము *agupadadamu,* (which signifies in Telugu *to take* in the sense in which it is used in such sentences as అదిధూమముగానాకుఅగపడింది *adi d,húmamugà nácu agupadindi, I* take *it to be smoke* - దానికినర్థముసాకగపడలేదు *dánikin art,hamu nác' agapada lédu, I do not* take, *or comprehend, the sense of it,* but in Tamil *to take* in general, *seize, obtain,* as குருவியெனக்ககப்பட்டது *curivi yenac' agapattadu, I have* caught *the bird*) the first member అగ *aga* or అగు *agu* has no separate meaning in Telugu, in Tamil அகம் *agam* signifies the *interior* and, in both languages, the root படு *padu to suffer.*

To shew that no radical connexion exists between the Sanscrit and Telugu, ten roots in alphabetic order, under the letters *A, C, P,* and *V,* have been taken from the common d,hátu-málà or list of roots, and with them have been compared ten Telugu roots, under the same letters taken from a Telugu d,hátu-málà compiled by Patáb,hi-ráma Śástri, the Head Sanscrit and Telugu Master at the College; these will be found in the following lists, the mere inspection of which will shew, that, among the forty Telugu roots, not one agrees with any Sanscrit root. To facilitate a comparison of the several languages treated on, each of which has a distinct alphabet, the Roman character is used throughout:

the orthography is generally that of Sir Wm. Jones, as explained in the 1st Volume of the Asiatic Researches, but the grave accent is used instead of the acute, to mark a naturally long syllable when final or formed by *Sand,hi,* and *K,* is occasionally substituted for *C,* before *i* and *e* in words belonging to the southern dialects only: other variations of trifling importance will be observed.

ROOTS UNDER THE LETTER

SANSCRIT.	TELUGU.
A.	
Ac *to mark-move-move tortuously.*	Accálu *to contract the abdominal muscles.*
Ag *to move-move tortuously.*	Agalu *to separate - break.*
Anca or Anga } *to mark.*	Aggu *to worship.*
Ag,h *to move - despise - begin - move quickly.*	Aggalu *to be insufferable - be excessive.*
Ag,ha *to sin.*	Ats *to give by compulsion - incur debt.*
Ach *to honour - serve.*	Ántu *to touch or stick - adhere - anoint the head.*
Anch *to move - speak unintelligibly - speak intelligibly.*	Ádangu *to be destroyed - submit - be subdued, or suppressed.*
Aj *to throw - move - shine.*	Ádaru *to shine - shoot at.*
Át or Át,h *to move.*	Ádalu *to weep bitterly.*
Ád *to occupy - undertake.*	Adu *to slap.*

ROOTS UNDER THE LETTER.

C.	
Cac *to hint desire - go.*	Caccu *to vomit.*
Cacc *to laugh.*	Cats *to play dice, chess &c.*
Cac,h *to laugh.*	Crats *to want.*
Cacc,h *to laugh.*	Cattu *to tie - build - become pregnant.*
Cag *to move.*	Cadúgu, *to wash.*

SANSCRIT.	TELUGU.
Cach *to tie - shine.*	Cadangu or Canangu *to swell, boil.*
Caj *to hiccup.*	Catacu or Cadagu *to lick as a dog.*
Cat *to move - skreen - rain.*	Cadaru *to call aloud - exclaim.*
Cat,h *to fear - recollect anxiously.*	Cadalu *to move or shake.*
Cad *to eat - rejoice - divide - preserve.*	Cadi *to approach - obtain.*

ROOTS UNDER THE LETTER

P.

SANSCRIT.	TELUGU.
Pach *to cook-explain-stretch.*	Pagalu, or Pangalu *to break - make forked.*
Pad *to shine - move.*	Panchu *to devide into shares - send away - appoint - divide by figures.*
Pat,h *to speak.*	Pattu *to seize - touch - begin - knead the limbs - understand - contain - unite intimately, as colour with that which is coloured, &c.*
Pan *to traffic - praise.*	Padu *to suffer - fall.*
Pat *to rule - move.*	Pandu *to reprove - produce - lie down.*
Pat,h *to move.*	Padayu *to obtain.*
Pad *to move - be fixed.*	Pantangu *to vow.*
Pan *to praise.*	Padaru *to act precipitately - speak nonsense - threaten.*
Pamb *to move.*	Pannu *to join steers to a plough - prepare.*
Parbb *to move.*	Panatsu *to send - employ.*

ROOTS UNDER THE LETTER

SANSCRIT.	TELUGU.
	V.
Vak *to be crooked - move.*	Vaga or Vagu } *to grieve - pretend grief consult.*
Vag *to be lame.*	Vagir *to speak deceitfully - bark as a dog.*
Vach *to speak - order.*	Vangu *to stoop.*
Vaj *to move - renew or repair.*	Vats *to come.*
Vat *to surround - share - speak.*	Vantsu *to bind - pour water from a vessel.*
Vata *to surround - share.*	Vrats *to divide.*
Vanta *to share.*	Vatu *to become lean.*
Vat,h *to go alone - be able.*	Vattu *to dry up.*
Vad *to shine - surround.*	Vattru *to shine.*
Van *to sound.*	Vaddu *to serve food.*

To shew that an intimate radical connection exists between the Telugu and other dialects of Southern India, fifteen roots have been taken in alphabetical order from the Dhâtu-mâla above mentioned, under the first vowel and first consonant, with which the correspondent roots of the Tamil and Cannadi are compared: the Tamil roots are from a list compiled by the Head Tamil Master at the College, compared with the Sadur Agarâdi and other dictionaries and the Cannadi roots are from an old list explained in Sanscrit.

TELUGU.	CANNADI.	TAMIL.
	Accarey *to feel affection for, love.* This root, in Telugu *accara* and in Tamil *accarei*, is used as a noun, only in these languages.	
Accalu *to contract the abdominal muscles.* This root is never used without the formative syllable intsu in Telugu, isu in Can. which gives an active sense to primitive roots, and a causal sense to the derivative themes of verbs.	Accalu *as in Telugu.*	
Aggalu *to separate.*	Agalu *as in Telugu*-also, *to become extended- to extend - lament.*	Agal *as in Telugu* - also, *to keep at a distance - pass beyond.* Agavu. *to call, play.*

TELUGU.	CANNADI.	TAMIL.
	Agáĺu *to dig.*	Agaźh *as in Cannadi* in which language the Tamil *źh* is usually converted into *ĺ*.
	Agey *to be afraid - be pleased.*	Agei *to beat - cut - break in two.*
Aggalu *to become insufferable - be excessive.*		
Aggu *to worship.*		Ahgu *to decrease.*
		Angar *to gape.*
Ats *to give by compulsion-incur debt.*	Atchu *as in Telugu.* The consonant in this root, which agrees with the first of the second series of consonants in the Sanscrit alphabet, is pronounced *tsa* and *cha* in Telugu; *cha* in Can. and *sa*, *sha*, *cha*, and *ja* in Tam. according, as it is final or medial, single or double.	
	Anju *to be alarmed - fear - frighten.*	Anju *as in Can.*
Ańtu *to touch - stick or adhere - anoint the head.*	Ańtu *to join - stick together.*	Ańtu *to join - adjoin - approach - befit.* This root, spelt with the same letters in the three dialects, is in Tamil pronounced *Ándu*.
Ádangu, Ánangu, Aańugu } *to be destroyed - submit - be subdued or suppressed.*	Ádagu or Ádangu } *to be contained - enclosed - subdued or suppressed - submit-recede.*	Ádangu *as in Can.*
Ádaru *to shine - shoot at.* In the second sense it takes the formative *intsu*.	Ádaru *to ascend - climb ride.*	Ádaru *to throng - press together - be connected.*
Ádalu *to weep bitterly.*		
Ádu *to slap.*	Ádu *to cook.* This root with a final *e ade*, means the same as in Telugu, and, also it *to obtain-move.*	Ádu *to join - be near - be connected - to kill - fight - cook.* With a final *ei* this root means, as in Can. *to obtain* and, also, to *tie-unite*.

NOTE. This root is the primitive of all those in the three languages commencing with the letters *ád*, in which the leading idea of *nearnes -junction*, variously modified, is very apparent : the several modes of forming the secondary root by inserting a nasal before the final syllable, as in Ańdu, or Ańtu, or by adding the syllables *ei* or *e, ar, al, gu, angu, &c.* as here exemplified, is common to them all. This formation of a number of secondary roots from a primitive by the adjuncts mentioned, is constantly observable under every letter of the alphabet: the primitive is found sometimes in Tam. sometimes in Can. and sometimes in Tel. sometimes it exists in all three, sometimes in none of them.

TELUGU.	CANNADI.	TAMIL.
Áḋugú *to ask - beg alms.*		
Áḋḋagu *to interrupt prevent.*	Áḋḋagu *as in Tel.*	
Caccu *to vomit.*	Caccu *as in Tel.*	Caccu *as in Tel.*
	Cangéḋu *to become lean.*	
	Çargu *to become black, by fire &c.*	Carugu *as in Can.*
Cats *to play dice, chess &c.*		Casa *to be modest, or diffident.*
		Casangu *to be bruised by the hand - squeezed.*
	Cachini *to join together two things of the same kind - pair.*	Casi *to be moist or damp- to weep - entreat.*
	Carchu *to bite-wash rice.*	Caḋa *to pass beyond.*
		Caḋavu *to pay - fulfil- give attention - reflect- nail up.*
Caťťu *to tie - build - become pregnant,* said of cattle only.	Caťťu *to tie - build.*	Cattu *as in Can.*
Cadugu *to wash off,* as dust from the hands - *wash out,* as stains from a cloth.		This root in Tamil is pronounced Cashavu; *ḋa* in Tel. and *ľa* in Can. are constantly substituted for the Tamil *Zh* ழ and roots of which the final is *gu* in the former end in the latter in *vu*; thus the root meaning to *stroke gently - caress* is in Tam. Taźhuvu in Tel. Taḋugu &c.
Cadangu or Cańangu } *to swell - boil or bubble.*	Caḋangu *as in Tel.* In both languages this verb is primarily used of water, and secondarily of the affections of the mind, in expresions similar to *the sea swells, his anger boils, his wealth overflows.*"	This root is not in Tam. but it is evidently the same in meaning and derivation with the two following, the last of which, Caḋu, is the primitive of all those commencing with Caḋ in the three languages.

TELUGU.	CANNADI.	TAMIL.
	Cadi *to cut - bite.*	Cadi *to cut - bite - guard- swell or be angry.*
		Cadu *to cut - plough - snatch or seize suddenly - steal - be angry.*
	Cadekey *to hurry - hasten.*	Cadagu *as in can.*
	Cadé *to churn.*	Cadei *to stir up with a stick &c. - to turn by a lath.*
	Canmalei *to think - conceive in the mind.* This is evidently a compound of the simple root *can*, but the second member, *malei*, has no separate meaning.	Can or Cani *as in Can. also to consider - mark - determine.*
	Cattu *to kill.*	Cattu *to call aloud - roar or bellow - croak.*
	Cadadu *to dissolve in liquids.*	
Cadaru - *to call aloud from any affection of the mind - to exclaim.*	Cadaru *to call or weep aloud - bellow as a beast.*	Cadaru *as in Can.*
Cadalu or Cadulu *to move or shake.*	Cadalu *as in Tel.*	Cadalu *as in Tel.*
	Cadi *to steal.*	Cadi *to sound - make a noise - be haughty.*
Cadiy *to approach - obtain.*		
Cadu *to draw gold or silver.*		
Cādumu *to push away.*		
		Caduvu *to be confused or perplexed.*
	Cadrucu or Cadruncu *to peck as a bird.*	

TLUGU.	CANNADI.	TAMIL.
Candu *to fade or decay as flowers and fruit by heat.*	Candu *as in Tel.*	Candu *as in Tel. & Can.* It has this meaning in Tam. when the last syllable is writen *ru* but pronounced *du*; when written with the same final consonant as in Tel. and Can. it signifies *to be spoiled - to perish* generally.
	Canam *to become rancid- to acquire a bad taste or smell by smoke or keeping.* This root is used as a noun in Telugu in the same sense.	
Canalu *to become angry - fade.*	Canalu *to kindle as fire - to become angry.*	Canal and Candal } *to become angry.* Used, as a noun, Canal means fire.
Canu *to see - to bring forth a child.*	In the first sense, *to see*, this root in the present and future of the Can. and Tam. is written with a long *a* and with the nasal of the third series of consonants *Cán* and *Cánu*; in the past it is short *Canden-Candenu*, as in Tel: the second sense is peculiar to the latter language; but *Candu a calf* in Tamil is evidently derived from it.	
Cappu *to cover.*	Cappu *to dig a pit - excavate - hollow out.*	This root is not used in Tam. either in it's Tel. or Can. sense, but it is evident that from it in the latter acceptation is derived the Tamil terms, *Capparu a hollow bason* carried by beggars, and *Cappel a ship.*

But though radical connection may be proved to exist between languages, their actual connection, as regards terms used for the expression of ideas, may not be intimate and it becomes necessary, therefore, to establish this point, to enter further into detail and compare the words of the three cognate dialects, as well as the roots whence they are derived. Mámidi Vencaya, the author of the Ánd,hra Dìpaca, an excellent Dictionary of the Telugu, has, in the preface to this work, introduced a concise analysis of the language, the substance of which, as affording the means of making this comparison, is translated in the following paragraph.

"The modes of derivation in the Ánd,hra language are four; they are Tatsaman, Tad,bhavan, Désyam and Grámyam.

" *OF PURE SANSCRIT TERMS RECEIVED IN TELUGU.*"

" Tatsamam consists of Sanscrit terms, pure as spoken in heaven, the Telugu terminations being substituted for those of the original language, of which the following are examples.

SANSCRIT.	TATSAMAM.	
Rámah	Rámandu	*a proper name.*
Vanam	Vanamu	*a forest.*
Gangá	Ganga	*the river.*
Harih	Hari	*a proper name.*
B, hagavatì	B, hagavati	*a goddess.*
'Sríh	'Srì	*prosperity.*
Sambuh	Sambuvu or Sambundu	*a proper name.*
Vad, huh	Vad, hu	*woman.*
Gauh	Govu	*a cow.*
Glau	Glau	*the moon.*
Vác	Váccu	*a word.*
Bishag	Bishacu	*a physician.*

SANSCRIT.	TATSAMAM.	
B, hub, hrüt	B, húb, hrüttu	*a king.*
Hanuman	Hanumá, hanumantudu and hanumánudu	*a proper name.*
Sampad	Sampadu and Sampattu	*wealth.*
Cshut...... and Cshud......	Cshuttu	*appetite.*
Ápah	Appu	*waters.*
Dyau	Divamu	*the heavens.*
Payah	Payasu	*milk.*
Anadwán	Anadwáhamu	*an ox.*

" *OF TERMS DERIVED FROM THE SANSCRIT.*

" Tadb,havam consists of terms formed, either from the Sanscrit direct, or through one of the six Pracrits, varied by the interposition of syllables, and by the substitution, increment, and decrement of letters, as explained in the Vaicrüta-chundrica: the several modes of derivation, here indicated, are exemplified in the following lists.

" *TADB,HAVAM TERMS DERIVED IMMEDIATELY FROM SANSCRT.*

SANSCRIT.	TADBHAVAM.	
Samudrah	Sandaramu	*the sea.*
Chandrah	Tsandurundu	*the moon.*
Cánanam	Cána	*a forest.*
Cudyam	Góda	*a wall.*

SANSCRIT.	TADBHAVAM.	
Yátrà	Dzatara	*pilgrimage.*
Áturam	Átramu	*hurry.*
Pangtih	Banti	*a line or row.*
C, huralí	Garidí	*a fencing school.*

" *TADB,HAVAM TERMS DERIVED FROM SANSCRIT THROUGH THE PRACRUTAM SPOKEN IN THE COUNTRY OF MAHARASTRA.*

SANSCRIT.	PRACRIT.	TELUGU.	
Chacravácah	Chaccaváyò	Dzaccavu	*a species of water fowl.*
Upád,hyáyah	Ojjháo	Oddza	*a preceptor.*
Brahmà	Bamhà	Bomma	*Brahma.*
Dwípah	Dívo	Dívi	*an island.*
Cámsyam	Camso	Cantsu	*bell metal.*
Yaśah	Jaso	Asamu	*fame.*

" *TADB,HAVAM TERMS DERIVED THROUGH SAURASENI, THE LANGUAGE OF THE COUNTRY OF SURASENA.*

SANSCRIT.	SAURASENI.	TELUGU.	
Yejuópavítam	Dzannóvídam	Dzannidamu	*the Brahminical thread.*
Prátijnyátam	Padinńádam	Pannidamu	*a vow.*
Hintálah	Hindálò	'Indu	*a date.*
Haritálah	Haridálò	Aridalamu	*orpiment.*
D,hátu	Dádu	Dzádu	*colour.*

" *TADB,HAVAM TERMS DERIVED THROUGH THE MAGAD,HI, SPOKEN IN THE COUNTRY OF MAGAD,HA.*

SANSCRIT.	MAGAD,HI.	TELUGU.	
Nédisht,ham	'Nédistam	Néstamu	*friendship.*
Géhast,hah	Géhastè	Gésta	*a householder.*
Cashtam	Castam	Casti	*difficulty.*
Rámà	Láma	Léma	*a woman.*

" *TADB,HAVAM TERMS DERIVED THROUGH THE PAISACHI, SPOKEN IN THE COUNTRIES OF PANDYA AND CECAYA.*

SANSCRIT.	PAISACHI.	TELUGU.	
Alactah	Alatto	Latuca	*lac-dye, prepared for painting the feet.*
'Sashculì	Sack,huli	Tsackilamu	*a contorted cake.*
Urnà	Unná	Unni	*wool.*
Trilingah	Tilingo	Telungu / Telugu / Tenugu	*the Telugu Language.*
Swernam	Sannam	Sonna	*gold.*
Nisréní	Nísena	Nittsena	*a ladder.*

" TADB,HAVAM TERMS DERIVED THROUGH THE CHULICA OR CHULICA-PAISACHI, SPOKEN IN THE COUNTRIES OF GANDARA, NEPALA AND CUNTALA.

SANSCRIT.	CHULICA.	TELUGU.	
Bründah	Pundo	Pindu	*an assemblage.*
Bud,hah *intelligent*	Puddo	Pedda	*great*; peddavańdu *a wise man &c.*
Swernam	Panaò	Ponnu	*gold.*
Mrügah	Mícò	Mécamu	*a beast.*
Brad,hnah	Paddo	Produ & Poddu	*sun rise.*

" TADB,HAVAM TERMS DERIVED THROUGH THE APAB,HRAMSA SPOKEN IN THE COUNTRY OF AB,HIRA AND THE COAST OF THE WESTERN OCEAN.

SANSCRIT.	APABHRAMSA.	TELUGU.	
Bráhmanàh	Bamb,hadu	Bápadu	*a Brahman.*
Abad,ham	Abadd,hu	Baddu	*an untruth.*
Stanam	Tanu	Tsannu	*the bosom.*
'Srutam *heard*	Sudu	Tsaduvu	*reading or learning."*

NOTE. Apabramśa means, literally, *corrupted language*; but the author says the word is not to be taken in this sense, but as the proper name of the dialect, and to this purpose quotes a verse from Appacavi; one of the commentators on the Nannayab,hattiyam, who states the same, and adds it was the speech of the goddess Saraswati in her youth, and that it's terms, therefore, are without exception, pure. Words which have passed through this dialect to the Telugu are, however, more frequently used by the 'Súdra tribes than by the Bráhmans.

The proportion of corrupt, or, more appropriately, permuted terms in Telugu of the several derivations above noticed, may be stated as follows; Sanscrit Tadb,havam *one half*; Prácrit, *one quarter*; Sauraséni *one tenth*; Mágad,hi *one twentieth*; the Paisáchi, Chúlicà, Apabramśa together *one tenth*. Mr. Colebrooke, in his dissertation on the Sanscrit and Pracrit languages, admits but of three distinctions; these two and the Magad,hi, or Apabramśa, which he considers the same. The six Prácrits here enumerated, however, are six distinct dialects, each formed, as to terms, according to it's own rules of permutation, but all following the idiom, collocation and, with special exceptions, the general grammar of the Sanscrit: in the Shadbáshà-chandricà by Lacshmid,hara, a joint grammar of the six Prácrits, after general rules applying to all, the Prácrit κατ᾽ ἐξοχὴν (*Pracrütam mahàrástr' ódb,havam*) is deduced immediately from the Sanscrit, the Saùrasénì from the Prácrit and Sanscrit and so on; the Mágadhi, Paisáchi, Chúclica - Paisáchi, and Apabramsa, each declining a degree in purity and the last varying more than any of the rest from the parent stock; this, however, the author does not allow to be, as Mr. Colebrooke considers it, "a jargon destitute of regular Grammar," for he says-*Apab,hramśas tu b,háshà syàd ab,hiràdi giráuchayah - cavi prayóg'ànerhetwàn n'àpasabdas sa tu cwachit, Apabramsa is the language spoken in Ab,hira and other countries, and, as it is used by the poets, it is not in any respect corrupted*—and he proceeds, accordingly, to detail it's grammatical rules.

The work here noticed is confined to these dialects, as they now exist in the Nátacas, and treats, therefore, only of Tatsamam and Tadb,havam terms of Sanscrit origin; it is expressly stated, however, that each possessed its proper Désyam, or native, terms, and it is probable, as many of these dialects prevailed in countries far distant from each other, that each was connected with Désyam words of various derivations, in conjunction with which they produced spoken languages differing considerably from each other; this in fact is declared to be the case with respect to Paisáchi in the following passage - *Pisácha désa niyatam Paisáchi dwitayam viduh - Pisácha desàstu vrüdd,hair uctáh-Pándya Cécaya Cháhlica Sahya Népála Cuntalàh Sud,hésha B,hóta Gánd,hára Haiva Canójanàs tat,hà- Etè paisácha désàs syus tad désyas tad guno b,havati.* The two Paisáchi dialects are said to prevail in all the countries here mentioned, commencing with Pándyam at the southern extremity of India, and extending to Canoj (*Canójána*) in the north, and Siam (*Sayha*) to the east, and it is added. *These are the Paisáchi countries, and the Désyam terms of each have their own particular quality.*

"Dèsyam, in other words 'And,hra, or Telugu, is of two kinds; the language which originated in the country of Telingana and Anya-désyam, or the language of foreign countries intermixed with it.

"*OF TERMS WHICH ORIGINATED IN TRILINGAM.*

"Previously to shewing what part of the language originated in Trilingam, the following stanzas from the Ad͵haravana Vyácaranam are here inserted, to describe the country to which this name applies."

A quotation from the Adharavana Vyácaranam is omitted: the author explains that part which relates to the boundaries of Trilingam as follows:

"As it is here said, in the country between Srisailum, the station of Bhímeswara at Dracharàmam, the greater Cálèswaram and, as the fourth, the mountain of Mahéndra, in these holy places were three Lingams, and the language which originated in the country known by the name of the Trilinga Désam, is that now under consideration; this is the *Atsu* or pure Telugu, and is thus described in the Appacavíyam.

VERSE.

"*All those words which are in use among the several races who are aborigines of the Country of A͵nd͵hra, which are perfectly clear and free from all obscurity, these shine forth to the world as the pure native speech of A͵nd͵hra (Sudd͵ha A͵nd͵hra Dés͵yam.)*

"*OF THESE THE FOLLOWING ARE EXAMPLES.*

Pálu	*milk.*	Nela	*the moon, a month.*
Perugu	*curdled milk.*	Vésavi and Vésaugi	*sultry weather.*
Ney	*clarified butter.*		
Rólu	*a mortar.*		
Róncali	*a pestle.*	Gudi	*a temple.*
Utti	*a long net for holding pots &c.*	Madi	*a field.*
		Puli	*a tyger.*
Pudami	*the earth.*	Tsali	*cold.*
Padatuca	*a woman.*	Madugu	*a natural pool or lake.*
Pasidi-paindi	*gold.*	U'ru	*a village.*
Bangáru	*gold.*		
Coducu	*a son.*	Magavandu	*a man.*
Códalu	*a daughter in-law.*	'Andadi	*a woman.*
Tala	*the head.*	Aluca	*vexation-displeasure.*

"*OF TERMS INTRODUCED INTO TELUGU FROM FOREIGN COUNTRIES.*

"The following verse is from the Appacavíyam.

"*O Césava, the natives of A'nd͵hra having resided in various countries, by using Telugu terms conjointly with those of other countries, these have become Ánd,hra terms of foreign origin.*

"The people of 'And,hra, otherwise called Trilingam, have, as Appacavi states above, frequented other countries and mixed their language with that of these several contries; of such Anya-dés yam terms the following are examples.

The examples are of Anya-dés yam terms in which aspirates, not belonging to the thirty letters proper to the Telugu, occur: such as, *b,halà* an eulogistic exclamation; *avad,háru* an exclamation of entreaty; *t,havu a place-station*; *d,háca a haughty, high spirited man*: of those which have a final long vowel; such as, *anà the sixteenth of a Rupee*; *navalà an excellent woman*; *códì a flag*; *jirà armour*: and, lastly, of difficult words, inappropriately ranked among Any-adés yam terms; such as, *calanu battle*; *toyyeli a woman*; *ménu the body*; *ullamu the mind.* Of the list given by the author as examples of the several kinds of Anya-désyam terms, the whole of the words in the first are of uncertain derivation: those in the second are either Hindustáni or they are terms the last syllable of which has been casually lengthened; thus *códì*, is the same as *códi* and *navalá* is either of Sanscrit derivation from *nava new*, or a native term from the Tamil *navam affection.* Most of those in the last list are common to the southern dialects; thus *calanu*, in Tamil *cal*, is derived from the root *cala to join*, common to the three dilalects; *toyyeli*, in Tamil *taiyel*, from *tai to beautify*, *ménu*, in Tamil *méni*, from *mêl upward-outward*, and *ullumu* from *ul inward-mind.*

" OF TERMS AND FORMS OF RUSTIC OR VULGAR SPEECH.

"Terms which cannot be subjected to the rules of Grammar, and in which an irregular increment or decrement of letters occur are called Grámyam; they are corruptions, and are described in the following verse from the Appacaviyam.

VERSE.

" *Such Tenugu words as are commonly used by rustic folk are known as Grámyam terms; these lose some of their regular letters and are not found in poetry, unless, as in abusive language, the use of them cannot be avoided, for example,*

Vastádà Hari Somulu
Destádà golladanti dittaca carunan
Tsústádà caungili nid'
Istádà tsepamannan ivi grámyóctul."

In this verse *vastádà* for *vatstsunnándà*; *testádà* for *tetstsutsunnándà*; *tsústádà* for *tsútsutsunnádà*; *istádà* for *itstsutsunnáudà* and *tseppamu* for *tseppumu*, are Grâmyam terms

In the preceding extracts, the auther, supported by due authority, teaches, that, rejecting direct and indirect derivatives from the Sanscrit, and words borrowed from foreign languages, what remains is the *pure native language of the land*: this constitutes the great body of the tongue and is capable of expressing every mental and bodily operation, every possible relation and existent thing; for, with the exception of some religious and technical terms, no word of Sanscrit derivation is *necessary* to the Telugu. This pure native language of the land, allowing for dialectic differences and variations of termination, is, with the Telugu, common to the Tamil, Cannadi, and the other dialects of southern India: this may be demonstrated by comparing the Désyam terms contained in the list taken by Vencaya from the Appacavíyam, with the terms expressive of the same ideas in Tamil and Cannadi. It has been already shewn that the radicals of these languages, *mutatis mutandis*, are the same, and this comparison will shew that the native terms in general use in each, also, correspond.

It would have been easy to have selected from the three dialects a far greater number of terms, than these, exactly agreeing with each other; but it is considered preferable to follow a work of known authority, and to which no suspicion of bias to any system can attach: the author, though a good Sanscrit scholar, was ignorant of all the dialects of southern India, his native tongue excepted.

TELEGU.	CANNIDI	TAMIL
Pálu *milk*	Hálu When *P* begins a word in Tamil or Telugu, it is in Cannadí changed to *H*, as Tamil *Palli* Tel; *Palle*, Can. *Halli asmall village* : but in the old Can. all such words may, also, be written with a *P*.	Pál.
Perugu *curdled milk*		Perugu.
Ney *clarified butter*	The Telugu term is not used by itself in Can. but is found in compounds as *Bennè, white ghee-butter.*	Ney. Of these terms the fist and last are common to the high and low Tamil, the second is confined to the high dialect.
Rólu *a mortar*	Orulu	Urul. High Tamil.
Róncali *a pestle*	Onake	Uroncali. H. Tam. The Telugu terms are contractions of these: many similar instances might be adduced, thus *ìra* night in Tamil becomes *rè* in Telugu, *irandu two rendu* ; *aven that man, iven this man become vandu and víndu.*
Utti *a long net for holding pots or other household utensils.*	This term may be used in Can. but nelu is more correct.	Uri In Tamil when the letter r̄ (ற) is doubled it, it is pronounced t̠ t̠ and in similar Tel. terms, is written t̃t (ట్ట)
Pudámi *the earth*	Podávi	Pudávi. H. Tam.
Padátuca *a woman* This term is probably a compound, but it is not easy to reduce it to its elements.		
Pasídi or Paindí *gold*	Pasaru or Hasaru with which the Telugu term is derivatively connected, is used in Can, in the acceptation of. *green colour* only.	Pasuppu *golden colour.* *Pasamei green colour,* whence this term is derived, means, also, *beauty-purity* ; *pasum*, the adjective derived from it is frequently contracted to *paim as pasumpon-paimpon pure gold* and from this contraction the second of the Tel. terms is derived.
Bangáru *gold*	Bangáru	Bangáru L. *Tam.*

TELUGU.	CANNDI.	TAMIL.
Cod́ucu *a son*........ } Cód́alu *a daghter in law*.......... }	....	Cuźhandi } Cuźhavi... } *H. Tam.* and Cozhandei *L. Tam.* signify *a child of either sex.* These are the same as the Tel. terms the anomalous letter z'h (ழ) being, as usual, changed to *d́* and the dialectic terminations added.
Tala *the head*	Tale.	Talei. A short *a* ends all words in Tel. which in Tamil end in *ei.*
Nela *the moon, a month*		Nilavu *the moon.*
Vésavi and Vésaugi } *sultry weather- the hot season*	Besagi. As usual in Cannadi the Telugu V is here changed to B.	This compound is not used as a noun in Tamil though it may be as in epithet, as *vésavi cálam* it is derived from *Vé* heat and *sari* light.
Guḋi *a temple*	Guḋi	Cuḋi or Guḋi. This used in Tamil signifies any *habita tion* ; *tiru-gudi*, or *dever-cudi* is *a temple* ; the first member of the lattercompound may be added or omitted in Tel.
Maḋi *a field*	Maḋi. In Can. this word properly means *beds in which vegetables are sown ; the subdivision of salt pans.*	Maḋi. This word may be used in the same sense as in Tel. but it means. derivatively *a section*, from the root *madu* to *devide into sections.*
Puli *a tiger*	Huli	Puli.
Tsali *cold*	Chali	....
Maḋugu *a natural pool or lake*	Muḋugu	Maḋu.
U'ru *a village*	U'ru	U'r.
Magavánḋu *a man*. *Vándu* is here merely the personal termination equivalent to *en* in Tamil ; without this termination the word means a male of any species, and *magaḋu* in the Mas. therefore, is *a husband*	Magenu. This word in Can. has exclusively the second of the Tamil meanings.	Magen. This word in Tamil means, first. *a man, amale of the human species,* secondly *a male child, a son.*

TELUGU.	CANNADI.	TAMIL.
Andadi *a woman.*	....	'Adável. The termination only differs; the nasal in the first syllable of the Telugu Word being scarcely heard in pronunciation.
Aluca *vexation - displeasure.*	....	Alappu. The only difference is the termination.

From the preceding extracts and remarks on the composition of the Telugu language, as respects terms, it results that the language may be divided into four branches, of which the following is the natural order. Dés'yam or Atsu-Telugu *pure native terms,* constituting the basis of this language and, generally, also, of the other dialects of southern India: Anya-dés'yam *terms borrowed from other Countries,* chiefly of the same derivation as the preceding: Tatsamam, *pure Sanscrit terms,* the Telugu affixes being substituted for those of the original language: Tadb,havam, *Sanscrit derivatives,* received into the Telugu, direct, or through one of the six Prácrits, and in all instances more or less corrupted. The Grámyam (literally the *rustic* dialect from *Grámam* Sans. *a village*) is not a constituent portion of the language, but is formed from the Atsu-Telugu by contraction, or by some permutation of the letters not authorized by the rules of Grammar. The proportion of Atsu-Telugu terms to those derived from every other source is *one half*; of Anya-dés'yam terms *one tenth*; of Tatsamam terms in general use *three twentieths*; and of Tadb,havam terms *one quarter.*

With little variation, the composition of the Tamil and Cannadi are the same as the Telugu and the same distinctions, consequently, are made by their grammatical writers. The Telugu and Cannadi both admit of a freer adoption of Tatsamam terms than the Tamil: in the two former, in fact, the discretion of the writer is the only limit of their use; in the high dialect of the latter those only can be used, which have been admitted into the dictionaries by which the language has long been fixed, or for which classical authority can be adduced; in the low dialect the use of them is more general—by the Bráhmans they are profusely employed, more sparingly by the Súdra tribes. The Cannadi has a greater and the Tamil a less proportion of Tadb,havam terms than the other dialects; but in the latter all Sanscrit words are liable to greater variation than is produced by the mere difference of termination, for, as the alphabet of this language rejects all aspirates, expresses the first and third consonant of each regular series by the same character, and admits of no other combination of consonants than the duplication of mutes or the junction of a nasal and a mute, it is obviously incapable of expressing correctly any but the simplest terms of the Sanscrit; all such, however, in this tongue are accounted Tatsamam when the alteration is regular and produced only by the deficiencies of the alphabet.

But, though the derivation and general terms may be the same in cognate dialects, a difference in idiom may exist so great, that, in the acquisition of one, no assistance, in this respect, can be derived from a knowledge of the other. As regards the dialects of southern India this is by no means the case, in collocation of words, in syntaxical government, in phrase, and, indeed, in all that is comprehended under the term idiom, they are, not similar only but the same. To demonstrate this and to shew how far they agree with, or differ from, the Sanscrit, the following comparative translations of examples taken from the section on syntax in Dr. Wilkins Sanscrit Grammar have been made into Tamil, Telugu, and Cannadi; from these, also, will appear the relation these languages bear to each other in the minuter parts of speech and in casual and temporal terminations.

SANSCRIT.

1 2, 3 4 5 6
Cumáràs seratè swairam rórúyantè cha náracàh
7 8 9 10 11
Jégiyantí cha gitajnyà mémriyanti rujájitàh.

TRANSLATION.

1 2 3 5 6 6 4 4 4
The children sleep freely and the infernal beings are continually crying;
9 7 7 7 8 11 11 11 11 10 10
The songsters are always singing, and those overcome by disease are always
10
dying.

TELUGU.

1 3 2 6 6 5 4
Cumárulu swéch,hagà nidrintsutsunnáru naracamulón undedivarunnu mickili
4 9 7 7 11 11 8
arutsutsunnáru gayaculu mickili pádutsunnáru rogamuchéta cottabaddavárunnu
10 10
bahu tsattsutsunnáru.

CANNADI.

1 3 2 6 6 4
Cumáreru yad,héchch,héyági nidrisut'táré naracadalli iruvarunnu héral'a
4 9 7 7 11 11
cúguttárè gayacaru ad,hicavági háduttárè rogadinda hodeyel-pattaverunnu
10 10
bahala sayittárè.

TAMIL.

1 3 3 3 2 6
Cuz'hendèigal' tam manadin padiacu nitterei-pannuckirárgal naragattil
6 5 4 4 9 7 7
ullavergálum nillámel cúppidugirárgal' páduvàr migavum páduckirárgal'
11 11 8 10 10
rogottinàl oducca-pattavergalum cureiyámel shágirárgal'.

The construction of the Sanscrit sentence is as follows. The figures throughout refer to the collocation of the Sanscrit.

1. A noun in the 1st case plural governing 2 a verb in the 3rd. per. plu. pres. of *sétè he sleeps.* 3 a noun in the 2d case neu. used adjectively, composed of *swa own* and *iram motion.* 4 the 3d per. plu. pres. of the reiterative form, medial voice, of *rauti he roars.* 5 a conjunction. 6 a derivative from *naracah* by the *tadd,hita* affix *an* with the meaning of the 7th or locative case, *being in a place.* 7 the same as 4 from *gáyati to sing.* 8 the same as 5. 9 a compound formed of *gítah* a song and *gnyah* part. past act. (*caprateya*) from *jánáti* to know. 10 the same as 4 from *mrityati to die.* 11 a compound from *rujà* disease fem. and *jitah* past part. pas. (*ctapratéya*) from *jayati to conquer.*

The construction of the Telugu sentence is ;

1. Sans. a noun in the first case plural. 3 an adverbial phrase, formed from *swéchch,ha,* of Sanscrit derivation, being from *swa own* and *ichch,hà desire,* and *gà,* changed from *cà* by *sandhi,* the inseparable part. from *cávadamu to be-become.* 2 the 3rd pers. plu. of the compound present, formed by *nidrintsutsu,* the gerund of the present tense, derived from *nidrà* Sans. *sleep,* and *unnáru,* the third per. plu. pres. of *undadamu to be-exist.* 6 Sans. a noun in the seventh

or locative case. 6. a compound formed by the aorist part. of *undádamu* and the plu. pro. *vádu he- that man.* 5 a conjunction; it is inseparably attached to the word it conjoins. 4 an adverb qualifying the following verb. 4 the same as 2 from the Telugu verb *aravádamu to roar.* 9 the same as 1. 7 an adverb. 7 the same as 2 from the Telugu verb *pádádamu to sing.* 11 Sans. a noun in the 3d, or instrumentive case. 11 a Telugu compound from *cótta* the inf. of *cóttádamu to beat, báddá,*by *sand,hi* for *páddá,* the past part. of *pádádamu to suffer,* used to form the passive voice, and the plu. of *vádu.* 8 the same as 5. 10 Sans. an adverb. 10 the same as 2 from the Tel. verb *tsávadámu to die.*

The construction of the Cannadi is exactly the same as the Telugu, one or two of the compounds only differing.

3 is composed of Sans. adverb *yathá as* and *ich,ha.* The verbs marked 2,4,7 and 10 are not compounds. 6 the 7th case is formed by the adjunct *alli place,* united to *naracadá* the genitive form of *naracam.* 7 is a compound used adverbially from *ad,hica excessive,* a Sans. crude noun, and *ági* the gerund of the past tense *agavadu to become.* The compound marked 11 is from the verbal noun *hodeyel the beating,* instead of the inf. as in Tel.

The construction of the Tamil is;

1 as in Tel. 3. the gen. plu. of the pronoun *tàn himself.* 3 the gen. of *manadu,* from the Sans. *mannas mind, will.* 3. the dat. of *padí a measure,* used as a preposition and signifying *according to.* 2 a hybrid compound formed from *nitterei,* the same as *nidrà* Sans. and *pánnudel to do-make,* the Tamil seldom allowing a simple verb to be formed from a Sanscrit word with a long final vowel. 6 as in Tel. 6 a compound formed by *ul'la,* indefinite part. of the defective verb *ul' to be- have,* and *avergal'* the plu. of the pro. *aven he- that man.* 5 as in Tel. 4 the neg. part. of *nilludel to stand-stay.* 4 this with 7 and 10 are simple verbs, as in Cannadi, not compounds, as in Tel. 9 an attributive noun from *pádudel to sing.* 7 the inf. of *migudel to increase,* with the conjunction *um* used adverbially. 7 as in Cannadi. 11 as in Telugu. 11 a compound from *oducca* the

inf. of *oduccudel to oppress* and *put ta* the same as in Tel. and Can. 8 as in Tel. 10 the neg. part. of *curēidel to lessen.* 10 as in Can.

In the preceding sentence the Sanscrit differs in every point from the southern dialects; in the following, the variation, except in the formation of cases, is not so great.

SANSCRIT.

1 2 3 4 5 6
Samyamáya s'rutam d,hattè narò dhermáya samyamam,

7 8 9 10 11 12
D,hermam mócsháya mèd,hávì d,hanam dànáya b,huctayé.

TRANSLATION.

9 4 3 2 2 1 6 5
A wise man keepeth the divine law for constraint, constraint for religion (and)

7 8 10 11 12
religion for salvation ; wealth for donation (and) for enjoyment.

TELUGU.

9 4 1 2 5 6
Méd,haviyaina narudu samyamamucoracu srutamunu dhermambucoracu samyama-

8 7 11 12 10
munu mócshambucoracu d,herrmamunu dánamucoracunu bhucticoracunu dhana-

3
munun dharintsutstunnádu.

CANNADI.

9 4 1 2 5 6
Méd,háviyáda manushyenu samy amaccóscara srutavannu d,hermaccóscara samya-

8 7 11 12
mavannu mócshaccóscara d,hermavanna dánaccóscaravágiyu b,huctigóscaravágiyu

10 3
d,hanavannu d,harisuttánè.

TAMIL.

9 4 1 2 5 8
Arivall'a manaden adaccattaccága vedatteiyun deramattuccágu adacatteiyum mattic-

7 11 12 10 3
cága derumatteiyum dánattuccágavum bógattaccàgavum danatteiyung càchirán.

CONSTRUCTION OF THE SANSCRIT.

1 a noun sub. neu. in the 4th or dative case. 2 the same in the 2d, or ac. governed by the following verb. 3 the third person sing. pres. medial voice, governing the several accusatives in the sentence. 4 noun sub. masc. in the 1st or nom. 5, 6, 7 and 8 the same as 1 and 2 respectively. 9 a noun of quality agreeing with *narah*; this word *méd,hávì,* has the force of an adjective, though it is actually, a substantive. 10 the same as 2. 11 and 12 the same as 1 &c.

CONSTRUCTION OF THE TELUGU.

9 a compound having the force of an adjective, formed by affixing, to the Sanscrit word, *aina* the past part. of *cávadamu to become.* 4 as in the Sans. formed by affixing the Tel. termination *udu.* 1 as in Sans. except that, in place of being declined, the case is formed from the sixth in *cu* by the adjunct *orucu for the sake of;* when *orucu* or *ósaram,* which has the same meaning, are added to this case the *drüttam* or nunnation, if interposed between the theme and affix is dropped; thus these compounds, though derived from *danamunucu,* become *danamuc' orucu* and *dánamuc' ósaram.* 2 as in the Sans. 5,6,8,7, 11 and 12, as in the Sanscrit, with the Tel. terminations and affixes; the two last are connected by the conjunction *nu and,* repeated after each. 10 as in the Sans. it takes the *drüttam* before the following *d,ha.* 3 the third person sing. pres. *of d,harintsadamu to dress - assume,* from the Sanscrit.

Note. The compound dative, answering to the Tádarthya chaturt, hi of the Sanscrit and to the noun governed by the proposition *for* in English, is formed in the three dialects from the fourth case in *cu* by the addition of the same or similar adjuncts; in Tel. by *ai, orucu* and *ósaram*; in Can. by *ági* and *óscaram,* and in Tamil by *ága* and *ósaram : ai* and *ági,* are the gerunds and *ága* is the inf. derived from the root *á be - become ; ósaram* in Tel. signifies *a side, inclination, bias,* but this and *orucu,* from *oray to join - obtain,* intimately correspond with the English term *sake,* as, like the latter, they are used only in the formation of this dative, the meaning of which may always be appropriately expressed by the phrase *for the sake of.*

The Canadi construction is exactly the same as the Tel. the datives are formed by adding *óscara for the sake of* to the fourth case in *cu.* 11 and 12 *ági,* the gerund of the past tense of *ágavadu to become,* is added to these datives, and the conjunction copulative *nu* is changed to *yu,* to mark their special connection with the following word.

CONSTRUCTION OF THE TAMIL.

9 a compound having the form of an adjective from *arivu knowledge* and *ul'lu* the part of the defective *ul' to have.* 4 as in Sans. 1 the dative case formed by adding *ága,* the inf. of *ádel to become,* to the dative of declension in *cu.* The sentence does not differ, otherwise than as here noticed, from the Telugu.

In the following short sentence and all similar constructions the Sanscrit agrees exactly with the southern dialects.

SANSCRIT.

1 2 3 4
Tasya bahu d,hanam esti.

TRANSLATION.

1 2 3 4
" *He possesses, or hath much wealth*: " or, nearer in Latin, *Illi multa res est.*

TELUGU.

, 2 3 4 , ,
Vániki bahu d,hanam unnœdi.

CANNADÍ.

1 2 3 4
Avenge héral'a d,hana vide.

TAMIL.

1 2 3 4 ,
Avenuccu micca porul' undu.

Again, in constructions like the following, when the *sati saptami,* or ablative case absolute, is used, as in Latin, or when the relative pronoun occurs, the Sanscrit idiom is totally different from that of the southern dialects; in these there is no relative pronoun, but the interrogative may, as these examples will shew, be used for it.

SANSCRIT.

1 3 4 5 6 7
Yas sa, servéshu b,hútéshu nasyetsu, na vinás'yeti.

TRANSLATION.

1 3 5 7 6 7 2 2
" *He who upon all things perishing does not perish*: " or in Latin *Ille qui,*
3 3 5 7
omnibus entibus periuntibus, non perit.

TELUGU.

1 4 5 1 67 2 ,
Samastamaina b,hùlamulu nasintsutsnudagà yevadu nas'intsadó ? vándu.

CANNADÍ.

1 4 5 1 , 2
Samasta b,hútangal' unasisuttirel ági yávenu nasisenò ? avenu.

TAMIL.

1 3 5 5 5 7 1 2
Bùtangal' ellámum násam adeiyum pozhudil násamadeiyán eveno ? avené.

In the Sanscrit sentence 3-4 and 5 have the form of the 7th or locative case and are in the grammatical connection denominated the ablative case absolute;

in Tel. this meaning is expressed by the gerund of the present tense of the verb *nasintsadamu,* united with the inf. of *undadamu to be,* and followed by the inseparable gerund of *Cávadamu to become*; literally *the destroying becoming to be.* The Can. is the same except that instead of the inf. the verbal noun *the being,* is used. The Tamil differs ; in this the future part. of the verb compounded of *násam* Sans. *destruction* and *adeidel to obtain-arrive* is followed by the 7th case of *poz,hadu time,* and the literal meaning, therefore, is *in the time in which* (*when*) *destruction shall have reached.* Again 1 and 2, the relative and it's antecedent, is in each of the southern dialects expressed by the interrogative pronoun *yevadu* with ò, the sign of dubitative interrogation, added, either to it, or to the verb it governs, followed by the words respecting which the doubt is expressed, or the question asked, so that the sense is *who may it be that is not destroyed? he.* The relative, however, may be as well, if not better, expressed, by any of the participles followed by the word which in the Sanscrit connection, would be the antecedent ; thus this example is properly in Telugu translated by
3 4 5 1-2-6 7
samastamaina bh,útamaulu nasintsutsundagá nasintsanivándu the last term being composed of *nasintsani* the negative of *nasintsadamu* united with the indicative pronoun *vándu.*

The preceding translations have been made into what may, not inappropriately, be called the Sanscrit dialect of the southern tongues; the terms employed being chiefly from that language, and, when they could be used without affectation, the same as in the original passages : in the translations of the following sentence, the pure native terms of the three dialects only are used.

SANSCRIT.

1 2 3 4 5 6
Dadátu sadbhyah sa suc,ham Haris smarát
7 8 9 10 11
Gopi ganó suyati cupyati irshàti,
12 13 14 15
Sma-róchetè druhyati tisht,hatè hnutè
16 17 18 19 20
'Slaghista yasmai spriihayaty as' apta cha.

TRANSLATION.

1 5 1 4 2 2 2 11 7 7
" *Let Hari grant happiness to the just, for whom the females of the cowherds,*

6 6 9 9 10 10 12 11 17
from desire, were calumnious, shewed anger, were pleasant, shewed malice,
15 13 16 18 20 19
waited, were sly and insidious, flattered, hoped & cursed."

NOTE. It will be observed that the English translation does not exactly express the meaning of the original, and, as this is carefully preserved in the other versions, it of course, disagrees with them.

TELUGU.

17 17 7 6 8 6 6 9
Yeveni gurinchi golla-ádavari gumpu tamacamu vella leni-tappul-encheno-
10 11 12 13 14 15 16
alegenò ortsaccapoyenò impayenò chedocórenò cátsiyundenò bonkenò pogadenò
18 19 3 5 2 1 2
córenò tit'tenò á Hari ped'dalacu hayn'itsugáca.

CANNADÍ.

17 17 7 8 6 9 10
Yávanan curittu gollatica gumpu soccuninda al'càjum-pattidò muniytó
11 12 13 14 15 16 18 19 3
sanasitò baitó keda-gorittó cădaconditló bonkitò hogal'itò gorittò baytò, antà
5 6 1 1
Hari val'l'evange sompannu codali.

TAMIL.

17 7 8 6 9 10
Evenuccága videiyàl' cùl'tam naseiyenàl az'haccàru-pattdidò munindadò
11 12 13 14 15
poràd'irundadó vinb'ànadò kèdaccorinadó càttucond'irundadó poccan-chon-
16 18 19 3 5 2
nadópugez'hndadò coradò túvinadò averri nellavugal' uccuchelvam coduccavum

The observations made on the preceding example, respecting the construction of the relative and antecedent in Sanscrit, and the modes of supplying it in the southern dialects, may be made on this. The original, in the work whence it is taken, exemplifies the government of the fourth or dative case by the several verbs which therein occur; in Telugu and Cannadí these verbs do not govern this case, but the *upapada dwitiya* of the Sanscrit with the *upaserga prati*; this, in these languages, is expressed by the accusative governed by *gurinchi or curitu-mark, determine,* used as a preposition : in Tamil these verbs may have the same government, or as in the translation into this language, they may govern the dative, as in the Sanscrit, with the preposition *for* as explained in the note on the foregoing example.

In translating this last sentence into the southern dialects, the difficulty has rather been in the selection of appropriate terms whereby to express the shades of meaning which the verbs, in tho original, convey; in general, however, it will be found difficult to express any sentiment clearly and precisely in Telugu or Cannadí, without using Sanscrit words in a greater or less proportion, while in Tamil, in the higher dialect (*Shen Tamiz'h*) especially, this may always be done with facility. Thus in the present examples, *smarah,* a name of the Indian Cupid, but signifying, the cause being put for the effect, *love,* is appropriately translated in Tamil *nasel sexual love* : in the other two dialects, however, there is no such native word, the Sanscrit *cámam* being used for it ; *tamacamu,* the word substituted in Telugu, means *lust* merely, and *soccu* in Cannadí *desire* in general. Again, *asapta* the third person of the past tense *lang* of *sapati he curses,* cannot be rendered strictly into any of the three dialects, except by a term from the same root ; *tittádámu* in Telugu, and *bayvadu* in Cannadí, mean to *vilify-abuse,* either of these, *v* being substituted for the *b* of the last, may be used in Tamil, but *túridel* is preferred, as it is more frequently applied when abuse by women is meant. Again *hnuti* in Sanscrit means to *dissemble* this is exactly rendered by *bonkadamu* in Tel. and Can. but *poccam* in Tam. though derived from the same root, scarcely extends to this meaning, nor is it in common use.

To enable a comparison to be made of the superior dialects of the southern languages with each other, and with the Sanscrit, the following versions of an English sentence have been made ; they are necessarily in verse as this is the appropriate style of the three dialects and, and with the preceding observations, will sffiuciently establish the positions maintained at the commencement of this note; relative to the affiliation of the Telugu.

1 2 3 4 5 6
When thou art an anvil, endure like an anvil ;
7 8
when a hammer, strike like a hammer.

TAMIL.

CURAĹ-VEŃBA.

6 5 4 41 2 3
Adeiyel'át't at'tel ád ngi ad'eiyelày
12 11 10 10
Suttiyel at't àt'tel ad i.

TELUGU.

DWIPADA.

6 5 4 1 2·3 10
Dáy velan an'igi diyyai venca
12 11
Tíyaca suttiya tiruna cot'tu.

CANNADI.

DWIPADA.

Ádiyallu sari boggi yági yà gallu.
Man'di tirasada chamalige saribadi.

SANSCRIT.

ANUSH'TUP, VRUTTAM.

Cútò b,hútwà cúta iva vinamya twam ayóg,hanah
B,hùtwà'yog,hanavad gad,ham d,hairyavàn prahara dwishah.

CHAPTER FIRST.

TELOOGOO ALPHABET.

THE letters in the Teloogoo, as in most other Indian alphabets, are apt, 1
on a first view, to appear unnecessarily numerous. Some syllables even seem admitted into the alphabet, as simple characters. The dipthongs are represented by separate signs, not, as in English, by the coalition of two vowels. There is one set of symbols for initial unconnected vowels; another for the same vowels when joined with consonants to form syllables; and in both of these, the long vowels are distinguished from the short. Among the consonants also, the aspirated letters are represented by distinct symbols, not by a combination, as in our own language; and the harsh are distinguished from the soft letters. But those who may at first question the utility of so many letters in the Teloogoo, will perhaps relinquish most of their objections, when they find that the variety of sound in this language is greater, and better represented, than in English. On the length of a vowel, on the harsh or soft pronunciation of a consonant, depends, in a thousand instances, the meaning of a word; and, consequently, it is of greater importance, in Teloogoo, that each different shade of sound should be accurately marked; than in our own language, in which, comparatively, few words materially resemble each other.

2 Notwithstanding the Teloogoo alphabet may be thought to contain some superfluous characters, it will readily be admitted that, in consistency, it is superior to our own. The sound attached to each letter remains constantly inherent in it: the coalition of words may cause one character to be changed for another, or may require the elision or the insertion of letters; but no association whatever can render any letter mute, nor can any change, or combination, give to one or more characters the sound belonging to another. The student, therefore, after once acquiring the correct sound of the Teloogoo letters, immediately pronounces every word with accuracy, and very little practice enables him to read with fluency and precision :—while a foreigner, who attempts to acquire a correct English pronunciation, scarcely ever arrives at the full attainment of his object. The proper pronunciation of our words, indeed, depends more upon the combination of our letters, than upon any fixed sound inherent in each separate character: and, in this respect, a person commencing the study of our language, for a long time, labors under the difficulties experienced by those, who are left to discover the meaning of the principal words in a sentence, without any other aid than what the context affords.

3 All Native Grammarians concur in reducing the number of letters in the Teloogoo alphabet to thirty seven ; by excluding from it forty four characters which they acknowledge to belong to the language, but will not admit into the alphabet. They reject nineteen letters as peculiar to words of Sanscrit origin; fifteen small connected vowels, as only abbreviated forms of the large initial unconnected vowels ; eight characters, as merely marks for certain consonants when doubled; and two, as contracted signs for certain letters which they have retained. But, in giving a general view of the Teloogoo alphabet, I shall insert all the letters which they have rejected ; for they belong to the language, as much as those which they have admitted ; and the whole are equally unknown to an English reader. Inclusive of these, the Teloogoo alphabet will be found to consist of no less than eighty one different symbols.

TELOOGOO ALPHABET.

VOWELS.

Initial unconnected vowels.	Connected vowels.	Powers.
అ	✓	u
ఆ	ా	a
ఇ	ి	i
ఈ	ీ	ee
ఉ	ు	ꝏ
ఊ	ూ	oo
ఋ	ృ	roo
ౠ	ౄ	roo
ఌ	ౢ	loo
ఎ	ె	ĕ
ఏ	ే	ē
ఐ	ై	ue
ఒ	ొ or ొ	ŏ
ఓ	ో or ో	ō
ఔ	ౌ	uo
15	15	

CONSONANTS.

Consonants.	Double forms of some consonants.	Powers.	Consonants.	Double forms of some consonants.	Powers.
క	్క	k	21	2	
ఖ		k,hu	న	్న	n
గ		g	ప		p
ఘ		g,h	ఫ		p,h
ఙ		gnu	బ		bu
చ		ts	భ		b,h
చ		ch	మ	్మ	m
ఛ		ch,h	య	్య	y
జ		dzu	ర	్ర	r
జ		ju	ల	్ల	lu
ఝ		j,h	వ	్వ	v
ఞ		nyu	శ		sh
ట		tu	ష		sh
ఠ		t,h	స		s
డ		d	హ		h
ఢ		d,h	ళ		l
ణ		nu	క్ష		ksh
త	్త	t	ఱ		rru
థ		t,h	ం		n or m
ద		d	ఁ		n
ధ		d,h	20 ః	6	h
21	2		41	8	

SIGNS.

ε— . . . . r

ε— . . . . n

2

15 Initial unconnected vowels.
15 Connected vowels.
41 Consonants.
8 Double forms of some consonants.
2 Signs.

81 Letters.

Of these eighty one letters, the initial vowels ఋ *roo*, ౠ *roo*, and ఌ *loo*, the ten aspirates ఖ *k,hu*, ఘ *g,h*, ఛ *ch,h*, ఝ *j,h*, ఠ *ṭ,h*, ఢ *ḍ,h*, థ *t,h*, ధ *d,h*, ఫ *p,h*, and భ *b,h*, the nasals ఙ *gnu* ఞ *nyu*, and the consonants శ *sh*, ష *sh*, క్ష *ksh*, and హ *h*, are the nineteen characters stated by Teloogoo Grammarians to be peculiar to words of Sanscrit origin. To these, the connected vowels ృ *roo*, and ౄ *roo*, should also be added. For, had not all the connected vowels been rejected from the alphabet, as marks instead of letters, a place would have been originally assigned to these two characters, in the list of symbols peculiar to Sanscrit derivatives. 4

Although the letter శ *sh*, is, as above stated, peculiar to Sanscrit, modern authors admit, that, Sanscrit derivatives excepted, all Teloogoo words which have the letter స *s*, followed by the connected vowels ి *i*, ీ *ee*, ె *ĕ*, or ే *ē*, may change the స *s*, into శ *sh*; hence, చేసి *chēsi*, or చేశి *chēshi*, *having done*. చేసెను *chēsĕnoo*, or చేశెను *chēshĕnoo*, *he, she or it, did.* సిగ్గు *siggoo*, or శిగ్గు *shiggoo*, *shame*. 5

The short initial vowels ఎ *ĕ*, ఒ *ŏ*, and their corresponding connected vowels ె *ĕ*, ొ *ŏ*, (excluded by Grammarians as being merely marks) together with the consonants ౘ *ts*, ౙ *dzu*, ళ *ḷu*, ఱ *rru*, and ఁ *ṇ*, are to be found in words of the pure Teloogoo only. 6

The other letters of the alphabet are common to all Teloogoo words, whether derived from the Sanscrit, or otherwise. 7

8 The letter క్ష *ksh* has been included in the Alphabet; but, as it is a compound of *s k* and ష *sh*, it is rejected by some authors.

VOWELS.

Initial Unconnected Vowels.

9 The fifteen initial vowels, అ *u*, ఆ *a*, ఇ *i*, ఈ *ee*, ఉ *oo*, ఊ *oo*, ఋ *roo*, ౠ *roo*, ఌ *loo*, ఎ *ĕ*, ఏ *ē*, ఐ *ue*, ఒ *ŏ*, ఓ *ō*, and ఔ *uo*, are *emphatically* termed by Teloogoo Grammarians ప్రాణములు. *lives*, or *living letters*; because they are supposed to possess, within themselves, a perfect and independent existence or sound. They are purely initial, and are always written separately, unconnected with consonants or other characters. Like our capital letters, the initial vowels are to be found at the commencement of a phrase or sentence only, and never, in grammatical compositions at least, at the beginning of each word; except when words are written by themselves, as in a dictionary or vocabulary; for in a correct Teloogoo sentence, each word coalesces with the following one; the whole becomes a chain of continued links; and there is no beginning, or place for an initial vowel, except at the commencement of the sentence itself.

10 In naming these characters, the Sanscrit word కారము *karumoo* is affixed to each; thus, అకారము *ukarumoo* u, ఇకారము *ikarumoo* i, and so on.

11 The initial vowels are written on a line with the consonants, never either below, or above them.

Connected Vowels.

12 When combined with consonants to form syllables, the abovementioned vowels take quite a different shape. In this new form they are inseparable from consonants; and, from their constantly preserving a servile connection with some of these characters, Teloogoo writers have been induced to view them, in this shape, rather as abbreviated forms of the initial vowels abovementioned, than as independent letters. They are here again exhibited, opposite the initial vowels which they respectively represent; and the particular appellation given to each is attached to it.

అ u in it's connected form becomes. ✓ u which in Teloogoo is named. తలకట్టు

ఆ a . . . . do. . . . . ా a . . . . . do. . . . . . . దీర్ఘము

ఇ i . . . . do. . . . . ి i . . . . . do. . . . . . . గుడి or గుడుసు

ఈ ee . . . . do. . . . . ీ ee . . . . do. . . . . . . గుడిదీర్ఘము

ఉ oo . . . . do. . . . . ు oo . . . . do. . . . . . . కొమ్ము

ఊ oo . . . . do. . . . . ూ oo . . . . do. . . . . . . కొమ్ముదీర్ఘము

ఋ roo . . . . . . do. . . . . ృ roo . . . . do. . . . . . . వట్రువసుడి

ౠ roo . . . . . do. . . . ౄ roo . . . do . . . . . . వట్రువసుడిదీర్ఘము

ఌ lω . . . . do. . . . ౢ lω . . . . do. . . . . . . ఌత్వము

ఎ ĕ . . . . do. . . . . ె ĕ . . . . do. . . . . ఎత్వము

ఏ ē . . . . do. . . . . ే ē . . . . do. . . . . ఏత్వము

ఒ ŏ . . . . do. . . . . ొ ŏ or ొ . do. . . . . ఒత్వము

ఓ ō . . . . do. . . . . ో ō or ో . do. . . . . ఓత్వము

ఐ ue . . . . do. . . . ై ue . . . do. . . . . . . ఐత్వము

ఔ uo . . . . . . do. . . . . ౌ uo . . . do. . . . . ఔత్వము

The connected vowels ✓ *u*, ా *a*, ి *i*, ీ *ee*, ె *ĕ*, ే *ē*, ొ *ŏ*, ో *ō*, and ౌ *uo*, are written above the consonants to which they are attached; ు *oo* ూ *oo* are written to the right of them; ృ *roo*, and ౄ *roo*, are placed partly to the right side of consonants, partly below them; and of ై *ue*, the upper part is written above, the lower part below the consonants. 13

When the initial vowels ఒ *ŏ*, ఓ *ō*, are represented in their connected forms, by a compound of the letters ె *ĕ*, and ు *oo*, ూ *oo*; thus, ొ *ŏ*, ో *ō*, the ె *e* is written above, and the ు *oo*, ూ *oo*, to the right side of the consonants. 14

The connected vowel ౢ *lω*, is always written below the consonant to which it is attached. 15

CONSONANTS.

With the view to facilitate the acquirement of the Teloogoo alphabet, the connected vowels have been separated from the consonants, to some of which they must invariably be joined. For the same reason, in arranging the conso- 16 nants, in the order in which they are usually placed by Grammarians, they are exhibited distinct from the connected vowels.

	Hard. పరుషలు		Soft. సరళలు		
	k	*k,hu*	*g*	*g,h*	*gnu*
Gutteral or కంఠ్యము......1st. Vurga	క	ఖ	గ	ఘ	ఙ
	ts ch	*ch,h*	*dzu ju*	*j,h*	*nyu*
Palatal or తాలవ్యము.... 2d. do.	చ చ	ఛ	జ జ	ఝ	ఞ
	tu	*t,h*	*d*	*d,h*	*nu*
Cerebral or మూర్ధన్యము 3d. do.	ట	ఠ	డ	ఢ	ణ
	t	*t,h*	*d*	*d,h*	*n*
Dental or దంత్యము..... 4th. do.	త	థ	ద	ధ	న
	p	*p,h*	*bu*	*b,h*	*m*
Labial or ఓష్ఠ్యము.... 5th. do.	ప	ఫ	బ	భ	మ

y	*r*	*lu*	*v*	*sh*	*sh*	*s*	*h*	*l*	*ksh*	*rru*
య	ర	ల	వ	శ	ష	స	హ	ళ	క్ష	ఱ

17 The consonants have not peculiar appellations, like the connected vowels; but are named in the same manner as the initial vowels; viz. by affixing to them the Sanscrit word కారము *karumoo;* thus, బకారము *bukarumoo* bee, దకారము *dukarumoo* dee, &c. To distinguish the letter ర *r* from ఱ *rru,* the term ఱకారము *rrukarumoo* is applied to the latter only; the ర *r* retains its original Sanscrit name, రేఫ *rēp,hu.*

18 The ten consonants ఖ *k,hu,* ఙ *gnu,* జ *dzu,* జ *ju,* ఞ *nyu,* ట *tu,* ణ *nu,* బ *bu,* ల *lu,* and ఱ *rru,* have the sound of the first vowel ˘ *u,* inherent; and are therefore represented in English characters by syllables; thus k,hu ju &c. but all the other consonants specified above, in order to obtain utterance, must be joined to some of the connected vowels. It is of much importance to the reader clearly to understand, that neither the consonants, nor the connected vowels, exactly correspond with what European authors call *a letter.* They have been separated from each other, merely with the view to facilitate the progress of the

early student: but this separation of them will lead to false ideas, unless it be at the same time borne in mind that, in Teloogoo, they are never so separated, and are not significant symbols except when compounded with each other. Indeed the consonants and connected vowels form together a set of inseparable syllabic characters, generally compared by Teloogoo writers to *animated bodies*; the life, or vowel, giving existence or articulation to the consonant, which, on separation from it, becomes a mere dead symbol, void of every sound. As Teloogoo words are composed chiefly of these syllabic characters, terminating with a vowel, a final consonant is seldom found in the language. When it does occur, the consonant cannot, as in English, stand alone. Without any sign, the ten letters before mentioned represent syllables ending in the vowel *u*, and the other consonants represent no articulation whatever. In the case of a final consonant, therefore, it is necessary to affix to it the sign ్, to denote that the sound is retained, but obstructed. Thus, final *k*, *k,h*, or *g*, must be written క్ ఖ్ గ్ never క ఖ గ without any sign, as before exhibited.

To form syllables, the connected vowels are added to the consonants, in the following manner. 19

ku.	*ka*	*ki*	*kee*	*kω*	*koo*	*krω*	*kroo*	*klω*	*kĕ*	*kē*	*kŏ*	*kō*	*kue*	*kuo*
క	కా	కి	కీ	కు	కూ	కృ	కౄ	కౢ	కె	కే	కొ	కో	కై	కౌ
k,hu	*k,ha*	*k,hi*	*k,hee*	*k,hω*	*k,hoo*	*k,hrω*	*k,hroo*	*&c.*	*&c.*	*&c.*				
ఖ	ఖా	ఖి	ఖీ	ఖు	ఖూ	ఖృ	ఖౄ							
gu	*ga*	*gi*	*gee*	*gω*	*goo*	*grω*	*groo*	*glω*	*gĕ*	*gē*	*gŏ*	*gō*	*gue*	*guo*
గ	గా	గి	గీ	గు	గూ	గృ	గౄ	గౢ	గె	గే	గొ	గో	గై	గౌ

It is not requisite to add the ✓ *u*, to the ten letters mentioned in No. 18; because the sound represented by that letter is already inherent in them. 20

In adding to the consonants the connected vowels ు *ω*, ూ *oo*, ృ *rω*, and ౄ *roo*, which are placed to the right of these letters, it is necessary previously to write the connected vowel ✓ *u*, above the consonants; except above those in which the sound of that character is inherent: because this sign, 21 which is termed తలకట్టు *bound to the head,* invariably retains it's place at the top of the consonants to which it can be attached, unless it's situation is occupied by another symbol.

22 For the same reason also, in adding to the consonants ఘ *g,h,* ఝ *j,h,* మ *m,* య *y,* and హ *h,* the long vowel ా *a,* which is affixed to the latter part of these letters, the ✓ affixed to the former part, is not removed; thus, మా *ma,* యా *ya,* &c: but as the consonant హ *h* already terminates with a symbol resembling ా *a,* when that vowel is added to this letter, it is written thus, హా the mark ఁ being substituted for ా *a.*

23 Instead of adding the long vowel ీ *ee,* to the consonants, ఘ *g,h,* ఝ *j,h,* ష *sh,* and స *s,* the short vowel ి *i,* with the symbol ా, is frequently used to represent it's sound; thus, we may write either సీ *see* or సిా *see.* In such cases, the symbol ా, which is named దీర్ఘము *long,* is to be considered as lengthening the short vowel ి *i,* rather than as representing the long vowel ా *a;* indeed this sign, in two other instances, is used to lengthen the short vowels; as ూ *oo,* from ు oo, and ౄ *roo,* from ృ *roo.*

24 In adding the long vowel ీ *ee,* to the letter మ *m,* it must always be written in the manner above mentioned; thus, మిా *mee,* never మీ: in adding it to the consonant హ *h,* it is written thus హిా *hee,* or హీ. The vowel ి *i,* or ీ *ee,* can never be added to the consonant య *y:* to express, in Teloogoo letters, the sounds *yi,* or *yee,* we write the consonant య *y;* in the former case, without the ✓ *u,* తలకట్టు, and in the latter, with the ా దీర్ఘము, and under it we place it's double form ్య *y,* thus నెయ్యి *nĕyi, ghee,* ఇయ్యీత చెట్టు, *Iyeeta chĕttoo, this date tree.*

25 In adding the short vowel ొ *ŏ* or ె ు *ŏ,* to the consonants ఘ *g,h,* ఝ *j,h,* మ *m,* and య *y,* it is invariably written in the latter form, never in the former shape; thus, మొ *mŏ,* యొ *yŏ,* &c. and in adding to these consonants the long vowel ో *ō* or ెూ *o,* it is also written in the latter form only; but, in this case, the last part of these consonants themselves are considered as representing the ు of ూ; and, therefore, instead of adding ూ to the consonant, the ా or దీర్ఘ

ము only is added; thus, మో *mō* యో *yō* &c. This latter rule is occasionally applicable to the consonants స *s*, and హ *h*, which, joined with long ూ ో *ō*, are frequently written thus సో *sō*, హో *hō*.

The letters న *n*, & స *s*, and వ *v*, & ప *p*, when separated from the connected 26
vowels, are respectively represented by the same characters; but, like the other consonants before mentioned, they are invariably accompanied by some connected vowel, and they are distinguished from each other, by the different modes in which the connected vowels are added to them; న *n*, and వ *v*, are always united with the vowels; thus ను *nu*, వు *vu*, వూ *vuo*, but స *s*, and ప *p*, have the connected vowels written separately from them; as in the syllables సు *su*, పు *pu*, పూ *puo*.

Thus also the shape of the letter ర *r*, as given in the foregoing list of the con- 27
sonants, is the same as that of ం *n* or *m*, hereafter noticed; the latter, however, is never joined with any of the connected vowels; as అంటె *untĕ*, a part of the verb అను *unco*, *to say*. పాపం *papum*, *sin*, &c. while the former is always found with some of them united to it, in the following manner; రు *ru*, రా *ra*, రొ *rŏ*, &c. The student, therefore, can have little difficulty in distinguishing the one from the other.

Though native Grammarians, in enumerating the letters of the alphabet, 28
consider చ *ts* to be different from చ *ch*, and జ *dzu* to be distinct from జ *ju*, they are respectively represented by the same characters; and, in fact, they are only two letters, each possessing two distinct sounds, which has induced Grammarians to consider them as four separate characters.

Following the arrangement of the Sanscrit, the twenty-five first Teloogoo 29
consonants have been classed by native writers in five *Vurgus* or classes, each containing five letters, as arranged above in horizontal lines. (see No. 16.)

The fifth consonant of each *Vurgu* or Class is a nasal; and, in Sanscrit deri- 30
vatives, if a nasal immediately precede another consonant, without the intervention of a vowel, it must be that particular nasal only which belongs to the same *Vurgu* as the consonant itself; for instance, in such words, if a nasal im-

mediately precede any of the 4 first letters in the 3d *Vurgu* it must be ఞ *nu* only, if it precede any of the 4 first letters in the 4th *Vurgu*, it must be ణ *n*, and, if it precede any of the 4 first letters in the 5th *Vurgu*, it must be మ *m*, and not any other nasal. But this rule does not apply to corruptions from the Sanscrit, or to words of the pure Teloogoo, or of the common dialect. The nasal before a consonant, without an intervening vowel, is, in such words, represented either by the sign of the letter ణ *n*, viz. ౯ *n*, or by the character ం *n* or *m*, or ఁ *n*, hereafter mentioned.

31 Besides this division of the first 25 consonants into *Vurgus* or Classes, according to the principles of Sanscrit Grammar, there is a classification of the consonants which is peculiar to the Teloogoo itself, and an intimate acquaintance with this arrangement of the alphabet, which pervades every part of the language, is of the highest importance to a correct grammatical knowledge of the Teloogoo. The chapter which follows, on the changes of the letters, (perhaps the most difficult and intricate part of the Grammar,) will be absolutely unintelligible, unless due attention be paid to this classification. It is as follows.

32 The first perpendicular line in the forgoing arrangement of the consonants (No. 16,) containing the first letter in each of the five *Vurgus*, Viz. క *k*, చ *ts* or *ch*, ట *t*, త *t*, and ప *p*, forms the first class; and these letters are denominated పరుషలు or *hard letters.*

33 The third perpendicular line in the above arrangement of the consonants (No. 16,) consisting of the third letter in each *Vurgu*, viz. గ *g*, జ *dzu* or *ju*, డ *d*, ద *d*, and బ *b*, which are termed సరళలు or *soft letters*, constitutes the second class.

34 The third class includes all the remaining consonants in the foregoing classification (No. 16.) The consonants in this class are termed స్థిరలు, or *fixed letters*; from their not being liable to those changes, to which, as hereafter explained, the letters of the other two classes are subject.

35 The letters ం *n or m*, ఁ *n*, and ః *h*, which conclude the list of consonants in the view of the whole alphabet given in page 4, are omitted from the foregoing

arrangement of the consonants in page 8; because the remarks which follow that arrangement do not apply to them. In contradistinction to all the other consonants, these three letters are never joined either to the connected vowels, or to any other characters whatever.

Double forms of some Consonants.

When a consonant is doubled, the one character is placed under the other, and 36
the lower of the two is written without any of the connected vowels, the subsequent vowel being attached to the upper one only; thus, పెద్ద *pĕddu, great.* This rule however does not apply to the following consonants, of which each has its respective double form. viz.

క	k in it's double form is written	్క
ట	t .... do.	్ట
న	n .... do.	్న
మ	m .... do.	్మ
య	y .... do.	్య
ర	r .... do.	్ర
ల	l .... do.	్ల
వ	v .... do.	్వ

These eight consonants, when doubled, are written first in their original 37
shape, and their second form is then written below them; thus, అక్క *ukku, an elder sister,* కట్టి *kutti, a knife.* అన్న *unnu, an elder brother.* అమ్మ *ummu, a mother, a respectful female appellation.* అయ్య *uyyu, sir, a respectful male appellation.* కర్ర *kurru, a staff.* ఇల్లు *illoo, a house.* అవ్వ *uvvu, a grand mother.*

If one consonant follow another without the intervention of a vowel, the 38
last is written below the first; and if the last be one of those abovementioned which has a double form, it is written in it's second or double form, not in it's original shape; thus, అష్ట *ushtu, eight.* ఆత్మ *atmu, the soul.*

When the double form of య *y*, namely ్య, follows another consonant, the 39
subsequent vowel, if ా *a*, ు *ω*, or ూ *oo*, may be attached either to the con-

sonant, or to the ్య ; thus న్యా *nya*, or న్యా *nya*, న్యు *nyoo*, or న్యు *nyoo*, న్యూ *nyoo*, or న్యూ *nyoo*. The same rule applies if the subsequent vowel be long ో or ొ ో *ō*; but, when this vowel is joined to the ్య *y*, the latter form only is used, and the ు of ూ being omitted, the ో దీర్ఘము alone is affixed to the ్య, the preceding ె ఎత్వము being written above the consonant; thus, న్యో *nyō* or న్యో *nyō*, or న్యో *nyō*. In all other cases where ్య or other double forms are used, the subsequent vowel is attached to the consonant only, never to the double form; thus, ర్యీ *ryee* &c.

SIGNS.

40 The consonants have two auxiliary signs, viz. ర్ *r* and న్ *n*: the former is used to represent the letter ర *r*, and the latter the letter న *n*, when these letters precede another consonant without the intervention of a vowel; but, though pronounced before the consonant, ర్ *r*, is written after it; thus, అర్కుడు *urkoondoo, the sun.* The న్ *n* also represents న *n*, at the end of a word, thus పోయెన్ *pōyen, he she* or *it went.*

PRONUNCIATION.

It is not difficult to communicate, to an English reader, the proper articulation of those Teloogoo characters, of which the pronunciation corresponds exactly with the familiar sound attached to some English letter; but it is scarcely possible to convey, in writing, a just conception of sounds altogether foreign to the ear. Grammar, by instructing us in the theory of a language, may enable us to read it with intelligence, and to write it with correctness; but no book can teach the practical use of a language, and the voice of an instructor is necessary, to communicate the full force and tone of a letter, representing some articulation altogether unknown to his pupil. A few concise rules, however, regarding the proper pronunciation of the most difficult Teloogoo letters, may assist the student; but, without the aid of a native instructor, they will fail to afford satisfactory information. I shall accordingly attempt to explain in the Roman character, the sound attached to each; and, in doing so, shall avail myself of the system of Dr. Gilchrist, not less because it is the best with which I am acquainted, than because most of those into whose hands this work may fall will probably have acquired a knowledge of it, by the perusal of some of that Gentleman's numerous and valuable publications, on the Hindoostanee, which is the universal language of the Mussulmans throughout the Peninsula.

VOWELS.

The duration of the sound of the vowels is divided into హ్రస్వ *short*, దీర్ఘ *long*, and ప్లుత *continuous*, the first occupying one, the second two, and the last three moments of time; and these measures of sound apply both to the initial and connected forms of the vowels. The vowels అ *u*, ఇ *i*, ఉ *ω*, ఋ *rω*, ఎ *ĕ*, and ఒ *ŏ*, have each three measures of sound; namely, the short, the long, and the continuous; the vowel ఌ *lω* has no intermediate sound, but the extreme short and continuous sounds only; and the vowels ఐ *ue*, and ఔ *uo*, are both long, and continuous, but not short. The short and long vowels are considered so different as to be represented by distinct letters, but it has not been thought necessary to distinguish the continuous measure of sound by separate characters. 41

The initial అ, and its connected form ‿, have the sound of *u*, as in *tun, sun*, or of the *o* in *come, done*. This sound must not be confounded with the other sound given to *u* in English, as in *cure, sure*, &c. 42

The initial ఆ, and its connected form ా, have the sound of *a*, as in *all, call, tall,*

do......ఇ......do......ి......do. short *i*, as in *fit, kill.*

do......ఈ......do......ీ......do. long *ee*, as in *feet, keel.*

do......ఉ......do......ు......do. short *ω*, as in *wool.*

do......ఊ......do......ూ......do. long *oo*, as in *moon, boon.*

do......ఋ......do......ృ......do. short *rω*, as in *rook.*

do......ౠ......do......ౄ......do. long *roo*, as in *room.*

do......ఌ......do......ౢ......do. short *lω*, as in *look.*

do......ఎ......do......ె......do. short *ĕ*, as in *they*, or as *ay* in *may say* &c.

do......ఏ......do......ే......do. long *ē*, as in the same words lengthened.

do......ఒ......do......ొ or ‿ do. short *ŏ*, as in *note.*

do......ఓ......do......ో or ‿ do. long *ō*, as in *no, lo.*

do......ఐ......do......ై......do *ue*, as the word *eye*, or as the *uy* in [*buy.*]

do......ఔ......do......ౌ......do. *uo* or *ou* in *thou* or of *ow* in *how.*

43 Each of the long vowels should be pronounced full and broad, and the voice should dwell upon them twice as long as upon the short vowels, which should be sounded as short as possible.

44 When the sound of the vowel ఇ *i* comes after another vowel, it is expressed by the consonant య *y*, (written without the ు *u*,) and that of ఈ by the character యీ; thus, రాయి *rai, a stone.* బోయీ *bōee a palanqueen-bearer.*

45 The long vowel ఏ and its connected form ే *ē* in some cases, which must be learned by practice, as they can scarcely be embraced by any rule, instead of the pronunciation before mentioned as that generally attached to them, take a sound nearly approaching to యా *ya*, and some what resembling the final sound produced by the bleating of sheep; hence, perhaps మేక *mēku* a *sheep*; thus also, నేల *nēlu, the ground*, and నేరము *nērumoo, a crime* are pronounced nearly as if written న్యాల *nyalu*, న్యారము *nyarumoo*; and, in the common dialect, they are often so erroneously written.

46 The sound above assigned to the vowels ఋ *roo*, ౠ *roo*, & ఌ *loo*; as well as to their connected forms, ృ *roo*, ౄ *roo*, and ౢ *loo*, is that which properly belongs to these characters in the Teloogoo language; and which is invariably given to them by all the natives in the northern provinces of the Peninsula. In the middle provinces, the *r* and *l* are pronounced with the tongue mor curved towards the roof of the mouth, and the *oo* less distinctly, with an inclination to the sound of the French *u*, and to the southward, these letters assume the sounds of ri-ree-and lee-given to them by Sanscrit Grammarians.

CONSONANTS.

47 It is chiefly in the pronunciation of the consonants that difficulty is experienced. ఖ *k,hu*, ఘ *g,h*, ఛ *ch,h*, ఝ *j,h*, ఠ *t,h*, ఢ *d,h*, థ *t,h*, ధ *d,h*, ఫ *p,h*, భ *b,h*, the ten aspirated consonants, peculiar to Sanscrit derivatives, are not, at the commencement of a word, familiar to an English ear; but they occur frequently in our language in the middle of compound terms; the sound of the *h* flowing, in an easy gentle manner, immediately after that of the *k, g, d*, &c. which precedes it, without the least articulation intervening; thus,

the sound of ఖ *k,hu* may be exemplified by that of the *k,h* in *ink,horn*.

do..... ఘ *g,h*......... do......... *g,h* in *dog,herd*.

do..... ఛ *ch,h*......... do......... *ch,h* in *church,hill*.

do..... థ *t,h*......... do......... *t,h* in *that,house*.

do..... ధ *d,h*......... do......... *d,h* in *ad,here*.

do..... భ *b,h*......... do......... *b,h* in *ab,hor*.

do..... ఫ *p,h*......... do......... *p,h* in *up,hill*, and so on.

క *k*, and it's double form ్క *k*, have the sound of the English *k*, as in *king*. 48

గ *g*, has the hard sound of *g* as in *go*, *gun*, &c. never it's soft sound as in *ginger* &c. 49

ఙ *gnu* has the peculiar nasal sound of *gn*, as in the French words *ignorance*, *digne* &c. 50

చ and జ have each two sounds. చ is pronounced either hard, as *ch* in *beach*; or soft, as *ts* in *beats*: and జ is sounded either hard, as *j* in *jar*; or soft, as *dz* in *torridzone*. The soft sounds *ts* and *dz* are peculiar to the Teloogoo; and therefore, when చ or జ occur in words of Sanscrit origin, they are invariably to be pronounced hard; thus, చంద్రుడు *chundrœndœ the moon*, జడుడు *judœndœ*, *a fool*, never can be pronounced *tsundrœndœ dzudœndœ*. In Teloogoo, both the hard and soft sounds are to be found; but the rule is simple for ascertaining which of the two is to be given to these letters; for if చ or జ be followed by the connected vowels ి *i*, ీ *ee*, ె *ĕ*, ే *ē*, or ై *ue* they are respectively pronounced hard, as *ch*, and *j*; thus, చేత *chētu*, *by*, జెట్టి *jĕtti*, *a wrestler*; but if followed by any other vowel, they always take the soft sounds *ts* and *dz*, as in చక్కెర *tsukkĕru*, *sugar*. చోటు *tsōtœ*, *a place*. జోడు *dzōdœ*, *a pair*. 51

ఞ *nya*, sounds like *n* before *y*, or as *ni* in the word *onion*. 52

ట *ṭ* డ *ḍ* and ణ *ṇ* are the harshest possible sounds of *t*, *d*, and *n*, formed by curving back the tongue, and forcibly striking the under part of it, against the roof of the mouth. 53

54 త *t* ద *d* and న *n* must be pronounced very soft, the tongue being protruded, in an easy manner, almost between the teeth; the sound of *t* in *tube*, of *d* in *duke*, and of *n* in *no*, will convey some idea of the proper pronunciation of these letters.

55 The pronunciation of త *t* ద *d* and న *n* is more soft, and that of ట *t* డ *d* and ణ *n̲* much harsher, than the sound of the English letters *t d* and *n*: but all endeavours to convey in writing an accurate idea of the correct pronunciation of these letters must, I fear, prove very inadequate to the purpose.

56 ప *p*, has the sound of *p*, as in *pure*.

బ *b*, has the sound of *b*, as in *bold*.

మ *m*, and its double form ్మ *m*, have the sound of *m*, as in *man*.

య *y*, ... do. . . . . ్య *y*, ... do. . . . . of *y*, as in *yet*.

ర *r*, ... do. . . . . ్ర *r*, ... do. . . . . of *r*, as in *river*.

ల *l*, ... do. . . . . ్ల *l*, ... do. . . . . of *l*, as in *billow*.

వ *v*, ... do. . . . . ్వ *v*, ... do. . . . . of *v*, as in *vain*.

57 శ. *sh* has a very soft smooth sound, between that of the *s* in the word *sing*, and of the *sh* in *shine*, but approaching more to the former, than to the latter sound.

58 ష *s̲h̲*, is the harshest sound of *sh*, as in *push*, *bush* &c.

59 స *s*, has the sound of *s*, as in *sister*; never as in *dismal*, *his*, *rosy* &c.

60 హ *h*, has the sound of *h*, as in *hair*. When this letter immediately precedes another consonant, as in the word బ్రహ్మ, it ought, according to the orthography, to be pronounced before it: but in Teloogoo so harsh a sound cannot be admitted, they therefore place the sound of the హ after that of the following consonant, and pronounce the word abovementioned *Brumhu*, instead of *Bruhmu*.

61 ళ *ḷ* partakes of the sound of both *l* and *r*, and is formed by the under part of the tongue curved back against the roof of the mouth: so far as regards the language of which we treat, this letter is to be considered as peculiar to the

pure Teloogoo; for though it occurs in the Sanscrit Védas, it is not to be found in any other Sanscrit work. It is common however to all the spoken dialects of the Peninsula.

క్ష *ksh* Is a compound of క *k* and ష *sh.* It is rather a harsh sound resembling the *ct* in the English words *fiction fraction* &c. &c. 62

ఱ *rru* is formed by a strong vibration of the tip of the tongue on that part of the roof of the mouth which is next the upper teeth, as in pronouncing the words *real, run,* the voice dwelling forcibly on the first letter. 63

The letter ం *n* or *m* never occurs except at the termination of a syllable; concluding the final syllable in a word it always represents the sound of *m*, as in *mum*; in every other situation it is pronounced *n*, as in *none;* except in Sanscrit derivatives, when it precedes a consonant included in any of the five Vurgus, it is then to be considered a mere abbreviation of the particular nasal which terminates the Vurgu to which the consonant belongs, and is to be pronounced accordingly. 64

ఁ *n* occurs only in pure Teloogoo words; and like ం *n* or *m*, is found always at the end of a syllable, it represents a very obscure nasal sound, which is perhaps peculiar to the language, and can therefore be only imperfectly illustrated by comparison with a slight indistinct pronunciation of the final *n* in the French words *bon, non,* &c. This letter is found only in studied composition; but, though omitted in common writings, the sound of this curious nasal may be discovered in the *pronunciation* of even the most ignorant natives. 65

The ం *n* or *m* is denominated పూర్ణానుస్వారము *full unooswarum* and the ఁ *n* అర్ధానుస్వారము *half unooswarum.* These are of two kinds, either radical in the word, or inserted or added by some grammatical rule. The ం *n* or *m* never can be changed into ఁ *n;* but if ఁ *n* be preceded by a short vowel, in order to render the quantity of this vowel long, the ఁ *n* may be changed into ం *n* or *m;* thus, మందు *mundoo medicine* never can become మఁదు; but కలఁగి *kulungi, possessing,* may become కలంగి; and రాముఁడు *Ramoondoo, Rama,* may become రాముండు. 66

67 ః *h* is peculiar to Sanscrit derivatives. In the middle of a word, it is pronounced like a strong aspirated *h* final; as అంతఃపురు, *untuhpooru*, but, at the end of a word, it takes after it the sound of the vowel which terminates the preceding syllable; thus, అంతః is pronounced *untuhu*, not *untuh* as above. In Teloogoo, it seldom occurs except in the middle of compound words derived from the Sanscrit; and therefore in general possesses only the first of the two powers here explained.

68 A clear, distinct, and correct pronunciation, and an easy deliberate manner of speaking, are acquisitions of importance in all intercourse with the Natives, by whom they are highly valued as marks of good breeding. Europeans are too apt to speak the Teloogoo in an abrupt, hurried, and consequently vulgar manner, and to disregard the great distinction between the long and short vowels, and the harsh and soft consonants; we are in consequenc often unintelligible, or at least very obscurely understood by the Natives, who are either too obsequious, or too timid, to explain their perplexity; and we are thus induced to blame their ignorance or stupidity, when our own attention alone is in fault.

ORTHOGRAPHY.

69 Founded on the principles above explained, nothing can be more nicely defined than the correct orthography of each Teloogoo word. The writers on this language, indeed, seem to delight in a refined minuteness and multiplicity of rule, unknown to European authors; and the last deviation from their established maxims would be considered an unpardonable error in any studied composition or literary work. But, in the colloquial use of the language, grammatical rule is more or less disregarded, even by the most learned persons; and as the Natives in familiar correspondence, or official business, write as they would speak, many irregularities in orthography are observable in common writings. The most general are the following.

70 The consonant య *y*, without any connected vowel, is improperly used instead of the initial vowel ఇ *i*.

The consonant య *y*, with the connected vowel ా *a*, viz. యా, is incorrectly used, instead of the initial vowel ఈ *ee*. 71

The consonant య *y*, with the connected vowel ె, viz. యె, is used for the initial vowel ఎ *ĕ*. 72

The letter య *y*, with the connected vowel ే *ē*, thus యే, is used instead of the initial ఏ *ē*. 73

The consonant వ *v*, with the connected vowel ు *œ*, *viz.* వు, is incorrectly used instead of the vowel ఉ. 74

The consonant వ *v*, with the connected vowel ూ, thus వూ, is improperly used instead of ఊ *oo*. 75

The consonant వ *v*, with the connected vowel ొ or ొ, thus వొ or వొ, is used for ఒ *ŏ*. 76

The consonant వ *v*, with the connected vowel ో or ో, thus వో or వో, is used instead of ఓ *ō*. 77

The vowel అ *u*, with య *y* above mentioned, thus అయ, is improperly used, at the commencement of Sanscrit words, for the vowel *ue* ఐ; but the use of అయ at the commencement of a pure Teloogo word is not incorrect. 78

The vowel అ *u*, with వు above mentioned, viz. అవు, is incorrectly used at the beginning of Sanscrit words for ఔ *uo*; although it's use at the commencement of pure Teloogoo words is proper. 79

The initial vowels, ఋ *rœ* & ౠ *roo*, and their connected forms ృ *rœ* & ౄ *roo*, which are peculiar to Sanscrit derivatives, are often confounded with the syllable రు, or with the double form of ర *r* (viz. ్ర *r*) and the connected vowel ు *œ*, thus, క్రుష్ణ *krœshnu* is erroneously written *krœshnu* కృష్ణ, and vice versa. 80

CHAPTER SECOND.

OF THE ELISION, INSERTION, AND PERMUTATION, OF LETTERS.

Possessing the refined and inexhaustible Sanscrit, as the established medium 81
for the communication of knowledge, to the few among whom it's dissemination is thought to be lawful; Teloogoo writers have had little inducement to give much attention to the cultivation of their own language. Their literature consists almost entirely of poetry; and their Poets, desirous only to please the ear, or to flatter the vanity of the reigning Prince, seem to have deemed the improvement of their style a secondary consideration. The cadence of their verses, and the tones of the words composing them, have occupied almost their exclusive attention. The consequence has been a neglect of the more important qualities of composition, and a studied conciseness of expression, which, though not inelegant in itself, has frequently the effect of rendering their sentences obscure. At the same time, by a judicious union of the sweetness of the original Teloogoo, with the majestic sounds of the sonorous Sanscrit, they have succeeded in giving to the language a pleasing variety of modulation, which distinguishes it from all others current in the Peninsula.

Another principal cause of this euphony is the extraordinary care that has 82
been taken to prevent any incongruity of sound arising from the conjunction of dissimilar letters. The numerous rules, for this purpose, are scattered, in a confused manner, through the works of many Grammarians; and, as the following is the first attempt to reduce them to methodical order, it may hereafter, perhaps, be found susceptible of great improvement.

I shall endeavour to explain, 1st the alterations which take place in letters at the *beginning* and *end* of words; and 2ndly, the changes which occur in the *middle* of words. But it is proper, in the first place, to apprize the Reader, that the following rules are by no means rigidly observed, except in studied compositions. In the common or colloquial dialect, many of the changes will occasionally be found: it is true that they are not there adhered to systematically, but even in that dialect they are seldom entirely neglected. The Student, however, may find it more convenient to refer occasionally to this chapter as he advances, than, at the very commencement of his labours, to enter into some of the most perplexing niceties of the language.

OF THE ALTERATION OF LETTERS AT THE COMMENCEMENT AND END OF WORDS,

83 In treating of this subject, the whole of the words in the Teloogoo language are divided into two classes; one termed కళలు *kululoo*, the other ద్రుతప్రకృతులు *drootuprukrootooloo*.

84 The class termed కళలు *kululoo* includes, 1st the singular and plural nominatives of all nouns and pronouns, (except నేను *I* and తాను *he she* or *it*) and the oblique case, or what I have termed the inflexion, of all nouns and pronouns, both in the singular and plural number.

2dly. The postpositions యొక్క or యొక *of*, కూర్చి or గురించి *towards, on account of*, పట్టుండి *through*, చేసి *from*, పట్టి *through*, విషయము *respecting*, నిమిత్తము *on account of*, కోసము or కోసరము *for, on account of*, నుండి or నుంచి *from, away from*.

3dly. The final significant letters ా or ా expressing interrogation, ే or ే denoting emphasis, and ొ or ో expressive of doubt.

4thly. Indeclinable particles, like అట, కద, మఱి, పలా, ఇంచుక, అంత, &c.

5thly. All Interjections, and vocative cases.

6thly. The words, ఇప్పుడు *now*, అప్పుడు *then*, ఎప్పుడు *when?*

7thly. Every part of the verb; except the first and third persons in the singular, and the third person neuter in the plural, of the first forms of the past and future tenses, and of the affirmative aorist; the first person singular of the negative aorist; the infinitive; and the present verbal participle terminating in చు; and, when followed by vowels only, the indifinite relative participle ending in టి or డు, or the root when used for this participle.

The Negative verbal participle, which always ends in క, is classed both in the కళలు *kululoo*, and the ద్రుతప్రకృతులు *drootuprukrootooloo*. 85

The nominatives నేను *I*, తాను *he she or it*, and the several parts of the verb mentioned above, as exceptions; together with all the other words in the language, not included in the foregoing specification of the కళలు *kululoo*, form the numerous class denominated ద్రుతప్రకృతులు *drootuprukrootooloo*. 86

Every Teloogoo word, whether included in the class of కళలు *kululoo*, or ద్రుతప్రకృతులు *drootuprukrootooloo*, naturally terminates in some one of the connected vowels. I shall first point out the changes which occur when any of these words is followed by another commencing with an initial vowel; and shall then explain the alterations that take place, when any of them is followed by another beginning with a consonant. 87

In Teloogoo, two vowels never can come in contact; therefore, when a word terminating in a connected vowel is followed by another commencing with an initial vowel, there is either the change termed by Grammarians *Sund,hi*, or a consonant is inserted between the two words; unless the initial vowel be one of the Sanscrit letters ఋ *roo*, ౠ *roo*, and ఌ *loo*, which at the beginning of a word, are to be considered the same as consonants. 88

The consonants inserted, when *Sund,hi* does not occur, are య *y* if the former of the two words be included in the class termed కళలు *kululoo*, and న *n* if it belong to the ద్రుతప్రకృతులు *drootuprukrootooloo*; but, which ever of these two consonants is inserted, it changes the following initial vowel into it's connected form, and, coalescing with it, forms, in conjunction with it, one syllable. 89

90 *Sund,hi* is the elision of the connected vowel terminating the first word, and of the initial vowel commencing the following word, and the substitution of the connected form of the latter vowel in lieu of both; as shewn in the examples hereafter given.

91 *Sund,hi* never takes place unless the first word terminates in one of the three short connected vowels ు *u*, ి *i*, or ృ *ω*, except in a few particular instances noticed hereafter.

FINAL. ు

92 It may be adopted as a general rule that a word terminating in ు followed by another commencing with an initial vowel, may *at option* have *Sund,hi*; thus, మేసిన *that grazed*, and ఆవు *a cow*, make మేసినావు *the cow that grazed*, by dropping the final ు in మేసిన and the initial ఆ in ఆవు, and substituting for both the connected form of ఆ viz. ా; which, uniting with the preceding న *n*, makes the syllable నా, by means of which the two words coalesce. But as the *Sund,hi* of final ు is *optional*, and మేసిన is included in the class of కళలు *kululoo*, మేసిన and ఆవు, when *Sund,hi* does not take place, become మేసిన యావు, by the insertion of య between the two words, and the change of ఆ in the latter to it's connected form ా, which, uniting with య, forms the syllable యా, by means of which the words coalesce, as above stated.

EXCEPTIONS.

93 Words of the class termed ద్రుతప్రకృతులు *drootuprukrootooloo*, ending in ు, never admit of *Sund,hi*. By rule 89, therefore, న *n* is always inserted after such words, when the following one begins with an initial vowel. The word ఇంక *more*, is excepted; for adding to it ఏమి *what?* we may say, either ఇంకనేమి *what more?* by inserting న *n*, or ఇంకేమి by *Sund,hi*.

94 Vocative cases ending in ు, and the nominative case singular of pure Teloogoo nouns denoting women, and terminating in ు, do not admit of *Sund,hi*, when followed by a word commencing with an initial vowel. Being of the class named కళలు *kululoo*, such words assume య *y* as explained in rule 89; thus, వెలఁత *a woman* and ఇచ్చెను *he she, or it gave*, make, వెలఁతయి

చ్చెను *a woman gave*, never నెలఁతిచ్చెను - కృష్ణుఁడ *O Krishtna!* and ఇక్క-డరమ్ము *come here*, make కృష్ణుఁడయిక్కడరమ్ము *O Krishtna! come here;* never కృష్ణుఁడిక్కడరమ్ము.

FINAL. ి

A word terminating in ి followed by another beginning with an initial 95
vowel, does not, in general, admit of *Sund,hi;* thus కత్తి a *knife*, and ఎక్కడ *where*; cannot by *Sund,hi* become కత్తెక్కడ, but make కత్తియెక్కడ *where is the knife?* by inserting య in the manner above explained, కత్తి being included in the class named కళలు *kululoo*.

EXCEPTIONS.

In the first form of the perfect tense of verbs, the second person singular 96
ending in తి or తివి, the first person plural terminating in తిమి, and the second person plural ending in తిరి, when followed by a word commencing with a vowel, *invariably* have *Sund,hi;* thus సేవించితివి *thou servedst*, and అమరుల *the gods*, make సేవించితివమరుల *thou servedst the gods*, by dropping final ి and initial అ, and substituting, in lieu of both, the connected form of అ viz. , which, joining with the preceding వ్ *v*, forms the syllable వ, by means of which the two words coalesce.

In the same tense, the first person singular terminating in తి, and the third 97,
person plural ending in రి, may, or may not, have *Sund,hi*, at pleasure; thus, మ్రొక్కితి *I have saluted*, and అచ్యుతుని the *Unperishable*, make మ్రొక్కితచ్యుతుని *I have saluted the Unperishable* (Vishtnoo) వచ్చిరి *they came*, and అమరులు *the Gods*, make వచ్చిరమరులు *the Gods came*; the *Sund,hi*, however, being *optional*, these phrases may have another form. We may say మ్రొక్కితి నచ్యుతుని *I have saluted the Unperishable* (Vishtnoo) వచ్చిరియమరులు *the Gods came*; here న *n* is inserted in the first phrase, because మ్రొక్కితి is included in the ద్రుతప్రకృతులు *drootuprukrootooloo;* and య *y* in the second sentence, because వచ్చిరి is of the class named కళలు *kululoo*.

The pronouns అది *that*, అవి *those*, ఇది *this*, ఇవి *these*, ఏది *which?* ఏవి 98
which? ఏమి *what?* the word మఱి *again, more*, and the postposition కి *to*, have

optional Sund,hi; thus, అది and ఏమి make అదేమి *or* అదియేమి *what is that?* అవి and ఏవి make అవేవి *or* అవియేవి *which are these?* in the same manner we may say, చేసినదేమి *or* చేసినదియేమి *what has been done?* మతేమి *or*, మతియేమి *what more?* రామునికిచ్చెను *or* రామునికినిచ్చెను *he, she* or *it gave to Rama*. In all these phrases, except the last, when *Sund,hi* does not take place, య *y* is inserted; because each of the first words are included in the class termed కళలు *kululoo*; but in the last sentence, న *n* is inserted after కి, because it is of the class named ద్రుతప్రకృతులు *drootuprukrootooloo*.

99 Words ending in ి, if followed by the word అయిన added to adjectives, or by ఎంత *how much?* have *Sund,hi at option*, thus; మేటి and అయిన make మేటయిన *or* మేటియయిన *chief*. In the same way, we say పిండెంత *or* పిండియెంత *how much flour?*

FINAL.

100 It may be taken as a general rule that words ending in ు, followed by others beginning with an initial vowel, *invariably* have *Sund,hi*; as రాముఁడు *Rama*, and ఇచ్చెను *he, she,* or *it gave*, become రాముఁడిచ్చెను *Rama gave*. Innumerable other instances might be given.

EXCEPTIONS.

101 The accusatives నన్ను *me;* నిన్ను *thee,* తన్ను *him, her,* or *it,* మమ్ము *us,* మిమ్ము *you,* తమ్ము *them,* the postpositions కొరకు *for,* కు *to,* అందు *in*; the words ఎందు *in which,* ఇందు *in this,* అందు *in that,* and the particle చు added to the roots of verbs to form the present verbal participle, have also *Sund,hi,* when followed by an initial vowel, but it is entirely *optional*; thus నన్ను *me,* and ఏలుము *rule thou,* make నన్నేలుము or నన్నునేలుము *rule thou me,* అను చు *speaking,* ఇట్లనియె *thus he, she,* or *it said,* make అనుచిట్లనియె or అనుచు నిట్లనియె *speaking, he, she,* or *it thus said,* చెప్పుచు *saying,* and ఉన్నాఁడు *he is* make చెప్పుచున్నాఁడు or చెప్పుచునున్నాఁడు *he is saying*. In these phrases, when *Sund,hi* does not take place, the first words being all ద్రుతప్రకృతులు *drootuprukrootooloo,* న *n* is inserted between them and the words which follow.

The first and third persons singular in the affirmative aorist, the indefinite 102
participle in చు, or the root used for that participle; and nouns in the accusative singular ending in ు *when deprived of their drootuprukrootica affixes,* never admit of *Sund,hi*; as వత్తు *I come, have come, or will come,* and ఇప్పుడు *now,* make వత్తునిప్పుడు *I come, have come, or will come now.* వచ్చు *he comes, has come, or will come,* and ఇప్పుడు *now,* make వచ్చునిప్పుడు *he comes, has come, or will come now.* పోషించు *that protects,* ఈశ్వరుని *the god,* and తలఁచినాను *I have meditated,* make పోషించునీశ్వరునిఁదలఁచినాను *I have meditated on the protecting God.* రాము the accusative of రాముఁడు *Rama,* deprived of it's drootuprukrootica affixes, and ఈక్షించెను *he, she, or it saw,* make రామునీక్షించెను *he, she, or it saw Rama.*

All words ending in any of the short vowels, invariably have *Sund,hi,* when 103
followed by ఎఁడు *full,* అంత *as much as,* ఏసి *at the rate of,* and ఆకు *a leaf;* or by the words అన్న *an elder brother,* అమ్మ *a mother,* అక్క *an elder sister,* అయ్య *a father,* అత్త *a mother-in-law,* అప్ప *a father,* అవ్వ *a grand mother &c.* when added to proper names to express familiarity or kindness; thus, చేర *the hand, held so as to contain any thing,* and ఎఁడు *full,* make చేరెఁడు *a handfull;* పోక *an areca nut;* and అంత *as much as,* make పోకంత *as large as an areca nut;* ఎనిమిది *eight,* and ఏసి *at the rate of,* make ఎనిమిదేసి *at the rate of eight;* సుబ్బి *Soobee,* the proper name of a woman, and అమ్మ *mother,* make సుబ్బమ్మ *friend Soobee!* తాటి *a Palmyra* (in the inflected case) and ఆకు *a leaf,* make తాటాకు *a Palmyra-leaf.*

Nouns of Sanscrit derivation, even ending in the short connected vowels ˇ, 104
ి, or ు, which in the nominative singular do not adopt the Teloogoo terminations ఁడు, ము, or వు, *never* admit of *Sund,hi*; thus, హంస, *a swan,* and ఏది *which?* make హంసయేది *which is the swan?* దర్భ *durb,ha, a kind of sacred grass,* and ఏది *which?* make దర్భయేది *which is the durb,ha?* హరి *the God Vishtnoo,* and ఏఁగెను *he, she, or it went,* make హరియేఁగెను *Vishtnoo went.* In all these instances, the first word is included in the class of కళలు *kululoo,*

and therefore, as *Sund hi* does not take place, య is inserted between it and the following word, according to rule 89.

105 Words ending in any of the long vowels *never* have Sund,hi, nor do the short vowels ు ూ ృ or ౄ admit of *Sund,hi*, except when followed by the words specified in rule 103. When followed by any other words beginning with an initial vowel, words of such terminations, if they be ద్రుతప్రకృతులు *drootu-prukrootooloo* insert న *n*, and if కళలు *kululoo* య.

As the first word in each of the following phrases belongs to the class termed కళలు, య is inserted between it and the word which follows.

నవలా *a woman*, and ఏది *where?* make నవలాయేది *where is the woman?* య being inserted between నవలా and ఏది changes the following initial vowel ఏ of ఏది to its connected form ే, and uniting with it, forms one syllable యే, by means of which the two words coalesce; పల్లకీ *a Palanqueen*, and ఎక్కెను *he, she,* or *it mounted*, make పల్లకీయెక్కెను *he, she,* or *it mounted the Palanqueen*; వన్నె *coloured*, and ఒల్లె *a garment* make వన్నెయొల్లె *a coloured garment*; రే *night*, and ఎండ *lustre*, make రేయెండ *moonshine*; మై *the body*, and ఒరపు *beauty*, make మైయొరపు *personal beauty*; రో *money*, and ఈవి *donation*, make రోయీవి *the donation of money*; గ్లౌ *the moon*, and ఉదయించెను *he, she,* or *it arose*, make గ్లౌయుదయించెను *the moon arose.*

The first word in each of the following phrases being of the class named ద్రుతప్రకృతులు *drootuprukrootooloo*, న *n* is inserted between it and the word which follows.

తిన్నఁగా *slowly*, and ఏఁగెను *he, she,* or *it* went, make తిన్నఁగానేఁగెను *he, she,* or *it went slowly*; న *n* being inserted between తిన్నఁగా and ఏఁగెను changes the following initial vowel ఏ of ఏఁగెను into it's connected form ే, and uniting with it, forms one' syllable నే, by means of which the two words coalesce; the accusative విధాతృ *the Creator*, and ఈక్షించెను *he, she,* or *it saw*, make విధాతృనీక్షించెను *he, she,* or *it saw the Creator*; జేజే *God*, in the accusative case, and ఈక్షించెను *he, she,* or *it saw*, make జేజేనీక్షించెను *he, she,* or *it saw God*; మాతౄ *the Goddess of learning*, (in the accusative case), and అడిగెను *he, she, or it asked,* make ముత్తోనడిగెను *he, she, or it asked the Goddess of learning ;* గ్లౌ *the moon* (in the accusative case) and ఆలోకించి *having seen,* make గ్లౌనాలోకించి *having seen the moon.* It must here be particularly observed that the accusatives abovementioned are, in the first place, for the sake of example, deprived of their *drootuprukrootica* affixes.

When a word, both ending and beginning with a vowel, is repeated, there 106
is *Sund,hi*; thus, అన్న *an elder brother,* when repeated, becomes అన్నన్న *brother! brother!* ఏమి *what,* in the same manner, becomes ఏమేమి *what! what!*

The pronoun అది *she or it,* when added, in composition, to other words, 107
frequently loses the initial అ ; thus, కాఁపు *a husbandman, a labourer,* and అది *she,* become, in composition, కాఁపుది *a female labourer,* by the elision of అ in అది ; but in consequence of కాఁపు ending in ఉ, *Sund,hi* also may take place, according to rule 100, and the two words in question will then become కాఁపది ; in the same way, కోమటి *a man of the Comtee cast,* and అది *she,* make కోమటిది *a woman of the Comtee cast,* but as the elision of అ is *optional,* we may also say కోమటియది by inserting య according to rules 95 and 89.

Inflexions ending in ఉ ఊ or ృ, though included in the class of కళలు 108
kululoo, affix న *n* when followed by postpositions, or prefixed in composition to other nouns commencing with an initial vowel, thus, రాము *Rama,* and ఎదుట *opposite,* make రామునెదుట *opposite Rama,* పాము *a serpent,* and ఎమ్ములు *bones,* make పామునెమ్ములు *a serpent's bones.*

Having thus endeavoured to explain the changes which take place, when a 109
word terminating in a connected vowel is followed by one commencing with an initial vowel, I shall proceed to state those which occur, when a word ending with a connected vowel is followed by one commencing with a consonant.

If a word beginning with a consonant be preceded by another included in 110
the class termed కళలు *kululoo,* there is no elision or insertion of letters and permutation takes place in the following instances only.

111 Nouns in the nominative case, even when used accusatively, and all parts of the verb ending in ను, దు, and ది together with the words అప్పుడు *then,* ఇప్పుడు *now,* ఎప్పుడు *when?* preceding a word beginning with any of *the hard letters* కచటతప, change them respectively to గసడదవ; thus, కలిమి *wealth,* preceding పోదు *she or it will not go,* changes the ప *p* of పోదు into వ *v*, and we say కలిమి వోదు *riches will not disappear*; in the same manner, పోవుచున్నాఁడు *he is going,* and కల్లరి *a robber,* make పోవుచున్నాఁడు గల్లరి *the robber is going*; పోవుచున్నది *she, or it is departing,* and చెలిమి *friendship,* make పోవుచున్నది సెలిమి *friendship is departing*; అప్పుడు *then,* and చనియెను *he, she, or it went,* make అప్పుడు సనియెను *he, she, or it then went*; ఇప్పుడు *now,* and పోయెను *he, she, or it went,* make ఇప్పుడు వోయెను *he, she, or it now went.*

112 But Sanscrit derivatives, preceded by pure Teloogoo words, are excepted from this rule, and are not subject to any change; because the nature of such words is considered so different, as to prevent their coalescing in orthography; thus, దొర *a master,* and కరుణించెను *he, she, or it was pleased,* make దొర కరుణించెను *the master was pleased*; never దొర గరుణించెను. వీఁడు *he, this man,* and పుణ్యాత్ముఁడు *a virtuous man,* make వీఁడు పుణ్యాత్ముఁడు *this is a virtuous man.* Nevertheless, if two words both of Sanscrit derivation come together, the general rule holds good; because, in that case, both the words are of the same kind, we therefore say రాముఁడు గరుణించెను never రాముఁడు కరుణించెను *Rama was pleased.*

113 When two pure Teloogoo substantives are joined together by a copulative conjunction, not expressed, but understood, and the latter word begins with any of *the hard letters* క చ ట త ప, these letters are severally changed to *గసడదవ; thus, కాలు *a leg,* and చేతులు *hands,* make కాలు సేతులు *legs and hands*; అన్న *an elder brother,* and తమ్ములు *younger brothers,* make అన్న దమ్ములు *elder and younger brothers.*

---

* Although క may be changed into గ - చ into స - ట into డ - త into ద and ప into వ, the reverse of this rule does not hold good, these letters are not *interchangable:* గ cannot by any means become క, nor స, చ &c. The first series may be converted into the second, but the second can never be converted into the first.

If a word commencing with any of the five *hard letters* క చ ట త ప, be preceded by another included in the class termed ద్రుతప్రకృతులు *drootupru-krootooloo,* both permutation and insertion of letters *invariably* take place; but if the latter word begin with any other consonant, there is insertion only, and it is *optional.* 114

When a word included in the ద్రుతప్రకృతులు *drootuprukrootooloo* precedes another word commencing with any of the *five hard letters* క చ ట త ప, it invariably changes these characters respectively, into *the soft letters* గ జ డ ద బ,* and if it end in ి ీ or ై it is requisite to insert ని between the two words, or ను if it terminate in any other letter; but if it already end in ని or ను, these terminations cannot again be affixed, for the repetition would be monotonous: at the same time, if the ద్రుతప్రకృతులు *drootuprukrootooloo* end in a short vowel, either ం or ఁ may be substituted for the ని or ను, but only ఁ if it terminate in a long vowel; thus, దేవతల (the accusative plural of దేవత *God*) deprived, for the sake of example, of all it's *drootuprukrootica* affixes, and కొలిచితిని *I served,* make దేవతలనుగొలిచితిని or దేవతలంగొలిచితిని or దేవతలఁగొలిచితిని *I served the Gods,* by changing the initial క of కొలిచితిని into గ, and inserting ను between the two words, or in consequence of the ల in దేవతల being short, substituting either ం or ఁ for ను. 115

Any of the ద్రుతప్రకృతులు *drootuprukrootooloo* preceding a word commencing with a consonant different from the five hard letters, without causing permutation, may at *option* affix ని if it end in ి ీ or ై, or ను if it end in any other vowel; but if it already terminates in ని or ను these affixes are not again to be added, because the repetition would be monotonous: either న *n* or ౯ may be affixed, in lieu of ని or ను, provided the consonants ర డ ఢ దధఝ are not the initials of the following word; and if the following word begins with గ జ బ మ ర డ ఢ ద ధ ఝ, in place of ని or ను, we may at option affix ం or ఁ, 116

* క is converted into గ - చ into జ - ట into డ - త into ద and ప into బ, but, as before observed of another rule, the reverse of these changes does not hold good.

provided the *drootuprukrootooloo* terminate in a short vowel, but if it end in a long vowel, we may insert ఁ *n* only ; thus, deprived for the sake of example of all *drootuprukrootica* affixes, the accusative అరి *an enemy*, and గెలిచితిని *I won or conquered*, make అరిని గెలిచితిని by affixing ని in consequence of అరి ending in ి ; or అరిన్గెలిచితిని or అరిఙ్ గెలిచితిని by affixing న *n* or ఙ్ ; or అరిం గెలిచితిని or అరిఁ గెలిచితిని by affixing ం or ఁ ; or as the whole of these affixes are optional, we may say simply అరి గెలిచితిని *I conquered the enemy:* thus also deprived, for the sake of example, of all *drootuprukrootica* affixes, the accusative రాక్షసుల *Giants*, and ఖండించినారు *they killed*, make రాక్షసులను ఖండించినారు by affixing ను, or రాక్షసులన్ఖండించినారు or రాక్షసులఙ్ ఖండించినారు by affixing న *n* or ఙ్ ; or as the whole of these affixes are *optional*, we may say simply రాక్షసులఖండించినారు *they killed the Giants*; but we cannot here affix ం or ఁ, and say రాక్షసులంఖండించినారు or రాక్షసులఁఖండించినారు, because ఖ follows, and the affixes ం or ఁ precede the letters గ జ బ డ ద డ ధ ద ధ క్ష only : deprived of all its *drootuprukrootica* affixes, the 3d person in the first form of the past tense of వచ్చు *to come* viz. వచ్చె *he, she, or it came*, and డాంభికుఁడు, *a coxcomb*, make వచ్చెను డాంభికుఁడు by affixing ను, or వచ్చెండాంభికుఁడు or వచ్చెఁడాంభికుఁడు by affixing ం or ఁ ; or, as the whole of these affixes are *optional*, we may say simply వచ్చె డాంభికుఁడు *a coxcomb came*, but we cannot affix *n* న or ఙ్, and say వచ్చెన్డాంభికుఁడు or వచ్చెఙ్ డాంభికుఁడు, because these affixes never precede the consonants ర డ క్ష ద ధ క్ష.

117 Certain masculine nouns in ు ఁడు form their accusative singular either by changing ఁడు into ని or by dropping ఁడు altogether ; thus, Nom : రాముఁడు *Rama*, Accus : రాముని or రాము : in the latter case, it must be observed, as an exception to rules 115 and 116, that to such accusatives in ు the drootuprukrootica affix ని is to be added, instead of the affix ను ; thus, రాము , one of the accusatives of Rama, and కొలిచితిని *I served*, make రామునిగొలిచితిని never రామునుగొలిచితిని *I served Rama.*

Nouns ending in ి యము change this termination optionally into ెము or 118
్యము; thus, ముత్తియము *a pearl*, కడియము *a bracelet*, మిరియము *pepper*, &c. make ముత్తెము or ముత్యము - కడెము or కడ్యము - మిరెము or మిర్యము, this rule is also applicable to nouns in ి య.

OF THE CHANGE OF LETTERS IN THE MIDDLE OF WORDS.

The changes which take place in the middle of words are few and easy, and consist chiefly of contractions which occur naturally in a quick pronunciation.

Present verbal participles ending in చు preceded by ను, optionally drop 119
the ు of ను, or sometimes change the ను into ం, thus, అనుచు *saying*, కనుచు *seeing*, వినుచు *hearing*, make అన్చు - కన్చు - విన్చు, or - అంచు - కంచు - వించు - చనుచు *going*, ఫ్రానుచు *entering*, and some other verbal paticiples do not change ను into ం, but they frequently drop the ు in ను.

Verbal Roots of more than two syllables, of which ను - లు - డు - రు or 120
ళు are medials, frequently drop the ు of these syllables; thus, పెనుచు *to plait, to twist*, often becomes పెన్చు and ఏడుచు *to weep, to cry*, ఏడ్చు; but if, in such roots, one short syllable only precede డు రు or ళు, no elision of the ు takes place; thus, తుడుచు *to wipe*, cannot become తుడ్చు, nor నడుచు *to walk*, నడ్చు.

The words ఇపుడు *now*, అపుడు *then*, ఎపుడు *when?* optionally drop the ు 121
of the middle syllable, and become respectively ఇప్డు - అప్డు - ఎప్డు.

Nouns of three syllables, of which the middle one is ను లు or డు, frequent- 122
ly drop the ు of these syllables; thus, చిలుక *a parrot*, కాలువ *a water-course*, make చిల్క - కాల్వ; and this elision of ు takes place even in other words; thus, కారుపోతు *a buffalo* కోలుపులి *a species of tiger*, sometimes become కార్పోతు - కోల్పులి.

గ in the middle or end of a word is often changed into వ; thus, ప్రోగు 123
an *ear-ring*, పగడము *coral*, become also ప్రోవు - పవడము.

124 Many Teloogoo words which have ్ర *r* in the first syllable, frequently lose it in the vulgar dialect; thus, ప్రోగు or ప్రోవు an *ear-ring*, is commonly both written and pronounced పోగు or పోవు.

125 The reader need not be surprized if, in the course of his studies, he should meet with some examples in opposition to the foregoing rules, supported by good authority. On no part of Grammar are the opinions of Teloogoo authors so much at variance, as with respect to the changes attempted to be explained in this chapter: the ingenuity and subtilty with which each combats the arguments of his opponent, have gained for every celebrated writer on Grammar some adherents; and as authors rigidly observe the precepts of the particular Grammarian whom they select for their guide, a comparison of almost any two books will exhibit some discrepancies not to be reconciled. Every endeavour has been used to select those opinions which are most generally received at present, but the subject itself is so intricate, and the opinions of native Grammarians respecting it so contradictory, that a foreigner who attempts to illustrate it must necessarily feel diffident of success.

CHAPTER THIRD.

The words of the Teloogoo language, formed of the letters treated of in 126
the foregoing pages, are classed by Sanscrit Grammarians under four distinct heads. 1st. దేశ్యము *Déshyumoo,* or, as it is more emphatically termed, అచ్చదేశ్యము *Utsu Déshyumoo,* the *pure* language of the land ; 2d. తత్సమము *Tutsumumoo,* Sanscrit words assuming Teloogoo terminations. 3d. తద్భవము *Tudbhuvumoo,* Teloogoo corruptions of Sanscrit words, formed by the substitution, the elision, or addition of letters ; and 4th. గ్రామ్యము *Grámyumoo,* Provincial terms, or words peculiar to the vulgar. To these we may also add the అన్యదేశ్యము, *Unyu Déshyumoo,* or words from other countries, somtimes given as a subdivision of the first Class, and comprizing, according to the definition of ancient writers, words adopted from the dialects current in the Canarese, Mahratta, Guzerat, and Dravida provinces only, but now also including several of Persian, Hindoostance, and English origin.

In each of the three following Chapters, which treat of substantive-nouns 127
and pronouns, of adjective-nouns and pronouns, and of the verb, the దేశ్యము will be distinguished from the తత్సమము words: but all observations regarding the తద్భవము and అన్యదేశ్యము words will be found in the Chapter respecting substantives ; because the words of the two last mentioned classes consist chiefly of substantives ; and the reader, reasoning from analogy, will find it easy to apply the rules given under that head, to adjectives, and verbs.

128 The గ్రామ్యము, or provincial terms, are contractions or corruptions of pure Teloogoo words, rather than a separate class of vocables; I have therefore deemed it better to offer, in the course of the work, such remarks respecting them as occasion has suggested, than to collect the rules regarding them under any separate head.

SUBSTANTIVES.

1ST OF THE POSTPOSITIONS.

Before entering on the subject of declension, a few preliminary observations are necessary, respecting that very useful class of words, by means of which the various cases of the substantive nouns and pronouns, in this language, are formed.

129 English substantives are declined by prefixing to them, in the singular and plural numbers, certain particles, termed *prepositions*. The cases of Teloogoo nouns and pronouns are formed in the same manner, except that the particles follow the noun, instead of preceding it; hence, I have termed them *postpositions*. In Teloogoo, we would not say *with swords, by men, of me;* but కత్తులతో - మనుష్యులచేత - నాయొక్క *swords with, men by, me of.*

130 When a preposition accompanies an English word which is liable to inflexion, the word cannot stand in the nominative case; it must assume it's inflected or oblique form: we cannot say *of I, to I,* &c. but *of me, to me,* &c. In the same manner, in Teloogoo, notwithstanding some nouns have nearly the same form in the inflexion, as in the nominative case, yet as all nouns and pronouns may be said to admit of inflexion, it may be laid down as a general rule, that when followed by postpositions, they cannot continue in the nominative case; by some of the postpositions, they are converted into their oblique form; by others, either into this simple inflected state, or into the dative; and by a few, derived from verbs, they are changed into the accusative case. The following is a list of the principal Teloogoo postpositions.

CONVERTING THE PRECEDING WORD INTO IT'S OBLIQUE FORM.

యొక్క - యొక ....*of*; the sign of the genitive case.
కి - కు ....*to, for ;* the sign of the dative case.
లో ....*in ;* the sign of the *local* ablative.
చే - చేత ....*by, by means of*; the sign of the *instrumental* ablative.

తో - తోడ - తోడుత........*with, along with* ; the sign of the *social* ablative.

న............................*in, by, with.*

లోపల.......................*within, inside.*

వల్ల - వలన...................*by, by means of, from.*

కొరకు - కై...................*to, for.*

నిమిత్తము........... ....*for, on account of, about.*

కోసము - కోసరము...... ...*on account of, for.*

విషయము....... ....*respecting.*

అందు......... ....*in.*

వలె........... ....*like.*

గుండా.............. ....*through.*

నుండి - నుంచి......... ... ..*from, away from.*

FOUND IN BOOKS ONLY.

అఱు - అఱుత......... ..... *with, along with.*

పొంటె.......... ....*with, together with, for.*

పారుడి...... ....*by, from.*

మై - మెయి...... ....*by, by means of.*

CONVERTING THE PRECEDING WORD EITHER INTO IT'S OBLIQUE FORM OR INTO THE DATIVE CASE.

బైట........ ....*out-side.*

పైన........... ....*upon, above.*

కింద...... ....*below, under.*

సందున - మధ్య - నడమ......*between.*

దగ్గిర - ఒద్ద...... ....*near.*

ముందర...... ....*before.*

వెనక ....behind, after.

వెంబడి........................behind.

ఎదురుగా - ఎదుట..........against, opposite.

CONVERTING THE PRECEDING WORD INTO THE ACCUSATIVE CASE.

కూర్చి - గురిచి - గురించి towards, on account of.

FOUND IN BOOKS ONLY.

పట్టుఁడి.......................through.

చేసి............................from, by.

పట్టి............................through.

131 Under the following rules, the whole of these words may be added to any noun or pronoun, placed in the particular case which the postposition is stated above to require.

132 The postpositions కి - కు, the signs of the dative case, are not used promiscuously with any inflexion; కి is added only to inflexions terminating in ి ీ or ై; thus, inflexion హరి *Vishtnoo*, dative హరికి *to Vishtnoo*; inflexion శ్రీ *The Goddess of prosperity*, dative శ్రీకి *to the Goddess of prosperity*; and కు to inflexions ending in any other letter, inflexion కట్టె *a stick*, dative కట్టెకు *to a stick*, inflexion దొర *a ruler*, dative దొరకు *to a ruler*, inflexion మగువ *a woman*, dative మగువకు *to a woman*: but it is requisite to insert the syllable న between కు and all inflexions ending in ు ూ or ృ; as, inflexion రాము *Rama*, dative రామునకు *to Rama*, inflexion అందము *beauty*, dative అందమునకు *to beauty*.

133 The postposition న is added only to the inflexions of nouns denoting inanimate things ending in ు; thus, we may say కాగితమున *in the paper*, because the inflexion కాగితము ends in ు; but we cannot add న to కోక *a female garment*, for it ends in ✓, nor to గుఱ్ఱము a *horse*, because it is an animate object.

134 Inflexions always terminate in some vowel, and the postpositions అందు, అఱు, అఱుత, ఎదుట, and ఎదురుగా commence with vowels; but, by the rules already given, two vowels cannot come in contact; a singular inflexion

terminating in ట టా or ౖ, although included in the class termed kululoo, when followed by these postpositions, affixes న n; thus, రాము నెదుట opposite Rama &c. (rule 108). When these postpositions, however, follow a singular inflexion ending in any other vowel, or plural inflexions which always end in ల, such inflexions being of the class named కళలు ku,luloo, యు is inserted between them and the postpositions in question, which, in consequence, become respectively యందు - యొఱు - యొఱుత - యెదుట and యెదురుగా; thus, దొర లయందు in rulers; at the same time, as all plural inflexions end in ల, and therefore have inherent the connected vowel ు, which before an initial vowel, may, by the rules before given, have *Sund,hi* at *option*, we may also say దొర లందు *in rulers* &c. &c.

పై or మెయి and చేసి are never subjoined to any words except verbal nouns, 135
or nouns denoting inanimate things; and పట్టి is used only after abstract nouns.

కూడిన - పట్టుకడి - చేసి and పట్టి always change into గూడిన - బట్టుకడి - జేసి 136
and బట్టి, when used as postpositions.

The nature and use of the foregoing words will be more fully explained in 137
the Syntax, where it will be shewn that many of them, though used as postpositions, are in fact parts of nouns, or forms of verbs. I have no doubt that the whole are derived from the same sources: at the same time, without a further knowledge of the ancient dialect than we now possess, it would be difficult to trace the origin of some pure Teloogoo derivatives, such as యొక్క the sign of the genitive, and కు or కి the signs of the dative case. This difficulty has led some to treat these, and similar words, rather as affixes inseparable from substantives, than as a separate class of vocables. But, whatever may be the history or etymology of these words; whether they are derived from nouns or verbs now obsolete, or are themselves original terms, there is no doubt that, in use, they are distinct from all others in the language, and precisely equivalent to our English prepositions. This, I think, justifies my classing them as a separate part of speech, and giving them the appellation by which I have endeavoured to distinguish them.

138. The articles *a* and *the* may be considered as inherent in the noun ; మనిషి according to the context, may mean either *a* or *the person.*

139 The indefinite article *a* is somtimes expressed by the numeral ఒక, vulgarly written వఖ, meaning *one* ; as, వఖమనిషి *one* or *a person*.

140 There is not any separate word to represent the definite article *the.* In the concise and nervous idiom which characterizes the Teloogoo, this article, together with the relative pronoun *who, which, that,* is incorporated with the verb, in that curious part of it termed the relative participles, which possess the combined force of the definite article, the relative pronoun, and the verb ; thus, in the sentence నన్నుజూచినమానిసి *the person who saw me* ; five English words are expressed by three Teloogoo terms, నన్ను signifies *me* మానిసి *person,* and జూచిన has the power of *the, who, saw.*

3d. OF THE DECLENSION OF SUBSTATIVE NOUNS.

141 The substantive nouns have two numbers ; the singular ఏకవచనము, and the plural బహువచనము ; and three genders, the masculine పుల్లింగము, including the gods and men only ; the feminine స్త్రీలింగము, comprizing the goddesses and women ; and the neuter నపుంసకలింగము, including inanimate things, and all animals, except the human species.

142 The cases are properly three only; the nominative, the inflexion, and the accusative ; but, in the following general remarks applicable to all nouns, the usual arrangement of six cases is observed.

S I N G U L A R.

143 It has already been mentioned that there are few words in the Teloogoo language which terminate in a consonant, among the nouns there's not one. In the nominative case singular, they all terminate in some of the following vowels ా ి ీ ు ూ ె ే ై or ో ; thus, దొర *a ruler,* వహా *a woman,* కల్లరి *a robber,* అందము *beauty,* శాలూ *a shawl,* కట్టె *a stick,* కై *the hand* &c.

144 The Inflexion singular varies with the declension, as explained hereafter.

The Genitive singular of all nouns is the same as the inflexion singular; but 145
iu books, and in conversation with Bramins, we occasionally find the postposition యొక్క or యొక of, added to the inflexion, to form the genitive.

The Dative singular is formed by adding కి to inflexions in ి ీ or ై - నకు 146
to inflexions in ు ూ or ృ, and కు to inflexions in all other terminations.

All nouns in the Accusative singular are the same as in the singular inflexion; 147
except that the inflexion is of the class termed కళలు *kululoo*, and the accusative of that named ద్రుతప్రకృతులు *drootuprukrootooloo.* That the reader may always bear in mind this distinction, the inflexion will hereafter be written in it's simple state, but to mark the accusative, the affix ని will be added to all inflexions in ి ీ or ై, (except to inflexions formed by changing the termination of the nominative into that syllable), and the affix ను to all those ending in any other letter, (except to those mentioned in rule 117) and an &c will be further added to all, to denote that although the affixes ని or ను are universal in the common dialect, and in correct language may, with propriety, be used before any consonants, yet others may be substituted in lieu of them, under the rules for *drootuprukrootooloo* ద్రుతప్రకృతులు, contained in the preceding chapter.

The Vocative singular is either the same as the nominative singular, or is 148
formed by merely lengthening the final vowel of that case; unless the nominative end in ు, when that vowel is changed into ా or ో.

The Ablative singular is formed by adding to the singular inflexion the 149
postpositions లోన్ - చేత - తోన్ &c. or న to the inflexion of nouns denotjng nanimate things ending in ు.

PLURAL.

The Nominative plural is formed, in various modes, from the nominative 150
singular, according to the declension to which the substantive belongs. It always ends in లు.

The Inflexion plural is formed by changing లు of the nominative plural into ల. 151

The Genitive plural of all nouns is the same as the inflexion plural; but 152
in books and in conversation with Bramins, we occasionally find the postpositions యొక్క or యొక of, added to the inflexion to form, the genitive.

153 The Dative plural is formed by adding కు to the inflexion plural in ల.

154 The Accusative plural is the same as the inflexion plural, both ending in ల; but the inflexion is included in the *kululoo*, and the accusative in the ద్రుతప్రకృతులు *drootuprukrootooloo*. To remind the reader of this material distinction, the inflexion will hereafter be written in it's simple state, without any of the additions peculiar to the ku,luloo; but ను, with an &c. will be added to all plural accusatives, for the reasons mentioned in treating of the accusative singular: ని is never affixed to plural accusatives, because they always end in ల, never in ి ు or ె.

155 The Vocative plural is formed by changing the final ు of the nominative plural into ారా or ారో.

156 The Ablative plural is formed by adding to the plural inflexion the post-positions. లోఁ - చేత - తోఁ &c.

157 The Vocative particles, ఓరి - ఓసి - ఓయి and ఓ, are often prefixed to the vocative case: the first is used in calling men of inferior rank only; the second in calling females inferior to oneself, among whom a wife is always included by the natives; and the third in calling men of equal rank with oneself; these three are prefixed to the vocative singular only: the last is prefixed to the vocative both in the singular and the plural number, and is used indifferently in calling superiors, inferiors, or equals.

158 It is of great importance that the reader should constantly bear in mind that, in nouns denoting inanimate things, the nominative is generally used for the accusative, and the accusative for the ablative, but that this is not the case with nouns denoting animate objects.

159 By the addition of the various postpositions to the different cases which they govern, the reader may form any number of other cases at pleasure.

160 The nouns belonging to the దేశ్యము, or language of the land, are more numerous than those of any other class; and, as the rules which regulate their declension extend also to nouns of the three other denominations, it seems proper to treat of them first.

OF REGULAR దేశ్యము NOUNS.

The regular nouns of this class are divided into three declensions. The first includes all masculine nouns, the nominative singular of which terminates in ఁడు; the second, all feminines or neuters of more than two syllables, having the nominative singular in ిము - ీము - or ాము; the third, nouns of all genders not included in either of the two foregoing declensions. The general rules, already given, explain the mode in which the different cases are formed from the nominative singular, the inflexion singular, or the nominative plural. It will be sufficient, therefore, to show how these three cases are formed in each declension. 161

FIRST DECLENSION IN ఁడు.

Many nouns denoting masculine agents have the nominative singular in ఁడు; but, as the letter ఁ is unknown to any, except the learned, the ఁ preceding డు is usually omitted *in writing,* and the nominative of this declension is consequently made to terminate simply in డు. The obscure nasal sound of ఁ before డు will notwithstanding be found in the *pronunciation* of even the most illiterate persons. 162

The singular inflexion of nouns belonging to this declension is formed by changing the final ఁడు of the nominative into ని; thus, nom. మగఁడు *a husband,* inflexion మగని. nom. తమ్ముఁడు *a younger brother,* inflex. తమ్ముని. But, with the exception of తమ్ముఁడు *a younger brother,* and అల్లుఁడు *a son in law,* all nouns of this declension, which have the vowel ు preceding ఁడు of the nominative singular, may also form the singular inflexion by merely dropping the termination ఁడు; the inflexion of మగఁడు *a husband,* is మగని only, never మగ; because ు does not precede the ఁడు of the nominative case; but, with the two exceptions abovementioned, all words which have ు before ఁడు of the nominative have two forms in the inflexion; thus, nom. బల్లిదుఁడు *a strong man,* inflex. బల్లిదుని or బల్లిదు. 163

The nominative plural is formed by changing ఁడు of the nominative singular into లు; thus, nom. sing. మగఁడు *a husband,* nom. plu. మగలు *husbands,* nom. sing. తమ్ముఁడు *a younger brother,* nom. plu. తమ్ములు *younger brothers.* 164

The other cases of this declension are formed according to the general rules given above; and, for the sake of illustration, a word of this declension is subjoined, declined according to the usual arrangement of six cases.

SINGULAR.

N. తమ్ముఁడు..........................*a younger brother.*

G. తమ్ముని or తమ్మునియొక్క ....*of a younger brother.*

D. తమ్మునికి..........................*to a younger brother.*

Acc. తమ్ముని &c.......................*a younger brother.*

V. తమ్ముఁడా..........................*o younger brother.*

Ab. తమ్ముని - లో - చేత - తో.......*in, by, or with a younger brother.*

PLURAL.

N. తమ్ములు..........................*younger brothers.*

G. తమ్ముల or తమ్ములయొక్క....*of younger brothers.*

D. తమ్ములకు..........................*to younger brothers.*

Acc. తమ్ములను &c.....................*younger brothers.*

V. తమ్ములారా.........................*o younger brothers.*

Ab. తమ్ముల - లో - చేత - తో.......*in, by, or with younger brothers.*

165 By rule 163, all words, except తమ్ముఁడు and అల్లుఁడు, which, in the nominative singular, have the vowel ు preceding the final termination ఁడు, may in the inflexion singular have two forms: such words, therefore, have likewise two forms in the genitive, dative, accusative, and ablative singular, which are formed from the inflexion; thus, nom. sing. బల్లిదుఁడు *a strong man*, inflex. sing. బల్లిదుని or బల్లిదు. gen. sing. బల్లిదునియొక్క or బల్లిదుయొక్క dat. sing. బల్లిదునికి or బల్లిదునకు, by the addition of కి to బల్లిదుని, or నకు to బల్లిదు, see rules 132 & 146. acc. sing. బల్లిదుని &c. or బల్లిము &c. see rule 117. abl. sing. బల్లిదుని - లో - చేత - తో or బల్లిదు - లో - చేత - తో; and even తమ్ముఁడు and అల్లుఁడు, which, in the other cases, are exceptions to this rule, in the dative

sigular, take two forms : viz· తమ్మునికి or తమ్మునకు - అల్లునికి or అల్లునకు. The plural however has no change of this kind.

In the *inferior* dialect, డి is substituted for ని in all the singular cases of 166
this declension, except the accusative, which is made to terminate in ణ్ని instead of ని ; thus, nom. sing. తమ్ముఁడు, inflexion sing. తమ్ముడి, dat. sing. తమ్ముడికి accus. sing. తమ్ముణ్ని &c. but these forms are never to be found in correct writings.

EXCEPTIONS.

Some words, of this declension, form the nominatve and inflexion plural, by 167
changing the final ఁడు of the nominative singular into ండ్రు and ండ్ర, or into ళ్లు and ళ్ల, instead of forming them regularly, by changing ఁడు into లు and ల respectively ; thus, గండఁడు *a robust man,* makes in the nominative plural గండండ్రు - ఒక్కఁడు *one man,* makes in the nom. plu. ఒక్కండ్రు - అల్లుఁడు *a son-in-law,* makes in the nom. plu· అల్లుండ్లు, and this rule applies to many other words of the same kind.

SECOND DECLENSION INCLUDING FEMININE OR NEUTER NOUNS, OF MORE THAN TOW SYLLABLES, IN ˇము - ాము or ాము.

There is a numerous class of neuter words of more than tow syllables end- 168
ing, in the nominative singular, in ˇము, and several in ాము and ాము : but పెండ్లాము *a wife,* is almost the only feminine noun of this declension.

The inflexion singular is the same as the nominative singular ; thus, nom. 169
sing. గుఱ్ఱము *a horse,* inflex. sing. గుఱ్ఱము.

The nominative plural is formed either by adding లు to the nominative singu- 170
lar ; or by changing the termination ము of the nominative singular into లు, and lengthening the preceding vowel, if not already long ; thus, nom. sing. గుఱ్ఱము *a horse,* nom. plu. గుఱ్ఱములు or గుఱ్ఱాలు *horses.*

The other cases are formed according to the general rules already given. 171
Subjoined is an example of this declension, according to the usual arrangement of six cases.

SINGULAR.

N.	గుఱ్ఱము…	*a hore.*
G.	గుఱ్ఱము or గుఱ్ఱముయొక్క…	*of a horse.*
D.	గుఱ్ఱమునకు…	*to a horse.*
Acc.	గుఱ్ఱమును &c…	*a horse.*
V.	గుఱ్ఱమా…	*o horse.*
Ab.	గుఱ్ఱము - లో - చేత - తో…	*in, by, or with a horse.*

PLURAL.

N.	గుఱ్ఱములు or గుఱ్ఱాలు…	*horses.*
G.	గుఱ్ఱముల or గుఱ్ఱములయొక్క… or గుఱ్ఱాల or గుఱ్ఱాలయొక్క…	*of horses.*
D.	గుఱ్ఱములకు or గుఱ్ఱాలకు…	*to horses.*
Acc.	గుఱ్ఱములను &c. or గుఱ్ఱాలను &c.…	*horses.*
V.	గుఱ్ఱములారా or గుఱ్ఱాలారా…	*o horses.*
Ab.	గుఱ్ఱముల - లో - చేత - తో or గుఱ్ఱాల - లో - చేత - తో…	*in, by, or with horses.*

172 All nouns in this declension, besides the dative singular as given above, may also form that case by changing ము of the nominative into ని, lengthening the preceding vowel, if not already long, and affixing the postposition కి instead of కు; thus, nom. sing. గుఱ్ఱము *a horse,* dative sing. గుఱ్ఱమునకు or గుఱ్ఱానికి nom. sing. లంచము *a bribe,* dative sing. లంచమునకు or లంచానికి.

173 The postposition న added to the singular inflexion of nouns ending in ు denoting inanimate things, is either affixed in the regular manner to inflexions of this declension, or the ము of the inflexion is changed into న, and the preceding vowel, if not already long, is lengthened; thus కాగిదమున or కాగిదాన *in paper.*

The nominative singular of nouns in this declension is often, in books, found changed, from ము, to మ్ము or ంబు; thus, nom. sing. గుఱ్ఱము *a horse*, is often found written గుఱ్ఱమ్ము or గుఱ్ఱంబు. This rule, however, does not apply to nouns which have the long vowel ా preceding the final ము; పెండ్లాము *a wife*, can never become పెండ్లామ్ము or పెండ్లాంబు. 174

In the *inferior* dialect, all the singular cases in this declension, (except the accusative), ending in ము, constantly change that termination into ం; thus, in conversation we frequently hear గుఱ్ఱం *gœrrum* used for గుఱ్ఱము *gœrrumœ*; but this practice is contrary to the genius of the language, which requires all words to terminate with a vowel. 175

The accusative, in the *inferior* dialect, is formed by changing ము of the nominative singular into ని, and lengthening the preceding vowel, if not already long; thus, nom. sing. గుఱ్ఱము *a horse*, acc. sing. గుఱ్ఱాన్ని nom. sing. లంచము *a bribe*, acc. sing. లంచాన్ని. 176

The following, with all other neuter or feminine nouns, of mor than two syllables, ending in ెము, ాము, or ాము, are declined like గుఱ్ఱము. 177

గడ్డము.................*the chin, a beard.*
అమ్మకము...........*sale.*
పెండ్లాము...........*a wife.*
వ్యాజ్యము...........*a dispute.*
సున్నము.............*lime, chalk.*
తాళము.............*a key.*
బీగము...............*the lock of a door.*
సీసము...............*lead.*
గంటము.............*an iron style.*
బియ్యము............*raw rice*
చక్కఁదనము.......*beauty.*
బెల్లము...............*jaggery.*

అంపము..............*a saw.*
జగడము...............*a fight, a battle.*
తగరము..............*tin.*
కాపురము............*residence.*
తొండము.............*an elephant's trunk.*
నేపము.................*an accusation.*
నేరము................*a crime.*
పందెము.........*a wager.*
కేడము.........*a shield.*
కళ్లెము.........*a bridle.*
టెక్కెము.......*a flag.*
బల్లెము.........*a spear.*

THIRD DECLENSION.

178 This declension includes all other regular nouns, of every gender, not comprized in the two foregoing declensions; it comprizes, therefore, all regular *neuters* in డు, all regular nouns in ము of two syllables only, or of more than two syllables when the ము is not preceded by ˘ ˉ or ˉ; in short, it comprizes every regular noun whether masculine, feminine, or neuter, provided it be not a masculine in ం డు, or a feminine or neuter, of more than two syllables, in ˘ము, ˉ ము or ˉము.

179 The inflexion singular is always the same as ths nominative singular; thus, nom. sing. బిడ్డ *a child,* inflex. sing. బిడ్డ. nom. sing. కత్తి *a knife* or *sword,* inflex. sing. కత్తి.

180 The nominative plural of nouns of this declension is formed by adding లు to the nominative singular, except to those ending in short ి which change the final ి into ులు; as, nom. sing. బిడ్డ *a child,* nom. plu. బిడ్డలు children; but as the noun కత్తి *a knife* or *sword,* ends in ి, it makes కత్తులు *swords,* in the nominative plural, never కత్తిలు.

181 The following is an example of this declension, declined according to the usual arrangement of six cases.

SINGULAR.		PLURAL.	
N. బిడ్డ	*a child.*	N. బిడ్డలు	*children.*
G. బిడ్డ or బిడ్డయొక్క	*of a child.*	G. బిడ్డల or బిడ్డలయొక్క	*of children.*
D. బిడ్డకు	*to a child.*	D. బిడ్డలకు	*to children.*
Acc. బిడ్డను &c.	*a child.*	Acc. బిడ్డలను &c.	*children.*
V. బిడ్డా	*o child.*	V. బిడ్డలారా	*o children.*
Ab. బిడ్డ - లో - చేత - తో	*in &c. do.*	Ab. బిడ్డల - లో - చేత - తో	*in &c. do.*

A few of the numerous words included in this declension are annexed. 182

అబ్బ . . . . . . *a father.*
తల . . . . . . *the head.*
గుంట . . . . . . *a pond, or tank.*
వెల . . . . . . *a price.*
గొల . . . . . . *a bunch.*
కొండ . . . . . . *a mountain.*
ఎలుక . . . . . . *a rat.*
జేన . . . . . . *a span.*
ఎముక . . . . . . *a bone.*
చీమ . . . . . . *an ant.*
కూర . . . . . . *curry.*
దవడ . . . . . . *the cheek.*
దూడ . . . . . . *a calf.*
కప్ప . . . . . . *a frog.*
పొగ . . . . . . *smoke.*
మెడ . . . . . . *the neck.*
మొగ్గ . . . . . . *a bud.*
నవలా . . . . . . *a woman.*
కొరడా . . . . . . *a whip.*
కల్లరి . . . . . . *a robber.*
చూపరి . . . . . . *a beautiful person.*
తలారి . . . . . . *a village-watcher.*
సోమారి . . . . . . *a lazy fellow.*
దాది . . . . . . *a nurse.*
చెవి . . . . . . *the ear.*
పని . . . . . . *business.*
పంది . . . . . . *a hog.*
కోతి . . . . . . *a monkey.*
బావి . . . . . . *a well.*

జెట్టి . . . . . . *a wrestler.*
పల్లకీ . . . . . . *a palanqueen.*
పట్టీ . . . . . . *a roll of beetle &c.*
పాము . . . . . . *a snake.*
చెరువు . . . . . . *an artificial lake.*
మడుగు . . . . . . *a natural lake.*
గొంతు . . . . . . *the neck.*
ముక్కు . . . . . . *the nose.*
అడుగు . . . . . . *a foot in length, a foot step.*
విందు . . . . . . *an entertainment.*
రొమ్ము . . . . . . *the breast.*
మందు . . . . . . *medicine.*
తావు . . . . . . *a place.*
ఎద్దు . . . . . . *a bull, an ox.*
పురుగు . . . . . . *an insect.*
పొద్దు . . . . . . *time.*
నిప్పు . . . . . . *fire.*
గుద్దు . . . . . . *a blow.*
తలుపు . . . . . . *a door.*
పాన్పు . . . . . . *bedding.*
తోపు . . . . . . *a grove.*
ఆకు . . . . . . *a leaf.*
పిడుగు . . . . . . *a thunder-bolt.*
జాబు . . . . . . *a letter.*
తుమ్ము . . . . . . *a sneeze.*
గిన్నె . . . . . . *a cup.*
గరిటె . . . . . . *a spoon.*
బూడిదె . . . . . . *ashes.*

గాడిదె .... *an ass.*
కిటికె .... *a window.*
తీగె .... *a creeping plant.*
పల్లె .... *a small village.*
బిందె .... *a large metal pot.*
ఈటె .... *a spear, or pike.*
పెట్టె .... *a box, a chest, a table.*
మై .... *the body.*

IRREGULAR PLURALS OF THE THIRD DECLENSION.

183 Many nouns ending in టి, టు, ట్టి, ట్టు, డ్డి, or డ్డు, which are regular both in the singular and plural, frequently drop the ు of the penultimate syllable in the plural number: thus, కోమటి *a person of the Comtee cast,* makes the nom. plu. కోమటులు or కోమట్లు; and if a double consonant precede the ు thus dropped, it is reduced to a single consonant in the nominative plural; thus, చెట్టు *a tree,* చెట్టులు or చెట్లు *trees,* బుడ్డి *a bottle,* nom. plu. బుడ్డులు or బుడ్లు *bottles.* గుడ్డు *an egg,* nom. plu. గుడ్డులు or గుడ్లు *eggs* &c.

184 Some nouns in డి or డు, regular in both numbers, form also an irregular plural, by changing the డి or డు of the nominative singular into ళ్లు; thus, nom. sing. పొడి *powder,* regular nom. plu. పొడులు, irregular nom. plu. పొళ్లు.

185 All nouns in this declension ending in డి or డు, which have the letter ఁ or ం immediately preceding these terminations, besides the regular plural, may have two irregular forms, viz. by changing the డి or డు of the nominative singular into either డ్లు or ళ్లు; thus, nom. sing. బండి *a carriage,* nom. plu. బండులు, irregular nom. plu. బండ్లు or బంళ్లు.

186 Many nouns having the termination of the nominative singular in లి or లు, in addition to the regular plural, form an irregular one in the manner mentioned in rule 184; thus, మొసలి *an alligator,* makes in the nom. plu. either మొసలులు or మొసళ్లు but nouns of two short syllables ending in లి or లు have the regular plural only, పులి *a tiger,* makes పులులు *tigers,* never పుళ్లు.

187 The noun పెండిలి *marriage,* makes in the nom. plu. పెండిండ్లు, or పెండింళ్లు or పెండిండులు *marriages.*

188 Some nouns, having the nominative singular in ను, change that syllable in the nom. plu. into ఁకులు; thus, కొలను *a tank,* nom. plu. కొలఁకులు; others

change the ను into ఁగులు; thus, గోను *the name of a tree,* nom. plu. గోఁగులు; others change the ను into లు in the nom. plu. as, మీను *a fish,* nom. plu. మీలు *fishes,* and others have the regular plural by adding లు to the nom. sing. thus, మేను *the body,* nom. plu. మేనులు *bodies,* కౌను *the waist,* nom. plu. కౌనులు *waists.*

The noun రేయి *night* makes the nom. plu. రేలు, and the noun ఆవు *a cow,* 189
makes in the nom. plu. either ఆవులు or ఆలు.

IRREGULAR దేశ్యము NOUNS.

As it is hardly possible to form any general rules for the declension of the 190
irregular దేశ్యము nouns: a list of most of them is subjoined, shewing the nominative singular, the inflexion singular, and the nominative plural of each. Except in the formation of these cases, the whole follow the general rules for declension laid down in rule 143 &c.

Most of the following nouns change the last syllable of the nominative sin- 191
gular into టి or ఁటి to form the inflexion singular, and into ండ్లు or ళ్లు to form the nominative plural, some of them also form the nominative plural, in the regular manner by adding లు to the nominative singular.

Nom. sing.		*Inflex. sing.*	*Nom. plu.*
ఎసరు	*Water boiled, for the purpose of dressing rice &c.*	ఎసటి	ఎసరులు or ఎసళ్లు
కుదురు	*Any thing placed under a round vessel, to prevent it's falling, such as a straw rope &c.*	కుదుటి	కుదురులు or కుదుళ్లు
నుదురు	*The forehead*	నుదుటి	నుదురులు or నుదుళ్లు
నోరు	*The mouth*	నోటి	నోరులు or నోళ్లు
పడమఱ	*The west*	పడమటి	పడమఱలు
ఏఱు	*A river*	ఏటి	ఏఱులు or ఏళ్లు
బైలు	*A plain, an open field, an empty space of ground, an esplanade, the outside.*	బైటి	బైలులు or బైళ్లు
అంగిలి	*The palate or throat*	అంగిటి	అంగిలులు or అంగిల్లు

Nom. Sing.		*Inflex. Sing.*	*Nom. Plu.*
అంబలి	*A kind of pap made of raggy.*	అంబటి	అంబలులు or అంబళ్లు
కౌఁగిలి	*The breast*, literally *the place of embrace*......	కౌఁగిటి	కౌఁగిలులు or కౌఁగిళ్లు
గుప్పిలి	*The fist*......	గుప్పిటి	గుప్పిలులు or గుప్పిళ్లు
చెక్కిలి	*The cheek*......	చెక్కిటి	చెక్కిలులు or చెక్కిళ్లు
పురుడు	*The imaginary pollution proceeding from the birth of a child*......	పురిటి	పురుడులు or పురుళ్లు
దోయిలి	*The palms of both hands joined together, to hold anything.*	దోయిటి	దోయిలులు or దోయిళ్లు
దోసిలి	*do ... do ... do*....	దోసిటి	దోసిలులు or దోసిళ్లు
నాగలి	*A plough*......	నాఁగటి	నాగలులు-నాగళ్లు or నాగండ్లు
పిడికిలి	*The fist*......	పిడికిఁటి	పిడికిలులు or పిడికిళ్లు
పుక్కిలి	*The interior of the cheek*......	పుక్కిటి	పుక్కిలులు or పుక్కిళ్లు
పుడిసిలి	*The palm of one hand, held in such a manner as to contain any thing placed in it*....	పుడిసిటి	పుడిసిలులు or పుడిసిళ్లు
పొక్కలి	*A number of loose bricks or stones, formed into a fire-place*......	పొక్కటి	పొక్కళ్లు or పొక్కండ్లు
పొక్కిలి	*The navel*......	పొక్కిటి	పొక్కిళ్లు
ముంగిలి	*The Court yard, the enclosed empty space of ground within a native house*......	ముంగిటి	ముంగిలులు or ముంగిళ్లు
రోకలి	*A large pestle*......	రోకఁటి	రోకలులు రోకండ్లు or రోకళ్లు
లోగిలి	*The interior*......	లోగిటి	లోగిళ్లు or లోగిండ్లు
వాకిలి	*An opening, a door-frame*...	వాకిటి	వాకిళ్లు or వాకిఁడ్లు
సందిలి	*The arm between the shoulder and the elbow*......	సందిటి	సందిలిలు or సందిళ్లు
గాడి	*A reservoir, a cistern, a manger*......	గాటి	గాడులు or గాళ్లు
కాడు	*A sepulchre, a place for burying or burning the dead.*	కాటి	కాళ్లు
కూడు	*Food*......	కూటి	కూడులు or కూళ్లు

Nom. Sing.		Inflex. Sing.	Nom. Plu.
కూరాడు	*The water in which rice has been washed, grown sour and boiled, vinegar.*	కూరాటి,	కూరాడులు or కూరాళ్లు
కోడు	*The leg of a bed-stead*	కోటి	కోడులు or కోళ్లు
త్రాడు	*A rope*	త్రాటి	త్రాడులు or త్రాళ్లు
చవుడు	*The earth on salt or barren ground, fuller's earth*	చవుటి	చవుళ్లు
తాడు	*The Palm tree*	తాటి	తాడులు or తాళ్లు
గూడు *	*A nest*	గూటి	గూడులు or గూళ్లు
నాడు	*A Country, or district; a general assembly: it also means a day, or time*	నాటి	నాళ్లు
పాడు	*Rising ground unfit for the cultivation of grain, in which tobacco and other plants of the same kind are grown.*	పాటి	పాడులు or పాళ్లు
పెరడు	*The back yard*	పెరటి	పెరడులు or పెరళ్లు
బీడు	*Pasture land*	బీటి	బీడులు or బీళ్లు
వీడు †	*A town*	వీటి	వీడులు or వీళ్లు

Most of the following nouns have the singular inflexion the same as the nominative singular, or form it by changing the last syllable of the nominative singular into టి; some however form the inflexion singular very irregularly. The nominative plural is formed either in the regular manner, by adding లు to the nominative singular, or by changing the last syllable of the nominative singular into ళ్లు or ళ్ళు. 192

Nom. Sing.		Inflex. Sing.	Nom. Plu.
కదురు	*A spindle*	కదురు or కదుటి-	కదురులు or కదుళ్లు
గోరు	*The nail or claw*	గోరు or గోటి	గోరులు or గోళ్లు
నీరు	*Water*	నీరు or నీటి	నీళ్లు
నెత్తురు	*Blood*	నెత్తురు or నెత్తుటి	నెత్తురులు
పన్నీరు	*Rose water*	పన్నీరు or పన్నీటి	

* గుడ్డు *an egg*, does not admit of any change of this kind, it is included in the 3d declension.

† The pronoun వీఁడు, *he, this man*, does not admit of any such change.

Nom. Sing.		*Inflex. Sing.*	*Nom. Plu.*
మున్నీరు	*(*మున్ *first and* నీరు *water, the first water,)* The *sea...*	మున్నీరు or మున్నీటి	మున్నీరులు
ఎదురు	*The front, that which is opposite*	ఎదురు or ఎదుటి	
కుందేలు	*A hare*........	కుందేలు or కుందేటి	కుందేలులు or కుందేళ్లు
నొసలు	*The forehead*........	నొసలు or నొసటి	నొసలులు or నొసళ్లు
మొదలు	*The beginning*........	మొదలు or మొదటి	మొదలులు or మొదళ్లు
తాబేలు	*A tortoise*........	తాబేలు or తాబేటి	తాబేలులు or తాబేళ్లు
రోలు	*A mortar*........	రోలు or రోటి	రోలులు or రోళ్లు
ఆఁకలి	*Hunger, appetite*........	ఆఁకలి or ఆఁకటి	ఆఁకళ్లు or ఆఁకండ్లు
ఎంగిలి	*Spittle*........	ఎంగిలి or ఎంగిటి	ఎంగిళ్లు or ఎంగిండ్లు
కొడవలి	*A sickle*........	కొడవలి or కొడవఁటి	కొడవళ్లు or కొడవండ్లు
పందిలి	*A pandal, or shed*........	పందిలి or పందిటి	పందిలులు or పందిళ్లు
పొంగలి	*Boiled rice mixed with milk, and seasoned with sugar and other articles, that give a high relish: this word is derived from the verb* పొంగు *to effervesce*........	పొంగలి or పొంగటి	పొంగలులు or పొంగళ్లు
గుద్దలి	*An instrument for digging, somewhat like a short hoe...*	గుద్దలి or గుద్దఁటి	గుద్దలులు or గుద్దండ్లు
గొడ్డలి	*An axe*........	గొడ్డలి or గొడ్డఁటి	గొడ్డలులు or గొడ్డండ్లు
బాణలి	*An iron plate upon which cakes are toasted*........	బాణలి or బాణఁటి	బాణండ్లు
చోటు	*A place*........	చోటు or చోటి	చోటులు or చోట్లు
కావడి	*A piece of wood, placed upon the shoulder for carrying a burden, like that used by milk-maids in England*........	కావడి or కావటి	కావడులు or కావళ్లు
జోడు	*A pair, a pair of shoes*........	జోడు or జోటి	జోడులు or జోళ్లు
తవుడు	*Bran, the substance on rice below the husk, the husk is called* ఊక	తవుడు or తవుటి	
పండు	*Fruit*........	పండు or పంటి	పండులు or పంళ్లు or పండ్లు
పుండు	*A boil or sore*........	పుండు or పుంటి	పుండులు-పుంళ్లు or పుండ్లు

Nom. Sing.		*Inflex. Sing.*	*Nom. Plu.*
ఒళ్లు	*The body*......................	ఒళ్లి or ఒంటి	ఒళ్లులు
ఊరు	*A village*......................	ఊరు or ఊరి	ఊరులు or ఊళ్లు
నూలు	*Thread*......................	నూలు or నూలి	
గూను	*A humped back*............	గూను or గూని	గూనులు
చేను	*A field producing grain*......	చేను or చేని	చేలు
మాను	*A tree, wood*..................	మాను or మాని	మాఁకులు or మానులు
మేను	*The body*......................	మేను or మేని	మేనులు
పేరు	*A name, an appellation*......	పేరు or పేరిఁటి	పేరులు or పేళ్లు
పాలు*	*A share*......................	పాలి or పాలిఁటి	పాలులు or పాళ్లు
కూఁతురు	*A daughter*............	కూఁతు or కూఁతురి	కూఁతురులు or కూఁతుండ్లు

The following nouns change the last syllable of the nominative singular 193
into ంటి to form the inflexion singular, and into ండులు, or ంళ్లు or ండ్లు to form the nominative plural: some of them also form the nominative plural in the regular manner, by adding లు to the nominative singular.

Nom. Sing.		*Inflex. Sing.*	*Nom. Plu.*
ఇల్లు	*A house*......................	ఇంటి	ఇల్లులు or ఇండులు or ఇంళ్లు or ఇండ్లు
పల్లు	*A tooth*......................	పంటి	పల్లులు or పండులు or పంళ్లు or పండ్లు
ముల్లు	*A thorn*......................	ముంటి	ముల్లులు or ముండులు or ముంళ్లు or ముండ్లు
విల్లు	*A bow*......................	వింటి	విల్లులు or విండులు or వింళ్లు or విండ్లు
కన్ను	*The eye*......................	కంటి	కన్నులు or కంళ్లు or కండ్లు
చన్ను	*A female's breast*......	చంటి	చన్నులు or చంళ్లు or చండ్లు
మన్ను	*Sand*......................	మంటి	మన్నులు
మిన్ను	*The sky, the atmosphere*	మింటి	మిన్నులు

The nouns noted below change the last syllable of the nominative singular 194
into తి in the inflexion singular, and into తులు in the nominative plural; and those which end in య్యి, with a short vowel preceding it, lengthen that vowel

* పాలు *Milk* does not admit of any such change: it is a plural noun of the 3d declension.

both in the inflexion singular and nominative plural, రాయి *a stone* makes in the nominative plural రాలు or రాళ్లు.

Nom. Sing.		*Inflex. Sing.*	*Nom. Plu.*
దాయి	*Any thing on which artificers place their work, an anvil, &c.*	దాతి	దాతులు
రాయి	*A stone*	రాతి	రాలు or రాళ్లు
వాయి	*The mouth*	వాతి	వాతులు
గొయ్యి	*A hole in the ground, a pit*	గోతి	గోతులు
చెయ్యి	*The hand*	చేతి	చేతులు
నుయ్యి	*A small well*	నూతి	నూతులు
నెయ్యి	*Ghee*	నేతి	నేతులు
రొయ్యి	*The ashes of wood*	రోతి	

195 The following nouns in ట్టు change that syllable into ట్టి to form the inflexion singular; they form the nominative plural either in the regular manner, by adding లు to the nominative singular, or by changing the last syllable of the nominative singular into ళ్లు.

Nom. Sing.		*Inflex. Sing.*	*Nom. Plu.*
అట్టు	*The neck*	అట్టి	అట్టులు or అళ్లు
కట్టు	*The plough share*	కట్టి	కట్టులు or కళ్లు
కొట్టు	*An iron or wooden spike on which criminals were impaled*	కొట్టి	కొట్టులు or కొళ్లు
గొట్టు	*A sowing machine*... ...	గొట్టి	గొట్టులు or గొళ్లు
మిట్టు	*Elevated ground*	మిట్టి	

196 The nouns noted below form the inflexion singular in లి or టి, and the nominative plural either in లులు or ళ్లు: some of them want the nominative.

Nom. Sing.		*Inflex. Sing.*	*Nom. Plu.*
	The left side	దాపలి or దాపటి	
	The inside	లోపలి or లోపటి	
	That side	ఆవలి	

Nom. Sing.		*Inflex. Sing.*	*Nom. Plu.*
	The further side......................	అవతలి	
	The right side..........................	వలపలి or వలపటి	
	This side.................................	ఈవలి	
	The nearer side.........................	ఇవతలి	
కాలు	*The leg*..................................	కాలి	కాలులు or కాళ్లు
కేలు	*The hand*................................	కేలి	
ప్రోలు	*A town*..................................	ప్రోలి	ప్రోలు or ప్రోళ్లు
వ్రేలు	*The finger*..............................	వ్రేలి	వ్రేలులు or వ్రేళ్లు

The singular inflexions, and the nominative, plural, of the following nouns 197
denoting time, are formed very irregularly.

Nom. Sing.		*Inflex. Sing.*	*Nom. plu.*
ఎన్నఁడు	*Every day, ever.* (ఎ *which ?* & న్నఁడు *corrupted from* నాడు *a day*).................	ఎన్నటి	
ఏఁడు	*A year*................................	ఏటి	ఏఁడ్లు or ఏఁడులు
నిరుడు	*Last year*............................	నిరుటి	
నేడు	*To day*................................	నేటి	
అప్పుడు	*That time, then*..................	అప్పటి	
ఇప్పుడు	*This time, now*...................	ఇప్పటి	
ఎప్పుడు	*Which time, when*...............	ఎప్పటి	
పొద్దు †	*Time*..................................	పొద్దుటి	
పగలు	*Day-time, noon*..................	పగటి	పగళ్లు
నిన్న	*Yesterday*...........................	నిన్నటి	
మొన్న	*The day before yesterday*......	మొన్నటి	
మాపు	*Night, evening*....................	మాపటి	మాపులు
రేపు	*Tomorrow, early in the morning*......................	రేపటి	రేపులు
సపు	*Time, in composition only ; as,* జాము సేపటికి *in 3 hours time.*		
తొల్లి	*Former - times*....................	తొంటి తొల్లిఁటి	

† when the noun పొద్దు affixes the postposition న, thus పొద్దున, it means *in the morning*.

198 కల్లు when it denotes the liquor extracted from the Cocoanut, Palmyra, or Date tree, is a regular noun of the 3d. declension ; but when it denotes *a stone,* it becomes in the sing. inflex. కంటి , and in the nom. plu. కండ్లు.

199 ఎఁడు *measure* is used only in composition with other nouns, and in the inflexion becomes ఎఁటి ; thus, ఎఁడు compounded with బార *a fathom,* makes the nominative singular బారెఁడు *the measure of a fathom, a fathom's length,* and the inflexion singular బారెఁటి.

200 Most of the irregular దేశ్యము nouns, which have the inflexion different from the nominative singular, by changing the final vowel of that inflexion into అ, form, in a manner peculiar to themselves, an inflected local or instrumental ablative ; they have also the regular form by the addition of the post-positions లో - చేత &c. thus, inflexion కంటి *the eye,* inflected ablative కంట, regular ablative కంటి-లో-చేత &c. *in* or *by, the eye* ; and many of these iflected ablatives are used as adverbs or postpositions ; thus from the inflexion బైటి comes బైట *in a plain* or *outside ;* from మొదటి, మొదట *in the beginning,* or *at first,* from లోపలి, లోపల *in the inside,* or *inside.*

201 The student will find it of great advantage to commit to memory the following list of nouns, denoting the several degrees of consanguinity and affinity, peculiar to the people of Telingana.

తండ్రి	*a father*............	*a mother*..................	తల్లి
		a step mother..............	సవతితల్లి
పెత్తండ్రి	*a father's elder brother*..	*his wife*..................	పెత్తల్లి
		also a mother's elder sister.	
పినతండ్రి	*a father's younger brother*	*his wife*..................	పినతల్లి
		also a mother's young sister.	
తాత	*a grand father*........	*a grand mother*............	అవ్వ
మామ	*a father in law*......	*a mother in law*..........	అత్త
మేనమామ	*a mother's brother*.....	*his wife*..................	మేనత్త
		also a father's sister.	

బావ { if older than oneself. if older than the husband. } { the son of a mother's brother, or of a father's sister, a man's brother in law. ... also a woman's brother in law. ... } { if younger than oneself. if younger than the husband. } మఱఁది

వదినె { if older than oneself. } the daughter of a mother's brother, or of a father's sister. { if younger than oneself. } మఱఁదలు

వదినె also denotes *the elder sister of a wife or husband, or an elder brother's wife.*

మఱఁదలు also denotes *the younger sister of a wife or husband, or a younger brother's wife.*

అన్న *an elder brother* .... *an elder sister* .... అక్క

తమ్ముఁడు *a younger brother* .... *a younger sister* ..... చెల్లెలు

మగఁడు - పెనిమిటి *a husband* .... *a wife* .... పెంద్లాము

బిడ్డ ... ... *a child*

కొడుకు *a son* ... ... *a daughter* ... ... కూఁతురు

మనమఁడు *a grand son* ... ... *a grand daughter* .... మనమరాలు

అల్లుఁడు *a son in law* ... ... *a daughter in law* ... ... కోడలు

మేనల్లుఁడు { *the son of a man's sister or of a woman's brother.* .... ⁞ *the daughter of a man's sister or of a woman's brother* .... } .... మేనకోడలు

సవతి *the wives of the same husband to each other.*

తోడికోడలు *the wives of two brothers to each other, joint daughters-in-law.*

సడ్డకుఁడు *the husbands of two sisters to each other.*

వియ్యంపురాలు *mothers in law to each other.*

వియ్యంకుఁడు *fathers in law to each other.*

All the words in the above list preceding తాత *a grand father*, and అవ్వ 202
a grandmother, and following తమ్ముఁడు *a younger brother*, and చెల్లెలు *a younger sister*, together with the words మఱఁది - మఱఁదలు - మేనత్త and మేనమామ, though expressing degrees of relationship, are never used in

addressing the person to whom they refer ; in speaking to such relations, the males are called నాయన - అన్నయ్య - కక్క - బాబు, and the females అమ్మ - పెద్దమ్మ or పిన్నమ్మ &c.

203 A native never addresses his wife by name, nor by the term denoting the degree of her affinity to him : but, in speaking to her, makes used of ఓసి and other words, equivalent to our phrases " I say, Hear you." &c. It is considered a great indelicacy, approaching almost to indecency, even to mention the name of one's wife or husband to any person.

204 Such nouns in the foregoing list, denoting females, as have the nominative singular in లు, form the singular inflexion by changing that termination to ఐ, and the nom. plu. by changing it to ండ్లు or ండ్రు.

OF NOUNS TERMED తత్సమములు OR SANSCRIT DERIVATIVES.

205 All Sanscrit * nouns may be adopted into this language ; but they appear in it under a new form, by assuming terminations and cases peculiar to the Teloogoo.

206 In explaining the derivation of Teloogoo nouns from the Sanscrit, Native Grammarians divide all the nouns in the sanscrit language into two classes, మహత్తులు, *the superior*, and అమహత్తులు *the inferior*. The మహత్తులు *or superior class* includes nouns of the masculine gender, and the అమహత్తులు *or inferior class* comprises those of the feminine, and neuter gender, as defined in rule 141.

207 The Sanscrit derivative is formed from the crude Sanscrit noun, and crude nouns, in the Sanscrit language, generally terminate in the vowels ా ీ ి ె ు ూ ృ, or in the consonants చ్ జ్ త్ ద్ ధ్ న్ ప్ భ్ మ్ ర్ వ్ శ్ ష్ స్ హ్

208 If the crude Sanscrit noun becomes a nominative singular in Teloogoo by affixing the termination ండు, it is declined like the nouns of the first regular దేశ్యము declension. If, in order to form the nominative singular, it assumes the Teloogoo affix ము, it follows the rules for the second regular దేశ్యము declension ; and if it is modified in any other manner, or is not changed at all, it

* The rules respecting sanscrit derivatives and corruptions apply to adjectives, as well as to substantives, borrowed from that language.

is declined like the nouns of the third regular దేశ్యము declension. It will suffice, therefore, to shew how the nominative singular in Teloogoo is formed from the crude Sanscrit noun; for, when that is known, this general rule will guide the student in declining it.

OF CRUDE SANSCRIT NOUNS ENDING IN VOWELS.

1st OF THOSE IN ✓

Crude Sanscrit nouns ending in short ✓ form the nominative singular, 209
in Teloogoo, by changing that termination into ుఁడు, if they be of the మహత్తులు *superior class*, and by merely affixing ము if they be of the అమహత్తులు *inferior class*; thus, in the మహత్తులు or *superior class*,

రామ *The God Rama* makes the nom. sing. in Teloogoo రాముఁడు
భాస్కర *the sun* literally *light-maker*.. ... ...do. ... ... భాస్కరుఁడు
హిమకర *the* † *moon* literally *snow-rayed*... ... ...do... ... ... హిమకరుఁడు

రాముఁడు &c. are declined precisely in the same manner as తమ్ముఁడు &c. see rule 164; and, as all Sanscrit derivatives ending in ఁడు have the vowel ు preceding ఁడు of the nominative singular, every noun of this description takes the two forms explained in rule 165.

thus, also in the అమహత్తులు *inferior class*.

వన *a garden, a forest* makes the nom. sing. in Teloogoo వనము
పర్వత *a mountain*.. ... ...*do*... ... ...*do*... ... ... పర్వతము
గృహ *a dwelling*.. ... ...*do*... ... ...*do*... ... ... గృహము
గజ *an elephant*... ... ...*do*... ... ...*do*... ... ... గజము
పాప *sin*.. ... ...*do*... ... ...*do*... ... ... పాపము
కమల *a lotus*... ... ...*do*... ... ...*do*... ... ... కమలము
వనము &c. are declined exactly in the same manner as . . . గుఱ్ఱము
see rule 172.

EXCEPTIONS.

The noun మిత్ర *a friend*, together with words used in composition to 210
imply eminence, as సింహ *a lion* వ్యాఘ్ర *a tiger* &c. are considered included

† The sun and moon are included in the మహత్తులు or superior class, because they are considered, or at least personified, by the Hindoos, as male divinities.

both in the superior and the inferior classes. Thus, we may say either మిత్రుఁడు or మిత్రము *a friend,* పురుషసింహము or పురుషసింహుఁడు *a man-lion, a noble person,* పురుషవ్యాఘ్రము or పురుషవ్యాఘ్రుఁడు *a man-tiger, a fierce person.*

211 The noun అపత్య *offspring* makes అపత్యము, never అపత్యుఁడు, and the word శరణ denoting, either *a house,* or a *protector, refuge* &c. when it has the latter meaning, takes in Teloogoo three forms, శరణము or శరణు or శరణుఁడు; but, when it means *a house,* it has the first form only.

212 The nouns ప్రౌఢ *an experienced person, and* దూత *a messenger, a spy,* included in the మహత్తులు or *superior class,* together with all nouns of the female gender, and the words కుశ *a kind of holy grass,* usually named *durb,ha,* చీర *a woman's garment,* హంస *a swan,* కోకిల *the Indian nightingale,* చరిత or చరిత్ర *a history,* భ్రమ *delirium, confusion,* అభిలాష *desire,* విజృంభణ *exaggeration,* or *enlargement,* కుండ *an earthen pot,* with some other nouns of the అమహత్తులు or *inferior class,* do not affix the terminations mentioned in the above rules, but, remaining unchanged, are declined according to the rules for the third regular దేశ్యము declension.

2d OF THOSE IN ి

213 Crude Sanscrit nouns of all genders ending in short ి, when brought into Teloogoo, do not undergo any change; and, therefore are all declined like దేశ్యము nouns in ి, of the 3d. declension.

హరి *The God Vishnoo* makes the nom. sing. in Teloogoo.........హరి

మతి *Mind*...................do...... ., ...do...... ....మతి

మణి *A precious stone*....do...............do.............................మణి

3d OF THOSE IN ు

214 Crude Sanscrit nouns in short ు, when adopted into Teloogoo, either undergo no change, or they form the nominative singular by affixing either వు or ఁడు if they be included in the మహత్తులు or *superior class,* but వు only if they be of the అమహత్తులు or *inferior class;* thus, in the మహత్తులు or *superior class,*

గురు *A spiritual guide* {makes the nom. sing. in Teloogoo........} గురు or గురువు or గురుఁడు

విష్ణు *The God Vishnoo*............*do*.......... విష్ణు or విష్ణువు or విష్ణుఁడు

భాను *The sun*... ... ...*do*... .... భాను or భానువు or భానుఁడు

విధు *The moon*.......... ... ...*do*..... .... విధు or విధువు or విధుఁడు

శత్రు *An enemy*... ... ...*do*.... ... ...శత్రు or శత్రువు or శత్రుఁడు

గురుఁడు &c. follow the rules for the 1st. declension.

గురువు &c. and గురు &c. are declined like nouns of the 3d. declension.

Thus, also, in the అమహత్తులు or *inferior class*.

తను *the body* makes the nom. sing. in Teloogoo తను or తనువు

మధు *wine, honey*........ *do*......... మధు or మధువు

అంశు *a ray*............ *do*........ అంశు or అంశువు

అంబు *water*........... *do*........ అంబు or అంబువు

ధేను *a cow*........... *do*........ ధేను or ధేనువు

తను &c. and తనువు &c. follow the rules for the 3d declension.

4th OF THOSE IN ఋ

Crude Sanscrit nouns, ending in short ఋ, form the nominative singular in Teloogoo by changing that termination into ‿; thus; భ్రాతృ *a brother* మాతృ *a mother* &c. make భ్రాత and మాత respectively, which are, of course, declined like nouns of the 3d declension. 215

EXCEPTIONS.

The nouns విధాతృ *the Creator*, సవితృ *the sun*, దాతృ *a giver*, and నేతృ *a leader*, with a few others, admit of another form, by affixing ఁడు; thus, we may say either విధాతృఁడు or విధాత *the Creator* &c. 216

5th OF THOSE IN ై ో AND ౌ.

The crude Sanscrit noun రై *money* ending in ై makes the nom. sing. in [Teloogoo రో

........*do*........ గో *a cow*......ో......*do*...... గోవు

........*do*...... నౌ *a ship*......ౌ......*do*.. నావ or నావి

........*do*...... గ్లౌ *the moon* has no change, the Teloogoo nom. sing. [being also గ్లౌ

No other crude Sanscrit nouns ending in ౄ or ఌ ౡ are ever found in Teloogoo works. It is, therefore, unnecessary to lay down any rules respecting them.

6th OF THOSE ENDING IN LONG VOWELS.

217 Except monosyllables, all crude Sanscrit nouns ending in the long vowels ీ or ూ, when adopted into Teloogoo, change these long terminations into the corresponding short vowels, ి and ు.

All nouns ending in long vowels, thus converted to short vowels, are considered as originally terminating in these short vowels; and, accordingly, form the nominative singular in Teloogoo, agreeably to the rules already given for crude Sanscrit nouns ending in short ి or ు respectively.

EXAMPLES.

విశ్వపా *The protector of the world,* being changed into విశ్వప, makes the [nom. sing. in Teloogoo విశ్వపుఁడు see 209.

స్వయంభూ { *self existent,* being changed into స్వయంభు do do } స్వయంభు or స్వయంభువు or స్వయంభుఁడు see 214.

రమా { *the wife of Vishnoo,* being feminine, is merely shortened into......... } రమ see 212.

వాణీ { *Suruswuttee* ...... *the goddess of learning,* } do.. do... వాణి see 213.

వధూ { *a woman,* makes the nom. sing. in Teloogoo either, } ......వధు or వధువు see 214.

218 భూ the *earth,* (భ్రూ) *an eye brow,* (స్త్రీ) *a woman* &c. being monosyllables, never shorten the last vowel; when adopted into Teloogoo, they remain the same as in Sanscrit, and are declined like the nouns of the 3d. regular దేశ్యము declension.

OF CRUDE SANSCRIT NOUNS ENDING IN CONSONANTS.

219 Crude Sanscrit nouns ending in the consonants చ్ జ్ ద్ ధ్ భ్ శ్ ష్ and హ్ form the nominative singular, in Teloogoo, either by changing చ్ and జ్ to క్కు - ద్ and ధ్ to త్తు - భ్ to ప్పు - శ్ and హ్ to ట్టు or క్కు - and ష్ to ట్టు for all genders-or, if masculine, by affixing ుండు, and if neuter, by adding ము.

EXAMPLES.

Masculine or feminine. *Masculine.*

పుష్పముచ్ makes పుష్పముక్కు or పుష్పముచుఁడు *one who strews flowers.*

వేదవిద్ .... do .. వేదవిత్తు .... or వేదవిదుఁడు ... *one skilled in the vedas.*

పాలితకకుభ్ do .. పాలితకకుప్పు or పాలితకకుభుఁడు *one who protects the cor- [ners of the world.*

ఘృతస్పృశ్ ... do .. ఘృతస్పృక్కు or ఘృతస్పృశుఁడు *one who touches ghee.*

విశ్ .... do..... విట్టు ...... or విశుఁడు ..... *a person of th 3d Hindoo [class.*

సురద్విష్.... do.... సురద్విట్టు ... or సురద్విషుఁడు *an enemy of the Sooras, [or angels; a gaint.*

అమృతలిహ్ do. .... అమృతలిట్టు ...or అమృతలిహుఁడు *one who feeds on nectar or ambrosia, an immortal person.*

Neuter.

త్వచ్ ..... do ... త్వక్కు .... or త్వచము ..... *skin, leather, bark.*

స్రజ్ ..... do ... స్రక్కు ...... or స్రజము ...... *a wreath.*

పరిషద్.... do ... పరిషత్తు ...... or పరిషదము .... *a society, an assembly.*

కకుభ్ .... do ... కకుప్పు .... or కకుభము ..... *a corner of the world.*

ప్రావృష్ . do ... ప్రావృట్టు ... or ప్రావృషము . *the rainy season.*

మధులిహ్ .. do ... మధులిట్టు .... or మధులిహము .. *a large bee.*

పుష్పముచుఁడు &c. follow the rules for the 1st. declension.

పుష్పముక్కు &c. are declined like the nouns of the 3d. declension.

EXCEPTIONS.

చ్

వాచ్ *speech, a word,* makes వాక్కు, but not వాచము. 220

ద్

సంపద్ *good fortune,* and ఆపద్ *adversity,* make సంపత్తు and ఆపత్తు or సంపద and ఆపద.

విపద్ *calamity* makes only విపత్తు.

ముద్ *joy* .... do ..... ముదము.

ధ్

The nouns క్షుధ్ *appetite,* &c. సమిధ్ *a sacrificial stick,* make either క్షుత్తు and సమిత్తు or క్షుధ and సమిధ - క్రుధ్ *rage* makes క్రుధ.

శ్

దృశ్ *an eye*, & దిశ్ *a side, or quarter*, make దృక్కు and దృశ, or దిక్కు and దిశ.

ష్

రుష్ *anger*, & త్విష్ *splendour*, make రుట్టు and రుష, or త్విట్టు and త్విష.

221 Crude Sanscrit nouns ending in త్ change it to త్తు, to form the nominative singular in Teloogoo; thus, వియత్ *the sky*, విద్యుత్ *lightning*, మరుత్ *wind*, గరుత్ *a feather*, &c. make వియత్తు - విద్యుత్తు - మరుత్తు - గరుత్తు which are, of course, declined according to the rules for the 3rd. declension.

EXCEPTIONS.

222 The nouns భగవత్ *the Deity*, and హనుమత్ *Hunooman*, have respectively the following irregular forms. భగవంతుఁడు - భగవానుఁడు - హనుమంతుఁడు - హనుమానుఁడు - హనుమ.

జగత్ *the universe* makes జగత్తు or జగము.

నీవృత్ *a village or country* makes నీవృత్తు or నీవృతము.

223 Crude Sanscrit nouns in న్ drop the final consonant, and then form the nominative singular in Teloogoo according to the rules for crude Sanscrit nouns ending in the particular vowel with which they terminate.

EXAMPLE.

అర్యమన్ *the sun* by dropping న్ is changed to అర్యమ and then becomes in [Teloogoo అర్యముఁడు see 209.

హేమన్ *gold* .... do .... do ... హేమ ...... do ... do హేమము see 209.

కరిన్ *an elephant* .... do... కరి .... do ... do కరి see 213.

శూలిన్ {*the trident bearer, the God Siva*} do. శూలి ....do ... do శూలి see 213.

EXCEPTIONS.

ఆత్మన్ *the soul, the supreme being*, becomes in Teloogoo ఆత్ముఁడు or ఆత్మము or ఆత్మ

రాజన్ *a king* .... do .... రాజు

బ్రహ్మన్ {when denoting *Brumha*, one of the three attributes of the divinity, personified in the Indian Trinity, becomes ....} do ... బ్రహ్మ.

బ్రహ్మన్ when denoting the *supreme being* himself, becomes either బ్రహ్మము or బ్రహ్మ.

Nouns ending in ిమన్ have also an irregular form.

EXAMPLE.

లఘిమన్ *lightness, smallness,* makes లఘిమ or లఘిమము.

Crude Sanscrit nouns ending in ప్ మ్ ర్ క్ are rarely adopted into the Teloogoo. 224

Crude Sanscrit nouns terminating with స్ form the nominative singular in Teloogoo, either by affixing సు or ు; or, after dropping the final consonant, by following the rules for crude Sanscrit nouns ending in the particular vowel with which they terminate. Masculine nouns in ‿స్ admit of a fourth form, by assuming ుఁడు without dropping the final స్ 225

EXAMPLES.

Masculine.

ఊర్ధ్వతేజస్ makes in Teloogoo ఊర్ధ్వతేజస్సు or ఊర్ధ్వతేజసు or ఊర్ధ్వతేజుఁడు or ఊర్ధ్వతేజసుఁడు *an anchorite.*

Feminine.

హేమతేజస్ do. . . . do. . . హేమతేజస్సు or హేమతేజసు or హేమతేజ [*a female resplendent as gold.*

Neuter.

మనస్ . . . . do. . . . . do. . . మనస్సు or మనసు or మనము *the mind.*
శిరస్ . . . . . do. . . . . do. . . శిరస్సు or శిరసు or శిరము *the head.*
ఉరస్ . . . . do. . . . . do. . . ఉరస్సు or ఉరసు or ఉరము *the breast.*
వక్షస్ . . . . do. . . . do. . . వక్షస్సు or వక్షసు or వక్షము *the breast.*
యశస్......... do. ... ... do. ... యశస్సు or యశసు or యశము *fame.*
తపస్ ... ...do. ... ... do. ... తపస్సు or తపసు or తపము *penance.*
తమస్... ... ...do. ... ... do. ... తమస్సు or తమసు or తమము *darkness.*
తేజస్... ... ... do. ... ... do. ... తేజస్సు or తేజసు or తేజము *lustre.*
ఆయుస్... ..... do. ... ... do.... ఆయుస్సు or ఆయుసు or ఆయు or ఆయువు *the* [*total period of life.*

EXCEPTIONS.

పయస్ *water* or *milk,* అయస్ *iron,* హవిస్ *a sacrificial fire-offering,* రక్షస్ *a giant,* చేతస్ *the mind,* మహస్ *lustre,* సరస్ *a lake,* అంహస్ *sin,* పాథస్ *water,* అంభస్ *water,* ఆగస్ *transgression,* and a few others, affix only the syllable సు as పయస్సు - అయస్సు &c. 226

When the noun వయస్ signifies *a bird* it makes వయస్సు, but when it signifies *the total period of life*, or *youth*, or *age*, &c. it makes either, వయసు or వయస్సు - అప్సరస్ *a nymph*, makes అప్సరస, or అప్సరస్సు; వేధస్, *the Creator*, *Brumha*, makes వేధ.

OF NOUNS TERMED తద్భవములు OR CORRUPTIONS OF THE SANSCRIT.

227 Besides the regular Sanscrit derivatives, there is in Teloogoo a class of words named తద్భవములు, or corruptions of the Sanscrit. These are formed from the crude Sanscrit noun by the substitution of one letter for another; by the elision, the insertion, or addition of letters; by subverting the order of the letters, or by doubling some of them. After these changes in the original letters of the crude Sanscrit noun, some of the Sanscrit corruptions affix Teloogoo terminations, in the same manner as the Sanscrit derivatives, and others take no affixes. In either case, the rules already given for the declension of the దేశ్యము nouns apply equally to the తద్భవము. It will, therefore, be sufficient to submit a few explanations respecting the manner in which the nominative singular is formed from the crude Sanscrit noun; at the same time, these, from the nature of the subject, must be necessarily very undeterminate.

OF THE CORRUPTION OF THE VOWELS IN CRUDE SANSCRIT NOUNS.

228 If the first syllable in the original crude noun terminate in the vowels ి or ు, these vowels are often, in Teloogoo, changed to ె or ొ. thus; దిశా *a quarter of the world*, makes దెస - వికటు *a pungent taste*, makes వెగటు - తువర *an astringent taste*, makes తొవర.

229 If the first syllable in the original crude noun end with ్య or ్యా these letters are respectively changed to ె and ే

EXAMPLES.

వ్యసన	*sorrow*	makes	వెసనము
వ్యథ	*pain*	do	వెత
వ్యయ	*expenditure*	do	వెయము
త్యాగ	*liberality*	do	తేగము
న్యాయ	*justice, propriety*	do	నేయము
ఖ్యాతి	*fame*	do	కేతి

The same rule applies to ్య or ్య terminating a syllable in the middle or 230
end of the original crude noun, provided the preceding syllable be short; in this case, however, the consonant preceding ్య or ్య is doubled; thus.

విద్యా ... ...*learning, art*... ... ...makes ......విద్దె
కన్యా ... ... *a young girl*. ... ...do... ....కన్నె
వ్యత్యాస ... *difference* ... ...do... ....వెత్తెసము

్వ—్వ terminating the first syllable in the original crude noun, are 231
changed to ొ or ో; thus,

జ్వర ... ... *fever* ... ... makes ...... జొరము
స్వర ... ... *the sound of the voice, a note* ... ...do... .... సొరము
ధ్వని ... ... *a sound*... ... ...do... .... దొని
ద్వాదశీ *the 12th day of the increase or decrease of the moon* do. .. దోదశి

The vowel ఋ in the original crude noun is sometimes changed to ి, ే, 232
ై. or రి; thus,

శృంగార ... . *beauty*..... ... ...makes... ... సింగారము
మృగ ... ... *a beast* ... ...do... ... ... మైకము
బృహస్పతివార . . *Thursday* ... ... do... ... బేస్తవారము
ఋక్ష ... ...*a star* ... ... do... ... ...రిక్క

THE CORRUPTION OF CONSONANTS IN CRUDE SANSCRIT NOUNS.

The consonants శ్, స్, are often changed to చ్; thus, 233

శుక్ర ... ... *the planet Venus*.. ... .makes... ....చుక్క
శర్కరా ... . *sugar* ... ...do... ... ..చక్కెర
కంస ... ... *a plate made of bell metal* ... ...do... ... ...కంచము

The consonants చ్, శ్, and ష్, in the original Sanscrit, are frequently 234
changed in Teloogoo to స్; as,

కాచ ... ... *a cash (the coin so named)* ... ...makes... ... కాసు
అంకుశ ... . *an elephant hook* ... ...do... ......అంకుసము
మోష ... . *danger, deceit* ... ...do... ......మోసము
భాషా ... ...*language*... ... ...do ... .బాస

235 ణ్ is somtimes changed to న్ ; as,

పూర్ణిమా ... ... *the day on which the moon is full*...makes......పున్నమ
గుణ... ... ...*disposition, quality*... ... ... do . . . . . .గోనము

236 య్, at the commencement of nouns, is frequently changed, in Teloogoo, to జ్ ; as,

యమ ... ... *Yama, the God of death* ... ... makes ... ... జముఁడు
యామ ... . *three English hours* ... ... do ... . జాము

237 క్ష్, preceded by another syllable, is changed in Teloogoo to చ్చ or క్క ; thus.

పక్ష ... ... *a side* ... ... makes . . . . . . పక్క
లాక్షా ... . *lac* ... ... do . . . . లక్క
అక్షర ... . *a letter or charactor* ... ... do . . . . అక్కరము
భిక్షా ... . *alms* ... ... do . . . . . . బిచ్చము
లక్షణ ... . *rule, definition* ... ... do . . . . లచ్చనము

238 జ్ఞ్ preceded by the vowel ˇ, is generally changed to న్న ; and preceded by ా, to న్ ; thus,

యజ్ఞ ... ... *a sacrifice* ... ... makes . . . . . . జన్నము
యజ్ఞోపవీత . . . *the sacerdotal thread*. . . . . do . . . . జన్నిదము
ఆజ్ఞా ... ... *a command, order, or adjuration*...do . . . . ఆన
ఆజ్ఞప్తి ... . *command, permission* ... ... do . . . . . . ఆనతి

but it is sometimes changed to ణ్ ; thus, రాజ్ఞీ *a Queen*, makes రాణి.

239 హ is changed in గ.

సింహ . . . . *a lion* . . . . makes . . . . సింగము
కంహ . . . . *a crane*. . . . . do . . . . కొంగ

240 The consonants of each vurga are interchangeable.

EXAMPLES.

ముఖ. . . . . *a face* . . . . makes . . . . మొగము
ఛాయా . . . . *colour* . . . . do . . . . చాయ
పీఠ . . . . *a seat*. . . . . do . . . . పీట
ఘటికా, ... *a Hindoo hour* . . . . do . . . . గడియ
అటవీ. . . . . *a forest* . . . . do . . . . అడవి
కథా . . . . *a history, a story*. . . . . do . . . . కత
మతి . . . . *the mind*. . . . . do . . . . మది
పఙ్క్తి. . . . . *a line* . . . . do . . . . బంతి
తాంబూల . . . . . *beetle nut*. . . . . do. . . . . తమలము

The consonants ర హ ష శ or స, when connected with other consonants 241
without the intervention of a vowel, are generally dropped, and the consonant with which they may be connected is sometimes doubled; thus,

ప్రయాణ ... ...*a journey* ....makes... ...పయనము

చిహ్న ... .*a mark*.......................... do.... .....చిన్నె

గోష్ఠ ... .*a cow-house*................ ....do... .....కొట్టము

అగ్ని ....*fire*...............................do........అగ్గి

రుక్మ ....*a piece of money*.................do... ......రూక

Some of the changes among the తద్భవము nouns are so little obvious, that 242
the reader may occasionally be inclined to doubt the existence of any connexion between the adulterated word and that stated to be it's original. Great deference, however, is due by a foreigner to the concurrent testimoney of native authors on this head; and when it is considered that most of the తద్భవము words have, in all probability, passed into Teloogoo, through the medium of the Pracrit, or other corrupt dialects of the Sanscrit, and have been naturalized in it for ages, the little resemblance now to be found between some of the original words, and their corruptions, ought not, alone, to invalidate the established etymologies of successive Grammarians.

OF NOUNS TERMED అన్యదేశ్యము OR FOREIGN.

In treating of the declension of the అచ్చదేశ్యము - తత్సమము and తద్భ 243
వము nouns, the peculiarities of the గ్రామ్యము or common dialect, have been duly pointed out. It remains, therefore, only to offer a few observations respecting foreign nouns.

The great facility with which the Teloogoo adopts and naturalizes foreign terms, must already have attracted the notice of the Student. The intercourse of the people of Telingana with the neighbouring provinces, has led to the introduction of a few terms from the Orissa, the Mahratta, the Guzerat, the Canarese or Carnataca, and the Dravida or Tamil: but, except from the Tamil and Canarese, with which the Teloogoo is radically connected, it has not borrowed extensively from any of these languages. Since the Mahommedan conquest of the Deccan, numerous technical revenue terms, and words connected with official business, derived from the Arabic, Persian, or Hindee, have been introduced into Teloogoo, through the medium of the Hindoostanee; but the use of many such words begins now to be superseded by that of corresponding English terms.

244 Nouns of foreign derivation are subject to the same rules as the దేశ్యము nouns of the third declension; thus, the Hindoostanee words.

ఖబురు...... *news.*
ఖజానా..... *a treasury.*
ములుకు ..... *a country, a district.*
ఫైసలా..... *arrangement, settlement.*
మిలాఖతు.... *a visit.*
పితూరీ..... *a disturbance, an intrigue.*
తజ్జీ........ *trouble, annoyance.*
కసుబా..... *the chief town in a district.*
సవారీ.... *a carriage of any kind, a palankeen &c. &c.*
సవాలు.............. *a question.*
జవాబు.............. *an answer.*
అర్జీ................ *a petition &c.*

and the English words.

నెంబరు..............*a number.*
ఇంకీ................. *ink.*
పేనా .... *a pen.*
పెన్సలు............ *a pencil.*
డిక్రీ................. *a decree.*
సమ్మను.............. *a summons &c.*

are declined like బిడ్డ *a child.*

4th. OF THE DECLENSION OF SUBSTANTIVE PRONOUNS.

245 The rules of politeness among the Hindoos, although very different from those in use among European nations, are so firmly established, and so scrupulously observed by the people, that the least deviation from the proper mode of address should be studiously avoided. Particular attention is therefore necessary to the correct use of the Teloogoo pronouns.

246 All the pronouns belong to that division of the Teloogoo termed దేశ్యము or *language of the land.*

247 There are no relative pronouns in Teloogoo: the idiom of the language renders the use of them superfluous; as will be fully explained hereafter.

The substantive pronouns have two numbers; the singular, and the plural.

248 The speaker, and the person addressed, being present, their sex is supposed to be obvious: the distinction of gender is therefore confined to the pronouns of

the third person, in treating of which, we shall explain the peculiar manner in which it is marked.

The substantive pronouns, like the substantive nouns, may be said to have properly only three cases; viz. the nominative, the inflexion, and the accusative; but they are here declined according to the arrangement adopted in the declension of the nouns. The vocative case is wanting in all the Teloogoo pronouns. 249

The genitive or possessive case, without యొక్క, is likewise the inflexion, which, with the addition of the postpositions, forms the different compound cases. The inflexions of the pronouns are of course included in the class termed కళలు *kululoo*, while the accusative cases belong to the ద్రుతప్రకృతులు *drootuprukrootooloo*; but, in addition to this general distinction, it will be observed, that the pronouns of the two first persons have the inflexion entirely different from the accusative. 250

THE PRONOUN OF THE FIRST PERSON. 251

	Singular.		*Plural.*	
N.	నేను	*I*	మేము	*We*
G.	నా - నాయొక్క	*of me*	మా - మాయొక్క	*of us*
D.	నాకు	*to me*	మాకు	*to us*
Acc.	నను or నన్ను	*me*	మము or మమ్ము	*us*
Ab.	నా - లో - చేత - తో	*in &c. me*	మా - లో - చేత - తో	*in &c. us.*

Men of rank, speaking of themselves, generally use the plural మేము *We*, for the singular నేను *I*: indeed, arrogance often induces inferior natives to apply the plural to themselves; but this is understood to be very improper when they address a superior. The Ratsawars and Velmawars in the Northern Circars, a bold warlike race of men, scarcely ever deign to speak of themselves in the singular number; even to a Bramin, their acknowledged superior in cast. 252

In the superior dialect, ఏను and ఏము are sometimes used for నేను and మేము. 253

THE PRONOUN OF THE SECOND PERSON. 254

	Singular.		*Plural.*	
N.	నీవు	*thou*	మీరు	*you*
G.	నీ - నీయొక్క	*of thee*	మీ - మీయొక్క	*of you*
D.	నీకు	*to thee*	మీకు	*to you*
Acc.	నిను or నిన్ను	*thee*	మిము or మిమ్ము	*you*
Ab.	నీ - లో - చేత - తో	*in &c. thee*	మీ - లో - చేత - తో	*in &c. you*

255 Although both the singular and plural inflexions of this pronoun end in ీ, they take, in the dative cases, కు instead of కి, in opposition to the general rules 132 - 146 & 153.

256 Addressing inferiors, or conversing familiarly with equals, నీవు *thou*, the nominative singular of this pronoun, may be used ; but, when we speak to superiors, or even to equals or inferiors, with any degree of kindness or respect, the plual మీరు *you*, is the only proper term of address. To be called నీవు *thou*, by a person decidedly his inferior, is an insult not be borne by the most meek Hindoo, he will resent it as studied disrespect, couched in the most bitter terms of reproach.

257 When much deference is paid to men of superior age, rank, or learning, the speaker uses the words తాము or తమరు *they*, దేవరవారు or స్వామి *Lord*, Which correspond with the English phrases, *Sir*, *My Lord* &c. &c.

258 In the superior dialect ఈవు and ఈరు are sometimes used for నీవు and మీరు.

259 The pronouns of the first and second persons have their respective plural numbers, మేము and మీరు, as given above, corresponding precisely with our words *we* and *you*. But the first of these two pronouns in Teloogoo has likewise another plural, applying to both persons jointly, which, from the want of a corresponding term in English, we are obliged also to translate *we*. This plural is declined as follows.

N..............మనము..................................*we*

G..............మన - మనయొక్క.....................*of us*

D..............మనకు ....*to us*

Acc............మనల or మనముల......................*us*

Ab..............మన - లో - చేత - తో...................*in &c. us*

There is a very material difference between మేము *we*, and మనము *we*: మేము is the plural of the first person only, it refers exclusively to those who speak ; but మనము is a plural, used by the first person, but applying to the first and second persons conjointly ; it refers exclusively to neither, but includes both those who speak and those who are addressed, each of whom may be either one, or more persons. For example, if two gentlemen, meeting several

Bramins, were to enquire who they were, they would not use the joint plural of the first and second persons and answer మనము బ్రాహ్మణులము *we* (who speak and are addressed) *are Bramins;* for, in that case, they would be understood to affirm that the gentlemen also were Bramins. Using the plural of the first person, they would say మేము బ్రాహ్మణులము *we* (who speak) *are Bramins.*

THE PRONOUNS OF THE THIRD PERSON.

The Teloogoo pronouns of the third person may be divided into two classes; 260
the definite, and the indefinite; the first referring to one or more particular defined objects, and the second referring to a number or collection of objects less defined. The first class consists of the demonstratives, and of the interrogative pronoun derived from them. The second class comprizes the collectives, and their interrogative.

The distinction of gender is confined to the pronouns of this person, and the 261
mode in which it is defined in the singular number, is different from the mode in which it is marked in the plural. In the singular, the masculine gender is distinct from the feminine and neuter, which are both represented by the same word. In the plural, the masculine and the feminine are the same, and the neuter is distinct from both. It is of importance that this peculiarity should be strongly impressed on the memory of the Student, for it will be found to pervade the verbs and adjectives, and materially to affect the construction of the language.

DEFINITE PRONOUNS.

262

DEMONSTRATIVE PROXIMATE.

Singular.

	M.	*F. & N.*	
N.	వీడు	ఇది	*he, she and it, this.*
G.	వీని or వీనియొక్క	దీని or దీనియొక్క	*of him, her and it, this.*
D.	వీనికి	దీనికి	*to him, her and it, this.*
Acc.	వీని	దీని	*him, her and it, this.*
Ab.	వీని .. లో - చేత - తో	దీని .. లో - చేత - తో	*in &c. him, her and it, this.*

Plural.

	M. & F.	*N.*	
N.	వీరు	ఇవి	*they, these.*
G.	వీరి or వీరియొక్క	వీటి or వీటియొక్క	*of them, these.*
D.	వీరికి	వీటికి	*to them, these.*
Acc.	వీరిని	వీటిని	*them, these.*
Ab.	వీరి..లో - చేత - తో	వీటి..లో - చేత - తో	*in &c. them, these.*

ఇది and ఇవి are vulgarly written యిది and యివి.

263 DEMONSTRATIVE REMOTE.

Singular.

	M.	*F. & N.*	
N.	వాఁడు	అది	*he, she and it, that.*
G.	వాని - వానియొక్క	దాని - దానియొక్క	*of him, her and it, that.*
D.	వానికి	దానికి	*to him, her and it, that.*
Acc.	వాని	దాని	*him, her and it, that.*
Ab.	వాని..లో - చేత - తో	దాని..లో - చేత - తో	*in &c. him, her & it, that.*

Plural.

	M. & F.	*N.*	
N.	వారు	అవి	*they, those.*
G.	వారి - వారియొక్క	వాటి - వాటియొక్క	*of them, those.*
D.	వారికి	వాటికి	*to them, those.*
Acc.	వారిని	వాటిని	*them, those.*
Ab.	వారి..లో - చేత - తో	వాటి..లో - చేత - తో	*in &c. them, those.*

264 It will be observed that the change of ీ *ee* to ా *a* and of ఇ *i* to అ *u*, in the first syllable of these pronouns, is the only difference between them.

265 Besides the plurals వీరు and వారు, these two pronouns, like some of the regular దేశ్యము nouns, occasionally take irregular plurals; thus, వీరు often becomes వీఁడ్లు or వీఁడ్రు and వారు is changed into వాఁడ్లు or వాఁడ్రు. In this case, they make the inflexion plural వీఁడ్ల or వీఁడ్ర, and వాఁడ్ల or వాఁడ్ర; and the accusative plural వీఁడ్లను or వీఁడ్రను, and వాఁడ్లను or వాఁడ్రను.

In the common dialect, the accusatives వీని and వాని are respectively written 266
వీణ్ణి and వాణ్ణి.

The singular numbers of the foregoing demonstrative pronouns, and their 267
irregular plurals, are never used, except when inferiors or equals are spoken of: when persons of very high rank are the subject of conversation, the plurals వారు and వీరు, are used to express the English words *he* or *she*. But if the speaker alludes to a person only in a trifling degree respected by him, instead of the pronoun వీడు, he uses ఇతడు to denote a male, and ఈబిడ or ఈపె to denote a female; and instead of the pronoun వాడు - అతడు for the masculine, and ఆబిడ or ఆపె for the feminine gender; or if he alludes to a person considerably superior to him, yet not of very high rank, instead of వీడు he uses ఈయన to denote a male, and ఈమె to denote a female, and instead of వాడు, ఆయన for the masculine, and ఆమె for the feminine gender. These pronouns have no plural number, ఇతడు and అతడు are declined like nouns of the first declension; thus.

N..........అతడు ....*he*.

G..........అతని - అతనియొక్క........ *of him*.

D..........అతనికి .... *to him*.

Acc........అతని .... *him*.

Ab... ... ...అతని...లో - చేత - తో......*in &c. him*.

ఈయన - ఈబిడ - ఈపె and ఈమె and ఆయన - ఆబిడ - ఆపె and ఆమె are declined like nouns of the third declension; thus,

N. ... .ఆయన ... ...*he*.

G. .... ఆయన - ఆయనయొక్క ... *of him*.

D. .... .ఆయనకు......................*to him*.

Acc. ...... ఆయనను..................*him*.

Ab. ...... ఆయన.. లో - చేత - తో *in &c. him*.

Instead of వీటి and వాటి, in the neuter plural of the demonstrative pronouns, 268
we sometimes find వీని and వాని used in books.

INTERROGATIVE.

Singular.

	M.	*F. & N.*	
N.	ఎవ్వఁడు	ఏది	*who? which?*
G.	ఎవ్వని - ఎవ్వని యొక్క	దేని - దేని యొక్క	*of whom? which?*
D.	ఎవ్వనికి	దేనికి	*to whom? which?*
Acc.	ఎవ్వని	దేని	*whom? which?*
Ab.	ఎవ్వని...లో - చేత - తో	దేని. లో - చేత - తో	*in &c. whom? which?*

Plural.

	M. & F.	*N.*	
N.	ఎవ్వరు	ఏవి	*who? which?*
G.	ఎవ్వరి..ఎవ్వరియొక్క	వేటి... వేటియొక్క	*of whom? which?*
D.	ఎవ్వరికి	వేటికి	*to whom? which?*
Acc.	ఎవ్వరిని	వేటిని	*whom? which?*
Ab.	ఎవ్వరి.. లో - చేత - తో	వేటి..లో - చేత - తో	*in &c. whom? which?*

269 Instead of ఏది, the word ఎవ్వతె, which follows the rules for the first declension, is often used, in the singular, to denote a female.

270 The initial ఎ & ఏ of the interrogative pronoun is constantly converted, in the common dialect, into యె & యే.

271 In the common dialect, వీడి - వాడి and యెవ్వడి are used, in the singular number of the definite pronouns, instead of వీని- వాని and ఎవ్వని; except in the accusative, which is made to terminate in ణ్ని instead of ని.

INDEFINITE PRONOUNS.

272 As the pronouns of this class refer to a number of objects, they have no singular, but are all of the plural number.

COLLECTIVES.

	M. & F.	*N.*	
N.	ఇందఱు	ఇన్ని	*so many.*
G.	ఇందఱి - ఇందఱి యొక్క	ఇన్నిఁటి - ఇన్నిఁటియొక్క	*of so many.*
D.	ఇందఱికి	ఇన్నిఁటికి	*to so many.*
Acc.	ఇందఱిని	ఇన్నిఁటిని	*so many.*
Ab.	ఇందఱి..లో - చేత - తో	ఇన్నిఁటి..లో - చేత - తో	*in &c. so many.*

The initial ఇ of this pronoun is constantly written యి, in the common dialect. 273

M. & F. .... *N.*

N. అందఱు...........................అన్ని...........................*all.*

G. అందఱి...అందఱియొక్క.......అన్నింటి...అన్నింటియొక్క *of all.*

D. అందఱికి...........................అన్నింటికి...........................*to all.*

Acc. అందఱిని...........................అన్నింటిని...........................*all.*

Ab. అందఱి....లో - చేత - తో .. అన్నింటి .. లో - చేత - తో ..*in &c. all.*

M. & F. .... *N.*

N. కొందఱు...........................కొన్ని...........................*a few.*

G. కొందఱి..కొందఱియొక్క..కొన్నింటి..కొన్నింటియొక్క *of a few.*

D. కొందఱికి...........................కొన్నింటికి...........................*to a few.*

Acc. కొందఱిని...........................కొన్నింటిని...........................*a few.*

Ab. కొందఱి..లో - చేత - తో....కొన్నింటి.. లో- చేత - తో *in &c. a few.*

INTERROGATIVE.

M. & F. .... *N.*

N. ఎందఱు...........................ఎన్ని...........................*how many?*

G. ఎందఱి .. ఎందఱియొక్క .... ఎన్నింటి .. ఎన్నింటియొక్క .. *of how many?*

D. ఎందఱికి...........................ఎన్నింటికి...........................*to how many?*

Acc. ఎందఱిని...........................ఎన్నింటిని...........................*how many?*

Ab. ఎందఱి .. లో - చేత - తో .... ఎన్నింటి..లో-చేత-తో.. *in &c. how many?.*

The initial ఎ of this pronoun is, in the common dialect, converted into యె. 274

None of the foregoing pronouns of the third person can be used more than once in a sentence, with reference to the same person or thing. If I say, వాఁడు *he,* వానితండ్రితో *with his father,* వచ్చినాఁడు *has come,* I should not be understood to express that he (the third person) has come with his own father, but that he (the third person) has come with the father of a fourth. If I ask వీఁడువీనియింటికిపోయినాఁడా *did he go to his house?* I ask whether he (the third person) went to the house of another, not whether he went to his own house. 275

276 This peculiarity in the use of the pronouns of the third person, has given rise to the reflective pronoun తాను, which is the same for all genders, and is always used with reference to some nominative of the third person preceding it.

Singular.

N.........................తాను................. *he, she, or it.*

G.........................తన-తనయొక్క ......*of him, her, or it.*

D.........................తనకు.....................*to him, her, or it.*

Acc.......................తను or తన్ను.........*him, her, or it.*

Ab.........................తన....లో-చేత-తో .. *in &c. him, her, or it.*

Plural.

N.........................తారు or తాము or తమరు *they.*

G.........................తమ or తమయొక్క.........*of them.*

D.........................తమకు.........................*to them.*

Acc.......................తము or తమ్ము..............*them.*

Ab.........................తమ....లో - చేత - తో.... *in &c. them.*

we say వాఁడుతనతండ్రితోవచ్చినాఁడు *he came with his (own) father.* వీఁడు తనయింటికిపోయినాఁడా *did he go to his (own) house?*

277 The pronoun ఏమి commonly written యెమి, *what?* is defective: its inflexion is ఏమిటి, or ఏటి, but it is seldom used, except in the nominative or dative case; thus, nom. sing. ఏమి, *what?* dat. sing. ఏటికి, or ఏమిటికి, *to* or *for what? why?*

278 The words ఇందు-అందు-ఎందు,when standing alone, are not to be considered pronouns, but adverbs, respectively denoting *in this place, in that place,* and *in what place?* but when the postpositions కు - లో - చేత - వల్ల - కంటెన, and a few others, are affixed to them, they are indeclinable pronouns, respectively denoting *this, that, what?* as ఇందులో *in this,* అందుచేత *by that,* ఎందుకు *to* or *for what? wherefore?*

CHAPTER FOURTH.

ADJECTIVES.

OF దేశ్యము ADJECTIVES.

The దేశ్యము adjectives are indeclinable, varying neither in gender, in num- 279
ber, nor in case; but dependent for these distinctions upon the substantive nouns or pronouns, to some of which they are invariably prefixed. The following list, containing a few of the most common, will shew that they generally terminate in the short vowels ✓ ి or ు.

చల్ల......*cold.*	గట్టి......*strong, hard.*
చిన్న......*small.*	మెత్త......*soft.*
పెద్ద......*great.*	మురికి......*dirty.*
పిన్న......*little.*	తడి......*damp, wet.*
తెల్ల......*white.*	గుడ్డి......*blind.*
నల్ల......*black.*	చేఁదు......*bitter.*
ఎఱ్ఱ......*red.*	అందము......*beautiful.*
పచ్చ......*yellow.*	పొడుగు......*tall, long.*
చెడ్డ......*bad.*	వదులు......*slack.*
పాఁత......*old.*	వెడల్పు......*broad.*
కొ్రత్త......*new.*	బరువు......*heavy.*
మగ......*male.*	తీపు......*sweet.*
ముసలి......*aged, old.*	పులుసు......*sour.*
పొట్టి......*short, small.*	నిజము......*true.*
మంచి......*good.*	చురుకు......*sharp.*

280 A number of దేశ్యము adjectives, ending in ◡ and denoting qualities which are the peculiar objects of sight, taste, or touch, when prefixed to substantive nouns or pronouns, may, at pleasure, affix the particle ని; thus, నల్ల *black*, తెల్ల *white*, ఎఱ్ఱ *red*, పచ్చ *yellow*, చామ *azure blue*, తియ్య *sweet*, పుల్ల *sour*, తిన్న or మెత్త *soft*, prefixed to substantives, either remain unchanged, or become నల్లని - తెల్లని &c. as తెల్ల or తెల్లనిబట్ట *a white cloth*, తియ్య or తియ్యని పండు *a sweet fruit*, మెత్త or మెత్తనిపత్తి *soft cotton.*

281 To all దేశ్యము adjectives, when prefixed to substantives, we may, at pleasure, affix the particles అగు-అయిన or అయినటువంటి from the verb అవు *to become;* but these affixes do not alter their meaning in any way whatever; thus, పెద్ద *great*, గొప్ప *large*, క్రొత్త *new*, గుడ్డి *blind*, పొట్టి *short*, వదులు *slack*, &c. make పెద్దగు-పెద్దయిన or పెద్దయినటువంటియిల్లు *a large house*, గొప్పగు-గొప్పైన or గొప్పైనటువంటిమనిషి *a great person*, and so forth; these particles, however, cannot be added to the adjectives mentioned above as assuming ని, until that affix is first inserted; thus, we cannot say నల్లైన but నల్లనైనబట్ట *black cloth:* it is at the same time to be remarked, that the addition of అగు-అయిన or ఆయినటువంటి to దేశ్యము adjectives is, in general, neither necessary nor elegant.

EXCEPTIONS.

282 The adjective చక్క *handsome* or *fine*, always affixes ని; thus, we say చక్కనిమనిషి *a handsome person*, not చక్కమనిషి.

283 వట్టి *empty*, మంచి *good*, and చిన్న *small*, take no affixes whatever: thus, వట్టిపెట్టె *an empty box*, మంచిమనిషి *a good person*, చిన్నగుఱ్ఱము *a small horse.*

284 The adjective సన్న *thin, small*, affixes, at pleasure, the syllable ము; to which అగు-అయిన or అయినటువంటి may be optionally added; thus, సన్నకాగిదము or సన్నమైనకాగిదము *thin paper:* when it assumes the syllable ము, it admits of another form, according to the following rule.

285 All దేశ్యము adjectives ending in ము, when prefixed to substantives, either affix అగు-అయిన, or అయినటువంటి, or change the final ము, to పు or ంపు;

thus, అందము *beautiful*, makes అందమగు-అందమయిన or అందమయినటు వంటి మోము or మోములు *a beautiful face* or *faces*, or అందపు or అందంపు మోము or మోములు *a beautiful face*, or *faces*.

All other దేశ్యము adjectives ending in ు when prefixed, without any of the affixes abovementioned, to substantives beginning with a vowel, require the insertion of ట, to prevent hiatus; thus, కఱకు *sharp*, and అమ్ము *an arrow*, make కఱకుటమ్ము *a sharp arrow*; నిగ్గు *pure*, and అద్దము, *a mirror*, make నిగ్గుటద్దము *a pure mirror*. 286

Some దేశ్యము adjectives are derived from substantives in the following manner. 287

SUBSTANTIVES.		ADJECTIVES.	
ఓడు	*a leak*	ఓటి	*leaky.*
కుంటు	*lameness*	కుంటి	*lame.*
జున్ను	*honey*	జుంటి	*honied.*
ఇనుము	*iron*	ఇనుప	*iron.*
జనుము	*hemp, flax*	జనుప	*hempen.*
చెముడు	*deafness*	చెవిటి	*deaf.*

It is necessary to apprize the reader that many దేశ్యము nouns are used both as adjectives and substantives, in the same manner as a number of terms in our own language; thus, we say తడినిండావున్నది *the damp is great*, and తడిబట్ట *a damp cloth*, the word తడి in Teloogoo, and *damp* in English, being used, in these sentences, first as a substantive, and afterwards as an adjective noun: thus, also, we find that చేదు means either *bitter* or *bitterness*, పొడుగు *tall* or *tallness*, వెడల్పు *broad* or *breadth*, బరువు *heavy* or *weight*, తీపు *sweet* or *sweetness*, &c. but అందము *beauty* or *beautiful*, and other words in ము, which are used either as adjectives or substantives, may be considered properly to belong to the latter class of nouns; for it will be observed that, by rule 285, they cannot be used in the former sense, without adding certain affixes, which as substantives they never assume. 288

OF తత్సమము ADJECTIVES.

289 The rules which have been given for the derivation of substantive nouns from the Sanscrit, apply equally to the derivation of adjectives from that language: తత్సమము adjectives, therefore, in opposition to దేశ్యము adjectives, admit of the distinctions of gender, number, and case.

Sanscrit.		*Teloogoo.*		
Crude.	*Adjective.*	*Masculine.*	*Feminine.*	*Neuter.*
ధన్య	*virtuous*	ధన్యుఁడు	ధన్య	ధన్యము
నిపుణ	*skilled*	నిపుణుఁడు	నిపుణ	నిపుణము
స్వతంత్ర	*independent*	స్వతంత్రుఁడు	స్వతంత్ర	స్వతంత్రము
పరతంత్ర	*dependent*	పరతంత్రుఁడు	పరతంత్ర	పరతంత్రము
ప్రియ	*dear*	ప్రియుఁడు	ప్రియ	ప్రియము
బధిర	*deaf*	బధిరుఁడు	బధిర	బధిరము
అంధ	*blind*	అంధుఁడు	అంధ	అంధము
బాల	*young*	బాలుఁడు	బాల	బాలము
వృద్ధ	*aged, old*	వృద్ధుఁడు	వృద్ధ	వృద్ధము
శ్రేష్ఠ	*excellent*	శ్రేష్ఠుఁడు	శ్రేష్ఠ	శ్రేష్ఠము
నిర్మల	*pure*	నిర్మలుఁడు	నిర్మల	నిర్మలము
అల్ప	*small, mean*	అల్పుఁడు	అల్ప	అల్పము
ఉన్నత	*lofty, tall*	ఉన్నతుఁడు	ఉన్నత	ఉన్నతము
హ్రస్వ	*short*	హ్రస్వుఁడు	హ్రస్వ	హ్రస్వము
దీర్ఘ	*long*	దీర్ఘుఁడు	దీర్ఘ	దీర్ఘము
దరిద్ర	*poor*	దరిద్రుఁడు	దరిద్ర	దరిద్రము
యోగ్య	*fit, proper*	యోగ్యుఁడు	యోగ్య	యోగ్యము
విశాల	*extensive*	విశాలుఁడు	విశాల	విశాలము
చమత్కారిన్	*dexterous*	చమత్కారి	చమత్కారిణి	చమత్కారి
అహంకారిన్	*arrogant*	అహంకారి	అహంకారిణి	అహంకారి

290 తత్సమము adjectives, when immediately prefixed to substantives, do not in general admit of declension. They usually require the particles అగు. అయిన.

or అయినటువంటి to be affixed to the nominative singular, if the substantive be neuter; and if the substantive be masculine or feminine, either to the singular or plural nominative, according as the substantive may be in the singular or plural number: feminine తత్సమము adjectives in ి, before affixing these particles, previously change the final ి into ురాలు in the singular, and ురాండ్రు or ురాండ్లు in the plural, from the word ఆలు, denoting a female; thus, సుందరమైనయిల్లు or యిండ్లు *a handsome house or houses*, సుందరుఁడైనపురుషుఁడు *a handsome man*, సుందరులైనపురుషులు *handsome men*, సుందరురాలైనస్త్రీ *a handsome woman*, సుందరురాండ్రయినస్త్రీలు or సుందరురాండ్లయినస్త్రీలు *handsome women*.

Neuter తత్సమము adjectives in ము, instead of affixing అగు-అయిన or అయినటువంటి, may, like the దేశ్యము adjectives, change the final ము, to పు orంపు; thus, we may say సరసపు or సరసంపుపలుకు or పలుకులు *a mellifluent expression* or *expressions* (literally, words full of quintessence.) 291

Sanscrit adjectives ending in the terminations వత్ and మత్, when adopted into Teloogoo, change them, in the masculine gender to వంతుఁడు and మంతుఁడు; in the feminine, to వంతురాలు and మంతురాలు, or వతి and మతి; and in the neuter gender, to వంతము and మంతము, or వత్తు and మత్తు. 292

EXAMPLES.

Crude.	Adjective.	Masculine.	Feminine.	Neuter.
బలవత్	strong	బలవంతుఁడు	బలవంతురాలు బలవతి	బలవంతము బలవత్తు
బుద్ధిమత్	sensible	బుద్ధిమంతుఁడు	బుద్ధిమంతురాలు బుద్ధిమతి	బుద్ధిమంతము బుద్ధిమత్తు
భాగ్యవత్	happy, rich	భాగ్యవంతుఁడు	భాగ్యవంతురాలు భాగ్యవతి	భాగ్యవంతము భాగ్యవత్తు

తత్సమము adjectives, preceding తత్సమము substantives, often drop all their Teloogoo terminations, and are compounded with the substantive in their uninflected or crude state, according to the rules of Sanscrit grammar; thus, 293

దుష్టుఁడు....*wicked* and.....రాక్షసుఁడు *a giant* may become దుష్టరాక్షసుఁడు [*a wicked giant*.

శ్రేష్ఠము....*excellent* and....అశ్వము...... *a horse* .... శ్రేష్ఠాశ్వము *an* [*excellent horse*.

అధికము.... *much*, and... ...ధనము......*money* .... అధికధనము [*much money*.

ధనవంతుఁడు *opulent*, and . ప్రభువు.....*a master* .... ధనవత్ప్రభువు [*an opulent master*.

294 In the common dialect, neuter adjectives in ము, of whatever class, are constantly prefixed, with the particles అగు-అయిన or అయినటువంటి, to substantives of all genders and numbers promiscuously; thus, సుందరమగు-సుందరమయిన or సుందరమయినటువంటి-పురుషుఁడు-పురుషులు-స్త్రీ-స్త్రీలు-ముఖము - ముఖములు &c. *a handsome man-men-woman-women-face,-faces, &c.*

295 The rules respecting తద్భవము and అన్యదేశ్యము substantives are also applicable to adjectives of the same descriptions.

OF ADJECTIVE PRONOUNS.

296 The adjective pronouns may be divided into the same classes as the substantive pronouns of the third person, viz. definite and indefinite, with the addition of the possessive pronouns.

POSSESSIVES.

297 The possessive pronouns consist of the possessive or genitive cases of the respective substantive pronouns, without the postposition యొక్క viz.

నా..............*my*	వాని............*his (remote)*
మా..............*our*	దాని............*her or its (do)*
మన..............*our*	వీరి..............*their M & F. (proximate)*
నీ..............*thy*	వీటి..............*their N. (do)*
మీ..............*your*	వారి............*their M. & F. (remote)*
వీని..............*his (proximate)*	వాటి............*their N. (do)*
దీని..............*her or its (proximate)*	తన..............*his, her, its*
	తమ............*their*

298 These pronouns are indeclinable; they are prefixed to nouns in the same manner as the దేశ్యము adjectives, but without affixes of any kind; thus నా యిల్లు *my house*, వారిగుఱ్ఱములు *their horses*, &c.

DEFINITE PRONOUNS.

Each of the definite adjective pronouns consists of one long vowel; viz. 299
the demonstrative proximate ఈ, or, as it is vulgarly written, యీ, meaning *this*; the demonstrative remote ఆ *that*; and the interrogative ఏ or, as it is commonly written, యే, *what?* When prefixed to substantives, these pronouns are sometimes converted into their corresponding short vowels, and the following consonant is then doubled; thus, ఈకమలము or ఇక్కమలము or, as it is commonly written, యీకమలము or యిక్కమలము *this lotus*, ఆకాలము or అక్కాలము *that time*, ఏకాలము or ఎక్కాలము or as it is vulgarly written యేకాలము or యెక్కాలము *what time?* When the vowel is shortened, the క is doubled, in each of these examples.

INDEFINITE PRONOUNS.

The indefinite adjective pronouns are prefixed to plural substantives, without any intermediate affix; they are merely the nominative cases of the indefinite substantive pronouns of the third person, viz. 300

M. & F.	*N.*	
ఇందఱు	ఇన్ని	*so many.*
అందఱు	అన్ని	*all.*
కొందఱు	కొన్ని	*a few.*
ఎందఱు	ఎన్ని	*how many?*

The indeclinable particle అంతే, commonly written అంతా, meaning *the whole, in full,* &c. affixed to substantives, has the same force as the pronouns అందఱు or అన్ని prefixed to them; thus, అందఱుమనుష్యులు or మనుష్యులంతే *all men*, అన్నివస్తువులు or వస్తువులంతే *all things.* 301

CHAPTER FIFTH.

VERBS.

Teloogoo verbs are of four kinds; neuter, active, passive, and causal. 302

These verbs are divided into two parts, the affirmative, and the negative; 303
and each of these two parts has an indicative mood, an imperative mood, participles, and a verbal noun. The affirmative verb has an infinitive, but the negative verb has none.

INDICATIVE.

The indicative mood, in the affirmative verb, has, properly, only four 304
tenses; the present, the past, the future, and the aorist. In the negative verb, the aorist is the only tense. Each of these tenses has two numbers, the singular and the plural; and in each number there are three persons; but there is no distinction of gender, except in the third person. In the singular number of most of the tenses, the third person masculine is distinguished from the third person feminine and neuter, both of which are the same. In the plural, the third person masculine and feminine are one; and the neuter is, in general, different from both. In a few cases, however, the third person is the same for all genders.

IMPERATIVE.

The imperative has two numbers; the singular and the plural. This 305
mood, in the affirmative verb, has two persons; the 2d in the singular, and the 1st and 2d in the plural. In the negative verb, it has the 2d person only in each number.

PARTICIPLES.

The participles are of two distinct kinds: the one we shall denominate 306
verbal, and the other *relative*, participles.

The affirmative verb has two verbal participles; the present and the past. 307

The negative verb has one only, indefinite as to time. These verbal participles require the addition of some personal termination, or of some tense of another verb, in order to distinguish number and person. They can never be used as adjectives, or substantives, like the English participles, in such phrases as, *the sounding shore, by promising, in speaking, &c. &c.* they must almost invariably be followed by a personal termination, or be governed by some tense of a verb; as in the phrases, *frowning she speaks, pleased he departed, wondering he stands.* The words *frowning, pleased,* and *wondering,* represent the Teloogoo verbal participle; and the words *speaks, departed,* and *stands,* the Teloogoo governing verb.

308 In the affirmative verb, there are three relative participles; the present, the past, and the indefinite; in the negative verb the indefinite only. They admit of no personal terminations, they can precede no verb, and are termed *relative* participles, because the power of the English relative pronoun *who, which, that,* is inherent in them: they therefore always refer to some noun or pronoun with which they agree, as adjectives; thus, *a tree which grows, a horse that leaps,* would be expressed in Teloogoo by the relative participles; viz. పెరిగేచెట్టు *a growing tree,* దుమికేగుఱ్ఱము *a leaping horse.* In order that the reader may recollect that our relative pronouns are inherent in this part of the Teloogoo verb, the relative *that* (selected, as agreeing promiscuously with all genders) will be prefixed to it in English; thus, *that leaps, that grows, &c.*

VERBAL NOUNS.

309 The verbal nouns are declinable substantives, expressing the action itself which is signified by the verb. Those terminating in ము follow the rules for the second declension; and those ending in any other syllable, are declined like nouns of the third declension.

310 The origin of every part of the Teloogoo verb may be traced to that crude form of it termed the ధాతు *root*; which is sometimes also an abstract noun, and, in the common dialect, is often the 2d person singular of the affirmative imperative. It always ends in ు; thus,

ఆలకించు.......................................*to hear, to listen.*
అడ్డగించు.......................................*to prevent, to oppose.*
ఊరడించు.......................................*to console, to comfort.*
ఎదిరించు.......................................*to oppose.*
కుమ్మరించు.......................................*to pour.*
తెగించు.......................................*to venture, to dare.*
దీవించు.......................................*to bless.*
పవ్వళించు.......................................*to lie down.*
చిగుర్చు.......................................*to bud.*
తలంచు.......................................*to think.*
ప్రేరేచు.......................................*to induce, to excite.*
ఎగియు.......................................*to fly.*
పెనయు.......................................*to be twisted.*
మెఱయు.......................................*to shine.*
కూయు.......................................*to make a noise, to bark.*
చేయు.......................................*to make.*
వ్రాయు.......................................*to write.*
కురియు.......................................*to rain.*
అడుగు.......................................*to ask.*
ఉఱుము.......................................*to thunder.*
ఎగురు.......................................*to fly.*
కడుగు.......................................*to clean, to wash.*
చదువు.......................................*to study, to read.*
తిఱుగు.......................................*to wander, to turn back.*
దుముకు.......................................*to leap.*
పెరుగు.......................................*to grow.*
వడుకు.......................................*to spin.*

It is necessary to remark that, although the Teloogoo root has been trans- 311
lated with *to*, the sign of the English infinitive, it is never used in an infinitive signification.

312 From the root thus terminating in ు , are formed the verbal participles, and the infinitive of the affirmative verb; and from these three principal parts of the verb, viz. the root, the verbal participles, and the infinitive of the affirmative verb, spring all the rest of it's parts, both affirmative, and negative, as shewn in the following table.

THE PRINCIPAL PARTS OF THE VERB.

From the root in ు, the present verbal participle is formed, by adding చు in the superior, and తు in the inferior dialect; thus, కొట్టు, *to beat*, makes కొట్టుచు or కొట్టుతు, *beating*. The participle ఉన్న from the root ఉండు *to be*, may be added, as an auxiliary, to each of these participles, which, by the rules for *Sund,hi*, make చున్న and తున్న respectively; hence కొట్టుచున్న and కొట్టుతున్న *beating*. 313

The past verbal participle is formed by changing ు of the root into ి; in other words, as expressed in the table, by adding ి to the root in ు, the final ు being dropped: thus, from కొట్టు, *to beat*, comes కొట్టి, *having beaten*. 31

The infinitive is formed by merely dropping the final ు of the root; thus, from the root కొట్టు comes కొట్ట, *to beat*. 315

INDICATIVE MOOD.

The present tense is derived from the present verbal participles; the past tense from the past verbal participle; the future and the affirmative aorist from the root, and the negative aorist from the infinitive, by the addition of the affixes shewn in the table, which consist partly of certain terminations defining the several persons singular and plural, partly of particles interposed between these personal terminations, and the principal parts of the verb, whence the tenses are derived. 316

PERSONAL TERMINATIONS.

The personal terminations of the verb are derived from the substantive pronouns. 317

The personal terminations of the first and second persons are, 318

		For all the tenses, except the first form of the past tense	*For the first form of the past tense.*
Singular	1	ను	ని
	2.	వు	వి
Plural	1	ము	మి
	2	రు	రి

319 Except the first form of the past tense, which merely converts the final ు to ి, the first person singular of all the tenses ends in ను, the termination of the pronoun నేను *I*; the second person singular, in the same manner, terminates in వు, the final syllable of నీవు *thou*; the first person plural ends in ము, the termination of మేము *we*; and the second person plural ends in రు, the termination of మీరు, *you*.

320 The personal terminations of the third person are not so regular: they stand thus.

		Present.	*Past.* 1st form.	*Past.* 2d form.	*Future.* 1st form.	*Future.* 2d form.	*Aorist.*	*Negative Aorist.*
Singular.	*M.*	డు	ను	డు	ని	ని	ను	డు
	F. N. & F.	ది	ను	ది	ని	ని	ను	దు
Plural.	*M. & F.*	రు	రి	రు	రు	రు	రు	రు
	N.	వి	ను	వి	ని	ని	ను	వు

321 In the present tense, in the second form of the past, and in the negative aorist, the third person singular ends, in the masculine, with డు, the final syllable of the pronouns వీడు or వాడు, *he*; in the feminine and neuter gender of the two first mentioned tenses, it terminates with ది, the final syllable of the pronouns ఇది or అది, *she* or *it*; but in the feminine and neuter of the last mentioned tense, it ends with దు. The first form of the past tense, and the affirmative aorist, have ను, and the two forms of the future ని, for all genders in the third person singular.

322 Except the first form of the perfect tense, which merely converts ు into ి, the third person plural of all the tenses in the masculine and feminine gendres ends in రు, the final syllable of the pronouns వీరు or వారు, *they*, in the neuter of the present tense, and of the second form of the past tense, it ends in వి, the final syllable of the neuter pronouns ఇవి or అవి, *they*; but the other tenses have the neuter plural the same as in the neuter singular, except the negative aorist, which terminates in వు.

INTERMEDIATE PARTICLES.

Before affixing the personal terminations above stated to the principal parts 323
of the verb, from which the tenses are derived; the affirmative tenses assume certain intermediate particles, which are the same for the first and second persons both singular and plural, but are liable to variation in the third person, as shewn below.

	1st and 2d persons singular and plural.	*3d person singular.* *M.*	*F. & N.*	*3d person plural.* *M. & F.*	*N.*
Present	ా	ా	న్న	ా	న్న
Past 1st form	ఇ	ె	ె		ె
Past 2d form	నా	నా	న	నా	న
Future 1st form	ెద	ెడి	ెడి	ెద	ెడి
Future 2d form	ే	ే or ె	ే or ె	తు	ే or ె
Aorist	దు			దు	

In the present tense, long ా (దీర్ఘము) is prefixed to all the personal 324
terminations, except the third person feminine or neuter in the singular, and the third person neuter in the plural, which prefix న్న.

In the first form of the past tense, ఇ is prefixed to all the personal termi- 325
nations, except to those of the third person, which take ె before them in the singular, and in the neuter plural: in the masculine and feminine plural, there is no prefix. In the second form of the past tense, నా is prefixed to all the personal terminations, except the third person feminine and neuter in the singular, and the third person neuter in the plural, which prefix న.

The first form of the future prefixes ెద to all the personal terminations, 326
except to those of the third person singular and the neuter of the third person plural, which prefix ెడి. The second form prefixes ే to all the personal terminations; but in the third person singular, and in the neuter of the third person plural, it may at pleasure be changed into ె

The affirmative aorist prefixes దు to all the personal terminations, except to 327
those of the third person singular, and of the neuter third person plural, which take no prefix.

328 The negative aorist does not assume any prefix before the personal terminations.

PRESENT TENSE.

329 The personal terminations, connected with the intermediate particles for the present tense, are exhibited in the table; thus, ాను-ావు-ాఁడు-న్నది. &c. When these affixes are added to the present verbal participle, in order to form the present tense, the final ు of the participle is dropped, and the present verbal participle, in all verbs, having four forms, viz. చు - తు- చున్న - and తున్న, the present tense, which is formed from the participles, has also four forms, viz. చాను - తాను - చున్నాను - తున్నాను &c. thus, the present verbal participles కొట్టుచు - కొట్టుతు - కొట్టుచున్న and కొట్టుతున్న *beating*, respectively, make కొట్టుచాను &c. కొట్టుతాను &c. కొట్టుచున్నాను &c. or కొట్టుతు న్నాను &c. *I &c. beat*; but it will be seen, from the table, that the third person feminine or neuter in the singular, and the third person neuter in the plural, are not added to the participles in చున్న or తున్న, but only to those in చు or తు: they have, therefore, only two forms; viz. చున్నది or తున్నది- చున్నవి or తున్నవి respectively; for the conversion in the singular of న్న to ం, in the common dialect, can hardly be reckoned a new form; thus, కొట్టుచు న్నది or కొట్టుతున్నది *she or it beats*, కొట్టుచున్నవి or కొట్టుతున్నవి *they beat*. The participles in చు and చున్న are both strictly grammatical, but those in తు and తున్న are generally used in the common dialect. Of the four forms of the present tense derived from these participles, that only which is derived from the participle in చున్న viz. చున్నాను &c. is strictly grammatical, the form derived from the grammatical participle in చు, viz. చాను, is vulgar, and it's use is confined chiefly to the religious bramins of the Northern districts: but the forms derived from the participles in తు and తున్న, viz. తాను and తున్నాను &c. are in common use, and should always be selected in preference to the other forms, when we speak the language.

PAST TENSE.

330 There is not any variation in the past verbal participle, from which the two forms of the past tense are derived; their formation, as shewn in the table, is

therefore very simple; కొట్టి *having beaten* makes in the first form కొట్టితిని *I have beaten*, కొట్టితివి *thou hast beaten* &c. The third person of the first form is కొట్టెను *he, she, or it has beaten*, the ఇ of కొట్టి being dropped when the termination ఎను, beginning with a vowel, is added to it. In the second form, కొట్టి *having beaten*, makes కొట్టినాను &c. *I have beaten &c.* Both of these forms are strictly grammatical, and both are equally in common use.

FUTURE.

All the terminations added to the root, to compose the two forms of this 331
tense, commence with vowels; the final ఉ of the root is therefore dropped, when they are added to it; thus, the root కొట్టు makes కొట్టెదను or కొట్టేను, *I will beat.* The second form of this tense is used by the vulgar only. The first person singular of the second form of this tense must not be confounded with the third person singular in the first form of the past tense. కొట్టేను *I will beat* is entirely distinct, in meaning, from కొట్టెను *he, she, or it has beaten*; but the only difference in writing or pronouncing them, is, that the ఎ before ను is long in the former, and short in the latter. It is of much importance to the reader to understand, that the two forms of the future tense are seldom used; the present or the aorist being commonly substituted for them.

AORIST.

The formation of the affirmative aorist from the root, and of the negative 332
aorist from the infinitive, by the addition of the affixes shewn in the table, is so simple, as scarcely to require explanation: the root కొట్టు makes it's affirmative aorist కొట్టుదును, *I do beat, have beaten, or will beat*; and from the infinitive కొట్ట comes కొట్టను, *I do not beat, have not beaten, or will not beat.*

IMPERATIVE, PARTICIPLES, AND VERBAL NOUNS.

AFFIRMATIVE VERBS.

The affiirmative imperative is formed by adding to the root ము or మీ for the 333
2d person singular; దము, or in the common dialect దాము, for the 1st person plural; and ండు or ండీ for the 2d person plural: the last mentioned termination, in the common dialect, is added to the infinitive, instead of the root; thus, from

కొట్టు come కొట్టుము or కొట్టుమీ *beat thou*; కొట్టుదము, or in the common dialect కొట్టుదాము, *let us beat*, కొట్టుఁడు or కొట్టుఁడీ, or in the common dialect కొట్టండి, *beat ye*; the reader, however, will bear in mind that, by rule 310, the root itself, in the common dialect, is often used as the 2d person singular of the affirmative imperative; instead of కొట్టుము or కొట్టుమీ, therefore, we constantly say కొట్టు *beat thou.*

334 The formation of the *verbal* participles, in the affirmative verb, has already been explained; see rules 313 and 314: it only remains, therefore, to shew the manner in which the *relative* participles are formed: the present relative participle is formed from the present verbal participles in న్నూ, by changing న్నూ into న్న: there are two verbal participles in న్నూ, viz. the grammatical participle in చున్నూ, and the common participle in తున్నూ; the relative participle, therefore, has also two corresponding forms, చున్న and తున్న; thus, from కొట్టుచున్నూ and కొట్టుతున్నూ *beating*, come కొట్టుచున్న and, in the common dialect, కొట్టుతున్న *that beats.* The past relative participle is formed by adding the syllable న to the past verbal participle; thus, from కొట్టి *having beaten*, comes కొట్టిన *that has beaten*; the indefinite relative participle is formed by adding to the root ‑ఎడు or ‑ఎడి in the superior, and ‑ఏ or ‑ఏటి in the common dialect, and as all these terminations commence with a vowel, the ఉ final of the root must be dropped when they are added: thus, the root కొట్టు makes its indefinite relative participle కొట్టెడు or కొట్టెడి in the superior dialect, and in the common dialect, కొట్టే or కొట్టేటి *that beats, has beaten, or will beat.* The root itself is somtimes, in books, used as the indefinite relative participle.

335 The affirmative verbal noun is formed by adding ట to the root, or in the common dialect, by adding డము to the infinitive; thus, from కొట్టు come కొట్టుట, or in the common dialect కొట్టడము *the beating.*

NEGATIVE VERB.

336 The negative imperative is formed by adding to the infinitive కుము or కుమీ, or in the common dialect కు, for the 2d person singular; and కుఁడు or కుఁడీ, or in the common dialect కండి, for the 2d person plural; thus, from కొట్ట *to beat*

come కొట్టకుము or కొట్టకుమీ or కొట్టకే beat not thou, and కొట్టకుఁడు or కొట్టకుఁడీ or కొట్టకండి beat not ye. By adding to the infinitive క, we form the negative verbal participle ; by adding to it ని, we form the negative relative participle ; and by adding to it మి, we form the negative verbal noun ; thus, from కొట్ట *to beat* come కొట్టక *without beating or having beaten* ; కొట్టని *that does not, has not, or will not beat* ; and కొట్టమి *the not beating.*

Neuter and active verbs are conjugated in the same manner : we shall, therefore, treat of them conjointly ; merely distinguishing the దేశ్యము from the తత్సమము verbs : we shall afterwards submit an example of the passive verb, and shall conclude this chapter with a few remarks on the causal verb. 337

OF దేశ్యము *VERBS.*

Roots in చు or యు undergo certain changes to which other verbs are not liable : we shall, therefore, divide the verbs in to three conjugations ; the first, including all verbs the root of which terminates in any other syllable than యు or చు ; the second, all those that have the root in యు ; and the third, all those of which the root terminates in చు ; and, in giving an example of each conjugation, we shall place first the correct grammatical form, the common forms following in order, as they more or less approach to it. 338

FIRST CONJUGATION.

All the roots that terminate in any other syllable than యు or చు belong to this conjugation ; and merely require the addition of the different terminations mentioned in the foregoing table. 339

The root కొట్టు *to beat,* is selected as an example of this conjugation. 340

Root...............కొట్టు *common.* *common.*

Present verbal participle...... } కొట్టుచున్న..కొట్టుచు..కొట్టుతున్న..కొట్టుతు *beating.*

Past...do.........కొట్టి...*having beaten.*

Infinitive.........కొట్ట...*to beat.*

AFFIRMATIVE VERB.

INDICATIVE MOOD.

PRESENT.

			common.	
Singular. 1st.		కొట్టుచున్నాను	కొట్టుచాను	*I beat.*
2d.		కొట్టుచున్నావు	కొట్టుచావు	*Thou beatest.*
3d.	*M.*	కొట్టుచున్నాఁడు	కొట్టుచాఁడు	*He beats.*
	F.&N.	కొట్టుచున్నది	కొట్టుచున్నది or కొట్టుచుంది	*She or it beats.*
Plural. 1st.		కొట్టుచున్నాము	కొట్టుచాము	*We beat.*
2d.		కొట్టుచున్నారు	కొట్టుచారు	*You beat.*
3d.	*M.&F.*	కొట్టుచున్నారు	కొట్టుచారు	*They beat.*
	N.	కొట్టుచున్నవి	కొట్టుచున్నవి	

		common.	*common.*	
Singular. 1st.		కొట్టుతున్నాను	కొట్టుతాను	*I beat.*
2d.		కొట్టుతున్నావు	కొట్టుతావు	*Thou beatest.*
3d.	*M.*	కొట్టుతున్నాఁడు	కొట్టుతాఁడు	*He beats.*
	F.&N.	కొట్టుతున్నది or కొట్టుతుంది	కొట్టుతున్నది or కొట్టుతుంది	*She or it beats.*
Plural. 1st.		కొట్టుతున్నాము	కొట్టుతాము	*We beat.*
2d.		కొట్టుతున్నారు	కొట్టుతారు	*You beat.*
3d.	*M.&F.*	కొట్టుతున్నారు	కొట్టుతారు	*They beat.*
	N.	కొట్టుతున్నవి	కొట్టుతున్నవి	

PAST.

Singular. 1st.		కొట్టితిని	కొట్టినాను	*I have beaten.*
2d.		కొట్టితివి	కొట్టినావు	*thou hast beaten.*
3d.	*M.*	కొట్టెను	కొట్టినాఁడు	*He has beaten.*
	F.&N.	కొట్టెను	కొట్టినది / కొట్టింది *common.*	*She, or it has beaten.*

Plural. 1st.	కొట్టితిమి	కొట్టినాము	*We have beaten.*
2d.	కొట్టితిరి	కొట్టినారు	*You have beaten.*
3d. M. & F.	కొట్టిరి	కొట్టినారు	*They have beaten.*
N.	కొట్టెను	కొట్టినవి	

FUTURE.

common.

Singular. 1st.	కొట్టెదను	కొట్టెను	*I shall beat.*
2d.	కొట్టెదవు	కొట్టేవు	*Thou will beat.*
3d. M. F. & N.	కొట్టెడిని	కొట్టేని / కొట్టీని	*He, she or it will beat.*
Plural. 1st.	కొట్టెదము	కొట్టేము	*We shall beat.*
2d.	కొట్టెదరు	కొట్టేరు	*You will beat.*
3d. M.&F.	కొట్టెదరు	కొట్టేరు	*They will beat.*
N.	కొట్టెడిని	కొట్టేని / కొట్టీని	

AORIST.

Singular. 1st. M.F.&N.	కొట్టుదును	*I beat, did beat, or shall beat.*
2d.	కొట్టుదువు	*Thou beatest, didst beat, or wilt beat.*
3d.	కొట్టును	*He, she, or it beats, did beat, or will beat.*
Plural. 1st.	కొట్టుదుము	*We beat, did beat, or shall beat.*
2d.	కొట్టుదురు	*You beat, did beat, or will beat.*
3d. M. & F.	కొట్టుదురు	*They beat, did beat, or will beat.*
N.	కొట్టును	

IMPERATIVE MOOD.

common.

Singular. 2d.	కొట్టుము	కొట్టుమీ	కొట్టు	*beat thou.*

common.

1st.	కొట్టుదము	కొట్టుదాము	*let us beat.*

common.

Plural. 2d.	కొట్టుఁడు	కొట్టుఁడీ	కొట్టండి	*beat ye.*

RELATIVE PARTICIPLES.

PRESENT.

common.

కొట్టుచున్న..............................కొట్టుతున్న....................*that beats.*

PAST.

కొట్టిన...*that has beaten.*

INDEFINITE.

common. common.

కొట్టు..కొట్టెడు..కొట్టెడి..కొట్టే..కొట్టేటి..*that beats, has beaten, or will beat.*

VERBAL NOUN.

common.

కొట్టుట...........కొట్టడము..*the beating.*

NEGATIVE VERB.

INDICATIVE MOOD.

AORIST.

Singular.	1st.	కొట్టను...............	*I do not, did not, or shall not beat.*
	2d.	కొట్టవు...............	*Thou dost not, didst not, or will not beat.*
	3d. *M.*	కొట్టఁడు...............	*He does not, did not, or will not beat.*
	3d. *F. & N.*	కొట్టదు...............	*She, or it, does not, did not, or will not beat.*
Plural.	1st.	కొట్టము...............	*We do not, did not, or shall not beat.*
	2d.	కొట్టరు...............	*You do not, did not, or will not beat.*
	3d. *M. & F.*	కొట్టరు...............	*They do not, did not, or will not beat.*
	3d. *N.*	కొట్టవు...............	

IMPERATIVE.

			common.	
Sing. 2d.	కొట్టకుము......	కొట్టకుమీ......................	కొట్టక...	*beat not thou.*
			common.	
Plu. 2d.	కొట్టకుఁడు......	కొట్టకుఁడీ......................	కొట్టకండి	*beat not ye.*

VERBAL PARTICIPLE.

కొట్టక.............................*without beating, or without having beaten.*

RELATIVE PARTICIPLE.

కొట్టని.............................*that does not, did not, or will not beat.*

VERBAL NOUN.

కొట్టమి.............................*the not beating.*

The following are a few examples of the numerous verbs in the first conjugation which, in all their forms, are similar to కొట్టు *to beat.* 341

Root.	Present verbal participle.	Past verbal participle.	Infinitive.	
పలుకు	పలుకుచున్న &c.	పలికి	పలుక	*to utter, to pronounce.*
అమ్ము	అమ్ముచున్న &c.	అమ్మి	అమ్మ	*to sell.*
అల్లు	అల్లుచున్న &c.	అల్లి	అల్ల	*to plait.*
ఆడు	ఆడుచున్న &c.	ఆడి	ఆడ	*to play.*
ఆరు	ఆరుచున్న &c.	ఆరి	ఆర	*to become cool, to be extinguished.*
ఈఁదు	ఈఁదుచున్న &c.	ఈఁది	ఈఁద	*to swim.*
ఈను	ఈనుచున్న &c.	ఈని	ఈన	*to bring forth, to produce, applied to cattle, or grain.*
ఉబ్బు	ఉబ్బుచున్న &c.	ఉబ్బి	ఉబ్బ	*to swell.*
ఊకొట్టు	ఊకొట్టుచున్న &c.	ఊకొట్టి	ఊకొట్ట	*to listen.*
ఊఁగు	ఊఁగుచున్న &c.	ఊఁగి	ఊఁగ	*to be roked.*
ఊను	ఊనుచున్న &c.	ఊని	ఊన	*to lean upon.*
ఎక్కు	ఎక్కుచున్న &c.	ఎక్కి	ఎక్క	*to mount.*
ఎండు	ఎండుచున్న &c.	ఎండి	ఎండ	*to dry.*
అదుము	అదుముచున్న &c.	అదిమి	అదమ	*to press.*
ఇఱుకు	ఇఱుకుచున్న &c.	ఇఱికి	ఇఱక	*to insert (in writing.)*
ఉడుకు	ఉడుకుచున్న &c.	ఉడికి	ఉడక	*to boil.*
ఉతుకు	ఉతుకుచున్న &c.	ఉతికి	ఉతక	*to wash, to bleach.*
ఉబుకు	ఉబుకుచున్న &c.	ఉబికి	ఉబక	*to overflow.*
కొఱుకు	కొఱుకుచున్న &c.	కొఱికి	కొఱక	*to bite.*
దొఱుకు	దొఱుకుచున్న &c.	దొఱికి	దొఱక	*to be found.*
నఱుకు	నఱుకుచున్న &c.	నఱికి	నఱక	*to cut.*
పగులు	పగులుచున్న &c.	పగిలి	పగల	*to break.*

EXCEPTIONS.

The undermentioned and a few other roots ending in ను, when followed by చు or దు, change నుచు or నుదు, at pleasure, into న్చు or ంచు, న్దు or ందు; and in these verbs, the syllables ని or ను, followed by త, are *invariably* changed into ం, the త being at the same time, converted into ద. 342

అను......................................to say.
కను......................................to see, to bring forth.
కొను......................................to buy, to take.
విను......................................to hear.
తిను......................................to eat.

343 For instance, కొను *to buy*, in order to form the present affirmative verbal participle, adds చు, and makes కొనుచు or కొన్చు or కొంచు *buying;* and in the affirmative aorist కొనుదును or కొన్దును or కొందును. In the second and third persons plural of the affirmative aorist, instead of కొందురు, we may, by a rule applicable to these verbs only, change the ు of దు, or the దు itself, into ఱ; thus, కొందురు or కొంఱు, *you or they buy, did buy, or will buy;* thus also కొను followed by తున్న, makes కొంటున్న *buying;* and, in the perfect tense, కొని, followed by తిని, makes కొంటిని *I have bought.*

344 The foregoing verbs, together with

చను..........*to go*..........	నగు..........*to laugh or smile.*
చెడు..........*to be corrupted*..........	తగు..........*to suit, to fit.*
పడు..........*to fall*..........	తెగు..........*to break.*
ఇడు..........*to place, to keep*..........	దిగు..........*to descend.*

may at option change ి, at the commencement of any of the terminations mentioned in the table, into ి యె; thus, కొనెను or కొనియెను *he has bought,* కొనెదను or కొనియెదను *I shall buy.*

345 All the roots mentioned above as exceptions, instead of forming the past relative participle of the affirmative verb in the regular manner, māy, at pleasure, form it by changing the final ు of the root into ్ and doubling the preceding consonant; thus, we say either కొనిన or కొన్న *that bought,* తగిన or తగ్గ *that fitted.*

346 The roots in ను specified in rule 342, together with the three roots in డు mentioned in rule 344, contract the second form of the past tense, in a manner peculiar to themselves; by doubling the consonant of the second syllable, which coalesces with the vowel of the third syllable, and rejecting both the

vowel of the second syllable, and the consonant of the third syllable; thus, కొనినాను *I bought,* becomes కొన్నాను, and పడినాను, *I fell,* becomes పడ్డాను.

The verb కొను, *to buy,* is here given at full length, as an example of the irregular verbs of this conjugation. 347

Root..........................కొను.

	common.		*common.*		
Present verbal participle....	కొనుచున్న....	కొంచున్న.....	కొనుచు......	కొంచు...	
		[కొంటున్న......	కొంటు..		*buying.*

Past........*do*..............కొని...*having bought.*

Infinitive......................కొన..*to buy.*

Verbs in ను, such as కొను, do not derive any form of the present tense from the participle in నుచు. 348

AFFIRMATIVE VERB.

INDICATIVE MOOD.

PRESENT.

Singular.	1st.	కొనుచున్నాను.........	కొంచున్నాను.............	*I buy.*
	2d.	కొనుచున్నావు.........	కొంచున్నావు............	*Thou buyest.*
	3d. M.	కొనుచున్నాఁడు........	కొంచున్నాఁడు...........	*He buys.*
	3d. F. & N.	కొనుచున్నది...........	కొంచున్నది..............	*She or it buys.*
Plural.	1st.	కొనుచున్నాము........	కొంచున్నాము............	*We buy.*
	2d.	కొనుచున్నారు.........	కొంచున్నారు............	*You buy.*
	3d. M. & F.	కొనుచున్నారు........	కొంచున్నారు....	......*They buy.*
	3d. N.	కొనుచున్నవి..........	కొంచున్నవి.......	

		common.	*common.*	*common.*	
Singular.	1st.	కొంచాను......	కొంటున్నాను......	కొంటాను......	*I buy.*
	2d.	కొంచావు......	కొంటున్నావు......	కొంటావు......	*Thou buyest.*
	3d. M.	కొంచాఁడు.....	కొంటున్నాఁడు.....	కొంటాఁడు....	*He buys.*
	3d. F. & N.	కొంచున్నది... or కొంచుంది.....	కొంటున్నది....... or కొంటుంది...........	కొంటున్నది or కొంటుంది....	*She or it buys.*

Plural.	1st.		కొంచాము...	కొంటున్నాము...	కొంటాము...	*We buy.*
	2d.		కొంచారు....	కొంటున్నారు....	కొంటారు...	*You buy.*
	3d.	M. & F.	కొంచారు....	కొంటున్నారు....	కొంటారు...	*They buy.*
		N.	కొంచున్నవి..	కొంటున్నవి.......	కొంటున్నవి	

PAST.

					peculiar.	
Singular.	1st.		కొంటిని......	కొనినాను........	కొన్నాను......	*I bought.*
	2d.		కొంటివి......	కొనినావు.........	కొన్నావు...	*Thou boughtest.*
	3d.	M.	కొనెను......	కొనినాఁడు.......	కొన్నాఁడు...	*He bought.*
		F. & N.	కొనెను...	కొనినది......... or *common.* కొనింది.........	కొన్నది........	*She or it bought.*
Plural.	1st.		కొంటిమి.....	కొనినాము........	కొన్నాము.....	*We bought.*
	2d.		కొంటిరి.....	కొనినారు..........	కొన్నారు......	*You bought.*
	3d.	M. & F.	కొనిరి........	కొనినారు..........	కొన్నారు......	*They bought.*
		N.	కొనెను......	కొనినవి..............	కొన్నవి.........	

FUTURE.

				common.	
Singular.	1st.		కొనెదను....................	కొనేను........	*I shall buy.*
	2d.		కొనెదవు....................	కొనేవు..........	*Thou wilt buy.*
	3d.	M. F. & N.	కొనెడిని....................	కొనేని...... or కొనీని......	*He she or it will buy.*
Plural.	1st.		కొనెదము....................	కొనేము.........	*We shall buy.*
	2d.		కొనెదరు....................	కొనేరు..........	*You will buy.*
	3d.	M. & F.	కొనెదరు....................	కొనేరు......	*They will buy.*
		N.	కొనెడిని....................	కొనేని........ or కొనీని........	

AORIST.

Singular.	1st.		కొనుదును...	కొందును...	*I buy, bought, or shall buy.*
	2d.		కొనుదువు..	కొందువు...	*Thou buyest, boughtest, or wilt buy.*
	3d.	M. F. & N.	కొనును..............		*He, she, or it buys, bought, or will buy.*

Plural. 1st. కొనుదుము..కొందుము..*We buy, bought, or shall buy.*

2d. కొనుదురు { కొందురు or కొండ్రు.. } *You buy, bought, or will buy.*

3d. M. & F. కొనుదురు..కొందురు.. or కొండ్రు... } *They buy, bought, or will buy.*
N. కొనును.............. }

IMPERATIVE MOOD.

common.

కొనుము...............కొనుమీ...............కొను...............*buy thou.*

common.

కొనుదము.............కొందము...............కొందాము.........*let us buy.*

common.

కొనుఁడు...............కొనుఁడీ...............కొనండి...........*buy ye.*

RELATIVE PARTICIPLES.

PRESENT.

common.

కొనుచున్న ....కొంచున్న...............కొంటున్న.......*that buys.*

PAST.

కొనిన..............................కొన్న.........................*that bought.*

INDEFINITE.

common. *common.*

కొను...కొనెడు...కొనెడి...కొనే...కొనేటి...*that buys, bought, or will buy.*

VERBAL NOUN.

common.

కొనుట..............................కొనడము..............................*the buying.*

NEGATIVE VERB.

INDICATIVE MOOD.

AORIST.

Singular. 1st. కొనను...................*I do not, did not, or shall not buy.*

2d. కొనవు...................*Thou dost not, didst not, or wilt not buy.*

3d. M. కొనఁడు...................*He does not, did not, or will not buy.*

F. & N. కొనదు...................*She or it does not, did not, or will not buy.*

Plural. 1st. కొనము...................*We do not, did not, or shall not buy.*

2d. కొనరు...................*You do not, did not, or will not buy.*

3d. M. & F. కొనరు................... }
N. కొనవు................... } *They do not, did not, or will not buy.*

IMPERATIVE MOOD.

			common.	
Sing. 2d.	కొనకుము..........	కొనకుమీ.........	కొనక......	buy not thou.
			common.	
Plu. 2d.	కొనకుఁడు..........	కొనకుఁడీ.........	కొనకండి..	buy not ye.

VERBAL PARTICIPLE.

కొనక ....*without buying, or without having bought.*

RELATIVE PARTICIPLE.

కొనని..........................*that does not, did not, or will not buy.*

VERBAL NOUN.

కొనమి...................*the not buying.*

SECOND CONJUGATION IN యు.

349 All verbs having the root in యు form the affirmative aorist and imperative, either in the manner explained in the table rule 312, or by changing యుదు of the affirmative aorist into తు, and యుద of the affirmative imperative into త; and, in these cases, if the vowel preceding యు be ఇ, it must be changed into అ; thus, from చేయు *to do* comes చేయుదును or చేతును *I do, did, or shall do.* చేయుదము or చేతము *let us do;* but the root తడియు, which has ఇ preceding యు, makes తడియుదును or తడుతును, and తడియుదము or తడుతము, never తడితును and తడితము.

350 In the common dialect, roots in యు form the second person of the affirmative imperative by changing the యు into యి; thus, చేయు *to do* makes చేయి *do thou.*

351 Roots in యు, when they affix ఇ or ఎ, or terminations beginning with these vowels, as shewn in the table, rule 312, *invariably* change the final syllable యు into సు or శు; thus, the root చేయు *to do,* when it adds ఇ to form the past verbal participle, makes చేసి or చేశి *having done,* and when it adds ఎదను to form the future, it makes చేసెదను or చేశెదను, &c. never చేయెదను &c. when followed by ట to form the verbal noun, and by ను in the third person singular of the affirmative aorist, such roots change the యు into సు *at option*

N. B.—The verb కొను has two irregular forms in the second person of the affirmative imperative, viz. కొమ్ము or కొమ్మీ *buy thou* కొండు or కొండీ *buy ye.*

only; as చేయుట or చేసుట *the doing,* చేయును or చేసును *he, she, or it does, did, or will do;* and if the vowel preceding the యు be ి, it must be changed into ు; thus, తడియు *to be damp,* makes తడుసుట *the being damp,* తడుసును *he, she, or it is, was, or will be damp,* never తడిసుట, and తడిసును.

Roots in యు, when followed by తున్న or తు, *invariably* change the syllable యు into the letter స, which coalesces with the త in it's doubled form ్త; thus, చేయు followed by తున్న or తు, to form the common present verbal participle always becomes చేస్తున్న and చేస్తు respectively, never చేయుతున్న and చేయుతు. 352

The following is an example of this conjugation. 353

			common.	common.	
Root	చేయు				
Present verbal participle	చేయుచున్న	చేయుచు	చేస్తున్న	చేస్తు	*doing.*
Past ... do	చేసి	చేశి			*having done.*
Infinitive	చేయ				*to do.*

Verbs of this conjugation do not derive any form of the present tense from the participle in యుచు.

AFFIRMATIVE VERB.

INDICATIVE MOOD.

PRESENT.

				common.	common.	
Singular.	1st.		చేయుచున్నాను	చేస్తున్నాను	చేస్తాను	*I do.*
	2d.		చేయుచున్నావు	చేస్తున్నావు	చేస్తావు	*Thou dost.*
	3d.	M.	చేయుచున్నాఁడు	చేస్తున్నాఁడు	చేస్తాఁడు	*He does.*
		F. & N.	చేయుచున్నది	చేస్తున్నది ... or చేస్తుంది	చేస్తున్నది. ... or చేస్తుంది	*She or it does.*
Plural.	1st.		చేయుచున్నాము	చేస్తున్నాము	చేస్తాము	*We do.*
	2d.		చేయుచున్నారు	చేస్తున్నారు	చేస్తారు	*You do.*
	3d.	M. & F.	చేయుచున్నారు	చేస్తున్నారు	చేస్తారు	*They do.*
		N.	చేయుచున్నవి	చేస్తున్నవి	చేస్తున్నవి	*They do.*

PAST.

Singular.	1st.	చేసితిని	చేశితిని	చేసినాను	చేశినాను	*I did.*
	2d.	చేసితివి	చేశితివి	చేసినావు	చేశినావు	*Thou didst.*
	3d. M.	చేసెను	చేశెను	చేసినాఁడు	చేశినాఁడు	*He did.*
	3d. F. & N.	చేసెను	చేశెను	చేసినది or *common.* చేసింది	చేశినది or *common.* చేశింది	*She or it did.*
Plural.	1st.	చేసితిమి	చేశితిమి	చేసినాము	చేశినాము	*We did.*
	2d.	చేసితిరి	చేశితిరి	చేసినారు	చేశినారు	*You did.*
	3d. M. & F.	చేసిరి	చేశిరి	చేసినారు	చేశినారు	*They did.*
	3d. N.	చేసెను	చేశెను	చేసినవి	చేశినవి	*They did.*

FUTURE.

				common.	*common.*	
Singular.	1st.	చేసెదను	చేశెదను	చేసేను	చేశేను	*I shall do.*
	2d.	చేసెదవు	చేశెదవు	చేసేవు	చేశేవు	*Thou wilt do.*
	3d. M. F. & N.	చేసెడిని	చేశెడిని	చేసేని or చేసీని	చేశేని or చేశీని	*He, she, or it will do.*
Plural.	1st.	చేసెదము	చేశెదము	చేసేము	చేశేము	*We shall do.*
	2d.	చేసెదరు	చేశెదరు	చేసేరు	చేశేరు	*You will do.*
	3d. M. & F.	చేసెదరు	చేశెదరు	చేసేరు	చేశేరు	*They will do.*
	3d. N.	చేసెడిని	చేశెడిని	చేసేని / చేసీని	చేశేని / చేశీని	*They will do.*

AORIST.

Singular.	1st.	చేయుదును	చేతును	*I do, did, or shall do.*
	2d.	చేయుదువు	చేతువు	*Thou dost, didst, or wilt do.*
	3d. M. F. & N.	చేయును	చేసును	*He, she, or it does, did, or will do.*
Plural.	1st.	చేయుదుము	చేతుము	*We, do, did, or shall do.*
	2d.	చేయుదురు	చేతురు	*You do, did, or will do.*
	3d. M. & F.	చేయుదురు	చేతురు	*They do, did, or will do.*
	3d. N.	చేయును	చేసును	*They do, did, or will do.*

IMPERATIVE MOOD.

Sing. 2d.	చేయుము	చేయుమీ	చేయి (common)	do thou.
Plu. 1st.	చేయుదము	చేతము	చేతాము (common)	let us do.
Plu. 2d.	చేయుఁడు	చేయుఁడీ	చేయండి (common)	do ye.

RELATIVE PARTICIPLES.

PRESENT.

చేయుచున్న.................చేస్తున్న (common).......................................that does.

PAST.

చేసిన..........................చేశిన...that did.

INDEFINITE.

చేయు..	చేసెడు..	చేశెడు..	చేసెడి..	చేశెడి	that does, did, or will do.
	common.	common.	common.	common.	
	చేసే	చేశే	చేసేటి	చేశేటి	

VERBAL NOUN.

చేయుట..............................చేసుట.................చేయడము (common).....the doing.

NEGATIVE VERB.

INDICATIVE MOOD.

AORIST.

Singular. 1st.	చేయను	I do not, did not, or shall not do.
Singular. 2d.	చేయవు	Thou dost not, didst not, or wilt not do.
Singular. 3d. M.	చేయఁడు	He does not, did not, or will not do.
Singular. 3d. F. & N.	చేయదు	She or it does not, did not, or will not do.
Plural. 1st.	చేయము	We do not, did not, or shall not do.
Plural. 2d.	చేయరు	You do not, did not, or will not do.
Plural. 3d. M. & F.	చేయరు	They do not, did not, or will not do.
Plural. 3d. N.	చేయవు	They do not, did not, or will not do.

IMPERATIVE.

చేయకుము............చేయకుమీ........చేయక (common)........do not thou.

చేయకుఁడు,...........చేయఁకుడీ...........చేయకండి (common)........do not ye.

VERBAL PARTICIPLE.

చేయక.............................*without doing, or without having done.*

RELATIVE PARTICIPLE.

చేయని.............................*that does not, did not, or will not do.*

VERBAL NOUN.

చేయమి.............................*the not doing.*

354 According to the common dialect, the syllables సి or శి, in this conjugation, when followed by the consonant *t* తి, are at pleasure changed into the letter *s* స, which coalesces with the *t* తి in it's doubled form ‿; thus, the 1st and 2d persons in the first form of the past tense of చేయు may become.

Sing.	1st.	చేస్తిని...	*I did.*
	2d.	చేస్తివి...	*Thou didst.*
Plu.	1st.	చేస్తిమి...	*We did.*
	2d.	చేస్తిరి...	*You did.*

355 The following, with all other verbs in యు, are conjugated under the foregoing rules.

Root.	Present verbal participle.	Past verbal participle.	Infinitive.	
అలయు.........	అలయుచున్న........	అలసి......	అలయ....	*to become fatigued or tired.*
అవయు.........	అవయుచున్న.......	అవసి......	అవయ....	*to become blind.*
నవయు.........	నవయుచున్న.......	నవసి......	నవయ....	*to linger in disease.*
పడయు.........	పడయుచున్న.......	పడసి.......	పడయ....	*to obtain.*
పెనయు.......	పెనయుచున్న......	పెనసి......	పెనయ..	*to twine.*
మొనయు......	మొనయుచున్న....	మొనసి....	మొనయ	*to attack in the field of battle.*
మొరయు......	మొరయుచున్న....	మొరసి....	మొరయ	*to make a noise, to sound.*
వలయు.........	వలయుచున్న......	వలసి.......	వలయ....	*to love, to desire.*
కోయు.........	కోయుచున్న.........	కోసి........	కోయ.....	*to cut.*
తీయు..........	తీయుచున్న.........	తీసి..........	తీయ......	*to take, to purchase, to pull.*
నేయు..........	నేయుచున్న.........	నేసి..........	నేయ....	*to weave.*
పూయు........	పూయుచున్న......	పూసి........	పూయ...	*to rub, to bloom.*

Root.	Present verbal participle.	Past verbal participle.	Infinitive.	
పోయు	పోయుచున్న	పోసి	పోయ	*to pour.*
మేయు	మేయుచున్న	మేసి	మేయ	*to graze.*
మోయు	మోయుచున్న	మోసి	మోయ	*to bear a burden.*
రోయు	రోయుచున్న	రోసి	రోయ	*to feel disgust.*
వ్రేయు	వ్రేయుచున్న	వ్రేసి	వ్రేయ	*to cast, to throw.*
కలియు	కలియుచున్న	కలిసి	కలియ	*to mix.*
కురియు	కురియుచున్న	కురిసి	కురియ	*to rain.*
జడియు	జడియుచున్న	జడిసి	జడియ	*to tremble with fear, to fear.*

Roots in యు of two syllables, of which the first ends in a long vowel, often shorten that vowel; and, in this case, double the య్; thus, the root చేయు may become చెయ్యు, the infinitive తీయ, తియ్య &c. &c. 356

THIRD CONJUGATION IN చు.

All verbs having the root in చు, form the aorist and imperative, either in the manner explained in the foregoing table, rule 312, or by changing చుదు in the affirmative aorist into తు, and చుద in the affirmative imperative into త. If the root has a double చ్చు, the తు and త are also doubled, into త్తు and త్త; thus, దీవించుదును or దీవింతును - దీవించుదము or దీవింతము, మెచ్చుదును or మెత్తును, మెచ్చుదము or మెత్తము. 357

In the common dialect, the terminations ము and మీ, in the second person singular of the affirmative imperative, are often dropped in this conjugation. 358

The undermentioned verbs terminating in చు, likewise deviate from the rules given in the foregoing table, (312) by forming the infinitive in వ, instead of చ, and taking వు instead of చు before the terminations for the affirmative imperative. 359

అఱచు.....*to make a loud or clamorous noise.*
ఏడుచు.....*to weep, to lament.*
కరచు *to bite.*
కాచు......only when it signifies *to protect.*
కుడుచు....*to suck, to eat.*
కొలుచు...*to measure, to serve.*
గడుచు....*to pass, or elapse.*
గెలుచు...*to win.*
నడుచు.....*to walk.*
నిలుచు......*to stand.*
పిలుచు......*to call.*
మఱచు......*to forget.*
మొలుచు...*to grow, to shoot.*
విడుచు......*to quit, to leave.*
లేచు.........*to rise.* (This verb has also an irregular form in the 2d person of the affirmative imperative, viz. లెమ్ము *rise thou,* లెండు *rise ye.*)

thus, పిలుచు *to call,* makes, in the infinitive పిలువ, never పిలుచ, and in the imperative పిలువుము never పిలుచుము.

360 The following, and a few other roots in చు, may at pleasure form the infinitive either in చ or వ, and may take either చు or వు before the terminations of the affirmative imperative.

ఈడుచు...*to draw, to drag.*
ఊడుచు...*to sweep.*
ఒలుచు...*to strip off any thing naturally attached to a substance.*
ఓరుచు...*to suffer.*
తరుచు...*to churn.*
తుడుచు...*to cleanse by rubbing, to efface.*
తొలుచు..*to perforate, to cleanse a pot or vessel, to carve wood.*
నులుచు..*to thresh.*
నలుచు...*to squeeze, to crush.*
పీలుచు...........*to draw up any thing with the breath,* as an elephant does water with his trunk.
ప్రోచు.........*to protect.*
మలచు..........*to cut, or carve stone; to separate sand from grain.*
మోచు.........*to bear a burden.*
వగచు...........*to grieve.*
వలచు..........*to love.*
వీచు............*to blow as the wind.*
వేలుచు.........*to sacrifice.*
వైచు...........*to place, or put.*

thus, ఊడ్చు *to sweep* makes, in the infinitive ఊడ్చ or ఊడ్వ, and in the affirmative imperative ఊడ్చుము or ఊడ్వుము &c.

361 The only deviations from the general rules given in the table, rule 312, of

which the following roots in చు admit, are those mentioned in the two first rules for this conjugation (357 & 358.)

ఎంచు ......*to reckon, to think.*

కాఁచు......*to attend.*

పంచు.......*to share, to divide.*

పొంచు......*to lurk, to lie in wait secretly.*

మించు......*to surpass, to go beyond.*

ఏచు..........*to harass, to torment.*

గీఁచు.......*to scrape, to scratch.*

తిగుచు......*to take, to receive.*

తోఁచు.....*to imagine, to think.*

దోఁచు.....*to rob.*

నోచు.....*to perform a ceremony in which a string is consecrated to a particular deity, and then tied round the arm or wrist; it is generally performed by females.*

తూచు......*to weigh.*

రాచు......*to rub.*

అచ్చు......*to owe.*

కచ్చు......*to move a piece,* as in a game [of chess, &c.

క్రచ్చు...*to love, to desire.*

గిచ్చు......*to claw.*

గ్రుచ్చు....*to string (pearls, &c.)*

గ్రొచ్చు...*to dig.*

త్రచ్చు.....*to churn.*

నచ్చు.......*to trust, to confide.*

పుచ్చు.......*to send, to command, to rot.*

మెచ్చు.....*to prefer, to approve.*

వ్రచ్చు...*to break in pieces.*

వాక్రుచ్చు.*to say.*

హెచ్చు......*to increase.*

All other roots in చు have the infinitive optionally either in చ or in ప, and, 362
when followed by చున్న to form the present verbal participle, by దు to form certain parts of the affirmative aorist, or by the terminations for the affirmative imperative, they may, at pleasure, convert చు into పు; thus, దీవించు, *to bless,* makes in the infinitive దీవించ or దీవింప, in the present verbal participle దీవించుచున్న or దీవింపుచున్న; in the aorist దీవించుదును or దీవింపుదును, and in the imperative దీవించుము or దీవింపుము.

The verbs of the class last mentioned being more numerous than any others, 363
in చు, one of them has been selected as an example of this conjugation.

Root ....దీవించు

Present verbal participle..........దీవించుచున్న......దీవింపుచున్న .....దీవించుచు

common. *common.*

[దీవించుతున్న .....దీవించుతు *blessing.*

Past..............*do*........ ....దీవించి.......................... .....*having blessed.*

Infinite.... ....దీవించ...........దీవింప.................*to bless.*

Verbs in this conjugation do not derive any form of the present tense from the participle in చుచు.

AFFIRMATIVE VERB.

INDICATIVE MOOD.

PRESENT.

Singular.	1st.	దీవించుచున్నాను	దీవింపుచున్నాను	*I bless.*
	2d.	దీవించుచున్నావు	దీవింపుచున్నావు	*Thou blessest.*
	3d. M.	దీవించుచున్నాఁడు	దీవింపుచున్నాఁడు	*He blesses.*
	3d. F. & N.	దీవించుచున్నది	దీవింపుచున్నది	*She or it blesses.*
Plural.	1st.	దీవించుచున్నాము	దీవింపుచున్నాము	*We bless.*
	2d.	దీవించుచున్నారు	దీవింపుచున్నారు	*You bless.*
	3d. M. & F.	దీవించుచున్నారు	దీవింపుచున్నారు	*They bless.*
	3d. N.	దీవించుచున్నవి	దీవింపుచున్నవి	*They bless.*

		common.	*common.*	
Singular.	1st.	దీవించుతున్నాను	దీవించుతాను	*I bless.*
	2d.	దీవించుతున్నావు	దీవించుతావు	*Thou blessest.*
	3d. M.	దీవించుతున్నాఁడు	దీవించుతాఁడు	*He blesses.*
	3d. F. & N.	దీవించుతున్నది or దీవించుతుంది	దీవించుతున్నది or దీవించుతుంది	*She or it blesses.*
Plural.	1st.	దీవించుతున్నాము	దీవించుతాము	*We bless.*
	2d.	దీవించుతున్నారు	దీవించుతారు	*You bless.*
	3d. M. & F.	దీవించుతున్నారు	దీవించుతారు	*They bless.*
	3d. N.	దీవించుతున్నవి	దీవించుతున్నవి	*They bless.*

PAST.

Singular.	1st.	దీవించితిని	దీవించినాను	*I blessed.*
	2d.	దీవించితివి	దీవించినావు	*Thou blessedst.*
	3d. M.	దీవించెను	దీవించినాఁడు	*He blessed.*
	3d. F. & N.	దీవించెను	దీవించినది or *common.* దీవించింది	*She or it blessed.*

Plural. 1st.		దీవించితిమి	దీవించినాము	*We blessed.*
Plural. 2d.		దీవించితిరి	దీవించినారు	*You blessed.*
Plural. 3d.	M.&F.	దీవించిరి	దీవించినారు	*They blessed.*
	N.	దీవించెను	దీవించినవి	*They blessed.*

FUTURE.

common.

Singular. 1st.		దీవించెదను	దీవించేను	*I shall bless.*
Singular. 2d.		దీవించెదవు	దీవించేవు	*Thou wilt bless.*
Singular. 3d.	M.F.&N.	దీవించెడిని	దీవించీని or దీవించేని	*He, she, or it will bless.*
Plural. 1st.		దీవించెదము	దీవించేము	*We shall bless.*
Plural. 2d.		దీవించెదరు	దీవించేరు	*You will bless.*
Plural. 3d.	M.&F.	దీవించెదరు	దీవించేరు	*They will bless.*
	N.	దీవించెడిని	దీవించీని or దీవించేని	*They will bless.*

AORIST.

Singular. 1st.		దీవించుదును	దీవింపుదును	దీవింతును	*I bless, blessed, or shall bless.*
Singular. 2d.		దీవించుదువు	దీవింపుదువు	దీవింతువు	*Thou blessest, blessedst, or wilt bless.*
Singular. 3d.	M.F.&N.	దీవించును	దీవించును	దీవించును	*He, she, or it blesses, blessed, or will bless.*
Plural. 1st.		దీవించుదుము	దీవింపుదుము	దీవింతుము	*We bless, blessed, or shall bless.*
Plural. 2d.		దీవించుదురు	దీవింపుదురు	దీవింతురు	*You bless, blessed, or will bless.*
Plural. 3d.	M.&F.	దీవించుదురు	దీవింపుదురు	దీవింతురు	*They bless, blessed, or will bless.*
	N.	దీవించును	దీవించును	దీవించును	*They bless, blessed, or will bless.*

IMPERATIVE MOOD.

దీవించుము	దీవింపుము *common.*	దీవించుమీ *common.*	*bless thou.*
దీవింపుమీ	దీవించు	దీవింపు	*bless thou.*
దీవించుదము *common.*	దీవింపుదము *common.*	దీవింతము *common.*	*let us bless.*
దీవించుదాము	దీవింపుదాము	దీవింతాము	*let us bless.*
దీవించుఁడు	దీవింపుఁడు *common.*	దీవించుఁడీ *common.*	*bless ye.*
దీవింపుఁడీ	దీవించండి	దీవింపండి	*bless ye.*

RELATIVE PARTICIPLE.

PRESENT.

దీవించుచున్న.....దీవింపుచున్న.........దీవించుతున్న (*common.*) *that blesses.*

PAST.

దీవించిన..*that has blessed.*

INDEFINITE.

దీవించు......దీవించెడు......దీవించెడి......దీవించే (*common.*)......దీవించేటి (*common.*)...*that blesses, blessed, or will bless.*

VERBAL NOUN.

దీవించుట...దీవించడము (*common.*)........దీవింపడము (*common.*)..........................*the blessing.*

NEGATIVE VERB.

INDICATIVE MOOD.

AORIST.

Singular.	1st.	దీవించను...దీవింపను...*I do not, did not, or shall not bless.*
	2d.	దీవించవు...దీవింపవు.....*Thou dost not, didst not, or wilt not bless.*
	3d. M.	దీవించఁడు.దీవింపఁడు....*He does not, did not, or will not bless.*
	3d. F. & N.	దీవించదు...దీవీంపదు....*She or it does not, did not, or will not bless.*
Plural.	1st.	దీవించము...దీవింపము....*We do not, did not, or shall not bless.*
	2d.	దీవించరు....దీవింపరు.....*You do not, did not, or will not bless.*
	3d. M. & F.	దీవించరు...దీవింపరు. *They do not, did not, or will not bless.*
	3d. N.	దీవించవు...దీవింపవు.. *They do not, did not, or will not bless.*

IMPERATIVE MOOD.

దీవించకుము.....దీవింపకుము..దీవించకుమీ
దీవింపకుమీ.....దీవించక (*common.*) .....దీవింపక (*common.*)
}.................*bless not thou.*

దీవించకుఁడు...దీవింపకుఁడు..దీవించకుఁడీ......
దీవింపకుఁడీ.....దీవించకొండి (*common.*)...........................
}.....................*bless not ye.*

VERBAL PARTICIPLE.

దీవించక.........దీవింపక.........*without blessing or without having blessed.*

RELATIVE PARTICIPLE.

దీవించని..........దీవింపని...................*that does not, did not, or will not bless.*

VERBAL NOUN.

దీవించమి........దీవింపమి........*the not blessing.*

In the common dialect, the syllables చు or చి, in this conjugation, when 364
followed by the consonant *t* త, may *at option* be changed into the letter *s* స, which coalesces with the *t* త, in its double form ్త. In this case, if ం precede చు or చి it is dropped; thus దీవించుతున్న becomes దీవిస్తున్న, and దీవించుతు దీవిస్తు; the two last forms of the present tense are accordingly converted into

			common.	*common.*	
Singular.	1st.		దీవిస్తున్నాను	దీవిస్తాను	*I bless.*
	2d.		దీవిస్తున్నావు	దీవిస్తావు	*Thou blessest.*
	3d.	*M.*	దీవిస్తున్నాఁడు	దీవిస్తాఁడు	*He blesses.*
		F. & N.	దీవిస్తున్నది	దీవిస్తున్నది	*She, or it blesses.*
Plural.	1st.		దీవిస్తున్నాము	దీవిస్తాము	*We bless.*
	2d.		దీవిస్తున్నారు	దీవిస్తారు	*You bless.*
	3d.	*M. & F.*	దీవిస్తున్నారు	దీవిస్తారు	*They bless.*
		N.	దీవిస్తున్నవి	దీవిస్తున్నవి	*They bless.*

and the first and second persons in the first form of the past tense become

Singular.	1st.	దీవిస్తిని	*I blessed.*
	2d.	దీవిస్తివి	*Thou blessedst.*
Plural.	1st.	దీవిస్తిమి	*We blessed.*
	2d.	దీవిస్తిరి	*You blessed.*

The follwoing, with many other verbs in చు, are conjugated under the 365
foregoing rules.

Root.	Present verbal participle.	Past verbal participle.	Infinitive.	
అప్పగించు.	అప్పగించుచున్న &c.	అప్పగించి..	అప్పగించ or అప్పగింప	*to deliver into one's charge.*
ఆరగించు..	ఆరగించుచున్న &c.	ఆరగించి...	ఆరగించ.. or ఆరగింప..	*to eat,* applied only to persons of distinction.
ఆవులించు..	ఆవులించుచున్న &c.	ఆవులించి..	ఆవులించ.. or ఆవులింప..	*to yawn, to gape.*

Root.	Present verbal participle.	Past verbal participle.	Infinitive.	
ఇగిలించు...	...ఇగిలించుచున్న &c...	...ఇగిలించి...	...ఇగిలించ or ఇగిలింప	*to grin.*
పెల్లగించు.	పెల్లగించుచున్న&c.	పెల్లగించి..	పెల్లగించ or పెల్లగింప	*to root out, to pluck out.*
మన్నించు..	..మన్నించుచున్న &c.	మన్నించి...	...మన్నించ or మన్నింప	*to forgive.*
రెట్టించు..	రెటించుచున్న &c.	రెట్టించి...	రెట్టించ... or రెట్టింప.	*to double.*
లెక్కించు.	లెక్కించుచున్న &c.	లెక్కించి......	లెక్కించ or లెక్కింప	*to calculate, to reckon.*
కూర్చు..	..కూర్చుచున్న &c.	కూర్చి..	..కూర్చ &c......	*to join, to sew.*
మార్చు	మార్చుచున్న &c.	మార్చి.	మార్చ &c......	*to change.*
తీర్చు...	...తీర్చుచున్న &c.	తీర్చి....	....తీర్చ &c......	*to settle, to decree.*
చేర్చు..	చేర్చుచున్న &c.	చేర్చి.....	....చేర్చ &c......	*to join, to unite.*
తలఁచు...	...తలఁచుచున్న &c.	తలఁచి...	...తలఁచ &c......	*to think.*
కాల్చు....	కాల్చుచున్న&c.	కాల్చి...	...కాల్చ &c......	*to burn.*
మాడ్చు...	...మాడ్చుచున్న &c.	మాడ్చి...	...మాడ్చ&c......	*to roast.*

EXCEPTIONS.

366 The following roots in చు are irregular in the infinitive, and in the second person of the affirmative imperative.

Root.	Infinitive.	Imperative. 2d person singular.		Imperative. 2d person plural.	
ఇచ్చు *to give.*	....	ఇమ్ము		ఇండు	
	ఇవ్వ.........	ఇవ్వుము		ఇవ్వుఁడు.......	ఇవ్వండి *common.*
	ఇయ్య.......	ఇయ్యుము..	ఇయ్యి *common.*	ఇయ్యుఁడు..	ఇయ్యండి. *common.*
	ఈవ........	ఈవుము		ఈవుఁడు	
	ఈయ......	ఈయుము		ఈయుఁడు	

Root.	Infinitive.	Imperative. 2d person singular.		2d person plural.	
వచ్చు *to come*	రా	రమ్ము	*common.* రా	రండు	*common.* రండి
తెచ్చు *to bring*	తే	తెమ్ము	*common.* తే	తెండు	*common.* తెండి
చొచ్చు *to enter*	చొచ్చ or చొర	చొచ్చుము / చొరుము	*common.* చొచ్చు	చొచ్చుఁడు / చొరుఁడు	*common.* చొచ్చుఁడి
నొచ్చు *to pain*	నొవ్వ / నోవ / నో	నొవ్వుము, / నోవుము	*common.* నొచ్చు / *common.* నొవ్వు	నొవ్వఁడు / నోవుఁడు.	*common.* నొవ్వండి
చచ్చు *to die*	చావ or చా.	చావుము	*common.* చావు	చావుఁడు	*common.* చావండి
చూచు *to see*	చూడ	చూడుము	*common.* చూడు	చూడుఁడు	*common.* చూడండి

These verbs are of course also irregular in all the tenses formed from the infinitive; thus, the negative aorist of వచ్చు is రాను &c. &c. 367

OF IRREGULAR దేశ్యము VERBS.

The following verbs are so irregular that they do not admit of being classed under any particular conjugation: on this account, and because most of them are in frequent use as auxiliaries, it has been thought proper to give them at full length. 368

Root.................................ఉండు

Present verbal participle...ఉండుచున్న......ఉండుచు......ఉంచున్న...ఉంచు

common. *common.*
[ఉంటున్న..ఉంటు...*being.*

Past............*do*............ఉండి..*having been.*

Infinitive..................ఉండ.......................................*to be.*

AFFIRMATIVE VERB.

INDICATIVE MOOD.

PRESENT.

Singular.

1st. ఉండుచున్నాను..............ఉంచున్నాను..................*I am.*

2d. ఉండుచున్నావు..............ఉంచున్నావు..................*Thou art.*

3d. M. ఉండుచున్నాఁడు..........ఉంచున్నాఁడు..............*He is.*

3d. F. & N. ఉండుచున్నది..............ఉంచున్నది..................*She or it is.*

Plural.	1st.		ఉండుచున్నాము	ఉంచున్నాము	We are.
	2d.		ఉండుచున్నారు	ఉంచున్నారు	You are.
	3d.	M.&F.	ఉండుచున్నారు	ఉంచున్నారు	They are.
		N.	ఉండుచున్నవి	ఉంచున్నవి	They are.

			common.	common.	common.	
Singular.	1st.		ఉంచాను	ఉంటున్నాను	ఉంటాను	I am.
	2d.		ఉంచావు	ఉంటున్నావు	ఉంటావు	Thou art.
	3d.	M.	ఉంచాఁడు	ఉంటున్నాఁడు	ఉంటాఁడు	He is.
		F. & N.	ఉంచున్నది. ఉంచుంది	ఉంటున్నది. ఉంటుంది	ఉంటున్నది. ఉంటుంది	She or it is.
Plural.	1st.		ఉంచాము	ఉంటున్నాము	ఉంటాము	We are.
	2d.		ఉంచారు	ఉంటున్నారు	ఉంటారు	You are.
	3d.	M.&F.	ఉంచారు	ఉంటున్నారు	ఉంటారు	They are.
		N.	ఉంచున్నవి	ఉంటున్నవి	ఉంటున్నవి	They are.

PAST.

Singular.	1st.		ఉండితిని	ఉండినాను	ఉంటిని	ఉన్నాను	I was.
	2d.		ఉండితివి	ఉండినావు	ఉంటివి	ఉన్నావు	Thou wast.
	3d.	M.	ఉండెను	ఉండినాఁడు	ఉండెను	ఉన్నాఁడు	He was.
		F.&N.	ఉండెను	ఉండినది, ఉండింది	ఉండెను	ఉన్నది, ఉంది	She or it was.
Plural.	1st.		ఉండితిమి	ఉండినాము	ఉంటిమి	ఉన్నాము	We were.
	2d.		ఉండితిరి	ఉండినారు	ఉంటిరి	ఉన్నారు	You were.
	3d.	M.&F.	ఉండిరి	ఉండినారు	ఉండిరి	ఉన్నారు	They were.
		N.	ఉండెను	ఉండినవి	ఉండెను	ఉన్నవి	They were.

FUTURE.

				common.	
Singular.	1st.		ఉండెదను	ఉండేను	I shall be.
	2d.		ఉండెదవు	ఉండేవు	Thou wilt be.
	3d.	M.F.&N.	ఉండెడిని	ఉండేని or ఉండీని	He, she or it will be.

Plural. 1st. ఉండెదము .... ఉండేము .... We shall be.

2d. ఉండెదరు .... ఉండేరు .... You will be.

3d. M.&F. ఉండెదరు .... ఉండేరు ....

N. ఉండెడిని .... ఉండేని .... or ఉండీని .... They will be.

AORIST.

common.

Singular. 1st. ఉండుదును.... ఉందును.......... I am, was or shall be.

2d. ఉండుదువు.... ఉందువు.......... Thou art, wast, or wilt be.

3d. M.F.& N. ఉండును....... ఉండును.......... He, she, or it is, was, or will be.

Plural. 1st. ఉండుదుము.... ఉందుము.......... We are, were, or shall be.

2d. ఉండుదురు.... ఉందురు.......... You are, were, or will be.

3d. M.& F. ఉండుదురు.... ఉందురు......

N. ఉండును....... ఉండును...... They are, were, or will be.

IMPERATIVE.

common.

Sing. 2d. ఉండుము....... ఉండుమీ.............. ఉండు........ be thou.

Plu. 1st. ఉండుదము..... ఉందము.............. ఉందాము.... let us be.

2d. ఉండుఁడు....... ఉండుఁడీ.............. ఉండండి..... be ye.

RELATIVE PARTICIPLES.

PRESENT.

common.

ఉండుచున్న.......... ఉంచున్న.......... ఉంటున్న..... that is.

PAST.

ఉండిన................ ఉన్న.............................. that was.

INDEFINITE.

common. common.

ఉండు... ఉండెడు... ఉండెడి... ఉండే... ఉండేటి...... that is, was, or will be.

VERBAL NOUN.

common.

ఉండుట .... ఉంట............ ఉండడము........ the being.

NEGATIVE VERB.

INDICATIVE MOOD.

AORIST.

Singular.	1st	ఉండను	I am not, was not, or shall not be.
	2d.	ఉండవు	Thou art not, wast not, or wilt not be.
	3d. M.	ఉండఁడు	He is not, was not, or will not be.
	3d. F. & N.	ఉండదు	She or it is not, was not, or will not be.
Plural.	1st.	ఉండము	We are not, were not, or shall not be.
	2d.	ఉండరు	You are not, were not, or will not be.
	3d. M. & F.	ఉండరు	They are not, were not, or will not be.
	3d. N.	ఉండవు	They are not, were not, or will not be.

IMPERATIVE.

				common.	
Sing.	2d.	ఉండకుము	ఉండకుమీ	ఉండక	be not thou.
Plu.	2d.	ఉండకుఁడు	ఉండకుఁడీ	ఉండకండి	be not ye.

VERBAL PARTICIPLE.

ఉండక........................*without being, or without having been.*

RELATIVE PARTICIPLE.

ఉండని........................*that is not, was not, or will not be.*

VERBAL NOUN.

ఉండమి........................*the not being.*

the fourth form of the past tense of this verb, ఉన్నాను &c. is constantly used as the present tense, in the common dialect.

Root.....................అవు

		common.	common.	commo
Present verbal participle...	అవుచున్న	అవుచు	అవుతున్న	అవుతు [*becoming.*

Past.........*do*.........అయి.............................*having be me.*

Infinitive....................కా.............................*to beco e.*

AFFIRMATIVE VERB.

INDICATIVE MOOD.

PRESENT.

			common.	
Singular.	1st.	అవుచున్నాను	అవుచాను	*I become.*
	2d.	అవుచున్నావు	అవుచావు	*Thou becomest.*
	3d. M.	అవుచున్నాఁడు	అవుచాఁడు	*He becomes.*
	3d. F. & N.	అవుచున్నది	అవుచున్నది / అవుచుంది	*She, or it becomes.*
Plural.	1st.	అవుచున్నాము	అవుచాము	*We become.*
	2d.	అవుచున్నారు	అవుచారు	*You become.*
	3d. N. M. & F.	అవుచున్నారు	అవుచారు	*They become.*
		అవుచున్నవి	అవుచున్నవి	

		common.	*common.*	
Singular.	1st.	అవుతున్నాను	అవుతాను	*I become.*
	2d.	అవుతున్నావు	అవుతావు	*Thou becomest.*
	3d. N. M.	అవుతున్నాఁడు	అవుతాఁడు	*He becomes.*
	3d. F. & N.	అవుతున్నది	అవుతున్నది	*She, or it becomes.*
		అవుతుంది	అవుతుంది	
Plural.	1st.	అవుతున్నాము	అవుతాము	*We become.*
	2d.	అవుతున్నారు	అవుతారు	*You become.*
	3d. N. M. & F.	అవుతున్నారు	అవుతారు	*They become.*
		అవుతున్నవి	అవుతున్నవి	

PAST.

			common.	
Singular.	1st.	అయితిని	అయినాను	*I became.*
	2d.	అయితివి	అయినావు	*Thou becamest.*
	3d. M.	అయ్యెను / ఆయెను	అయినాఁడు	*He became.*
	3d. F. & N.	అయ్యెను	అయినది	*She, or it became.*
		ఆయెను	అయింది	

Plural.	1st.	అయితిమి	అయినాము	*We became.*
	2d.	అయితిరి	అయినారు	*You became.*
	3d. M. & F.	అయిరి	అయినారు	*They became.*
	3d. N.	అయ్యెను, ఆయెను	అయినవి	*They became.*

FUTURE.

common.

Singular.	1st.	అయ్యెదను	అయ్యేను	*I shall become.*
	2d.	అయ్యెదవు	అయ్యేవు	*Thou wilt become.*
	3d. M. F. & N.	అయ్యెడిని	అయ్యేని or అయ్యీని	*He, she, or it will become.*
Plural.	1st.	అయ్యెదము	అయ్యేము	*We shall become.*
	2d.	అయ్యెదరు	అయ్యేరు	*You will become.*
	3d. M. & F.	అయ్యెదరు	అయ్యేరు	*They will become.*
	3d. N.	అయ్యెడిని	అయ్యేని or అయ్యీని	*They will become.*

AORIST.

Singular.	1st.	అవుదును	*I become, became, or shall become.*
	2d.	అవుదువు	*Thou becomest, becamest, or wilt become.*
	3d. M. N. & F.	అవును	*He, she, or it becomes, became, or will become.*
Plural.	1st.	అవుదుము	*We become, became, or shall become.*
	2d.	అవుదురు	*You become, became, or will become.*
	3d. M. & F.	అవుదురు	*They become, became, or will become.*
	3d. N.	అవును	*They become, became, or will become.*

IMPERATIVE.

common.

Sing.	2d.	కమ్ము	అగుము	కా	*become thou.*

common.

Plural.	1st.	అవుదము	అవుదాము	*let us become.*
	2d.	కండు	కండి	*become ye.*

RELATIVE PARTICIPLES.
PRESENT.

	common.	
అవుచున్న	అవుతున్న	*that becomes.*

PAST.

అయిన .... *that became.*

INDEFINITE.

			common.	*common.*	
అవు	అయ్యెడు	అయ్యెడి	అయ్యే	అయ్యేటి	*that becomes, became, or will become.*

VERBAL NOUN.

	common.	*common.*	
అవుట	కావడము	అయ్యేది	*the becoming.*

NEGATIVE VERB.
INDICATIVE MOOD.
AORIST.

Singular.	1st.	కాను	*I do not, did not, or shall not become.*
	2d.	కావు	*Thou dost not, didst not, or wilt not become.*
	3d. M.	కాఁడు	*He does not, did not, or will not become.*
	3d. F. & N.	కాదు	*She, or it, does not, did not, or will not become.*
Plural.	1st.	కాము	*We do not, did not, or shall not become.*
	2d.	కారు	*You do not, did not, or will not become.*
	3d. M. & F.	కారు	*They do not, did not, or wll not become.*
	3d. N.	కావు	

IMPERATIVE MOOD.

				common.	
Sing.	2d.	కాకుము	కాకుమీ	కాక	*become not thou.*
Plu.	2d.	కాకుఁడు	కాకుఁడీ	కాకండి	*become not ye.*

VERBAL PARTICIPLE.

కాక .... *without becoming or without having become.*

RELATIVE PARTICIPLE.

కాని .... *that does not, did not, or will not become.*

VERBAL NOUN.

కామి .... *the not becoming.*

Root. .... పోవు

Present verbal participle ... పోవుచున్న ... పోవుచు ... పోచున్న ... పోచు

	common.	*common.*	
	[పోతున్న	పోతు	*going.*

Past. .... *do* .... పోయి .... *having gone.*

Infinitive. .... పో ... పోవ .... *to go.*

AFFIRMATIVE VERB.

INDICATIVE MOOD.

PRESENT.

Singular.	1st.	పోవుచున్నాను	పోచున్నాను	*I go.*
	2d.	పోవుచున్నావు	పోచున్నావు	*Thou goest.*
	3d. *M.*	పోవుచున్నాఁడు	పోచున్నాఁడు	*He goes.*
	3d. *F.&N.*	పోవుచున్నది	పోచున్నది	*She, or it goes.*
Plural.	1st.	పోవుచున్నాము	పోచున్నాము	*We go.*
	2d.	పోవుచున్నారు	పోచున్నారు	*You go.*
	3d. *M.&F.*	పోవుచున్నారు	పోచున్నారు	*They go.*
	3d. *N.*	పోవుచున్నవి	పోచున్నవి	

		common.	*common.*	*common.*	
Singular.	1st.	పోచాను	పోతున్నాను	పోతాను	*I go.*
	2d.	పోచావు	పోతున్నావు	పోతావు	*Thou goest.*
	3d. *M.*	పోచాఁడు	పోతున్నాఁడు	పోతాఁడు	*He goes.*
	3d. *F.&N.*	పోచున్నది	పోతున్నది	పోతున్నది.	*She or it goes.*
		పోచుంది	పోతుంది	పోతుంది.	
Plural.	1st.	పోచాము	పోతున్నాము	పోతాము	*We go.*
	2d.	పోచారు	పోతున్నారు	పోతారు	*You go.*
	3d. *M.&F.*	పోచారు	పోతున్నారు	పోతారు	*They go.*
	3d. *N.*	పోచున్నవి	పోతున్నవి	పోతున్నవి	

PAST.

Singular.	1st.	పోతిని	పోయితిని	పోయినాను	*I went.*
	2d.	పోతివి	పోయితివి	పోయినావు	*Thou wentest.*
	3d. *M.*	పోయెను		పోయినాఁడు	*He went.*
	3d. *F.&N.*	పోయెను		పోయినది .... *common.* పోయింది	*She, or it went.*

Plural. 1st.		పోతిమి	పోయితిమి	పోయినాము	*We went.*
Plural. 2d.		పోతిరి	పోయితిరి	పోయినారు	*You went.*
Plural. 3d.	N. M. & F.	పోయిరి		పోయినారు	*They went.*
		పోయెను		పోయినవి	

FUTURE.

			common.	
Singular. 1st.		పోయెదను	పొయ్యేను	*I shall go.*
Singular. 2d.		పోయెదవు	పొయ్యేవు	*Thou wilt go.*
Singular. 3d.	M. F. & N.	పోయెడిని	పొయ్యేని or పొయ్యీని	*He, she, or it will go.*
Plural. 1st.		పోయెదము	పొయ్యేము	*We shall go.*
Plural. 2d.		పోయెదరు	పొయ్యేరు	*You will go.*
Plural. 3d.	N. M. & F.	పోయెదరు	పొయ్యేరు	*They will go.*
		పోయెడిని	పొయ్యేని or పొయ్యీని	

AORIST.

Singular. 1st.		పోదును	పోవుదును	*I go, went, or shall go.*
Singular. 2d.		పోదువు	పోవుదువు	*Thou goest, wentest, or wilt go.*
Singular. 3d.	M. F. & N.	పోను	పోవును	*He, she, or it goes, went, or will go.*
Plural. 1st.		పోదుము	పోవుదుము	*We go, went, or shall go.*
Plural. 2d.		పోదురు	పోవుదురు	*You go, went, or will go.*
Plural. 3d.	N. M. & F.	పోదురు	పోవుదురు	*They go, went, or will go.*
		పోను	పోవును	

IMPERATIVE MOOD.

Sing. 2d.	పొమ్ము	పోవుము	పొమ్మీ	పోవుమీ (common.)	పో ... *go thou.*
Plu. 1st.	పోదము	పోవుదము	పోదాము (common.)		*let us go.*
Plu. 2d.	పొండు	పొండీ	పోవుండు	పోవుండీ	పొండి (common.) ... *go ye.*

RELATIVE PARTICIPLES.

PRESENT.

పోవుచున్న .... పోచున్న .... పోతున్న .... *that goes.*

PAST.

పోయిన..that went.

INDEFINITE.

common. common.

పోవు...పోయెడు...పోయెడి...పొయ్యే......పొయ్యేటి...*that goes, went, or will go.*

VERBAL NOUN.

common.

పోవుట..............పోవడము........................పొయ్యేది..............*the going.*

NEGATIVE VERB.

INDICATIVE MOOD.

AORIST.

Singular. 1st.	పోను......పోవను...	*I do not, did not, or shall not go.*
Singular. 2d.	పోవు........పోవవు....	*Thou dost not, didst not, or wilt not go.*
Singular. 3d. *M.*	పోఁడు.......పోవఁడు...	*He does not, did not, or will not go.*
Singular. 3d. *F. & N.*	పోదు.........పోవదు...	*She or it does not, did not, or will not go.*
Plural. 1st.	పోము........పోవము.....	*We do not, did not, or shall not go.*
Plural. 2d.	పోరు.........పోవరు....	*You do not, did not, or will not go.*
Plural. 3d. *M. & F.*	పోరు......పోవరు..	*They do not, did not, or will not go.*
Plural. 3d. *N.*	పోవు......పోవవు..	*They do not, did not, or will not go.*

IMPERATIVE MOOD.

common.

Sing. 2d. పోకుము..పోవకుము...పోకుమీ...పోవకుమీ...పోక........*go not thou.*

Plu. 2d. పోకుఁడు..పోవకుఁడు..పోకుఁడీ....పోవకుఁడీ.....పోకండి...*go not ye.*

VERBAL PARTICIPLE.

పోక.............పోవక.......................*without going, or without having gone.*

RELATIVE PARTICIPLES.

పోని............పోవని..........................*that does not, did not, or will not go.*

VERBAL NOUN.

పోమి...................................*the not going.*

OF తత్సమములు OR VERBS OF SANSCRIT DERIVATION.

369 All Sanscrit verbs cannot, at pleasure, be adopted into Teloogoo; those only the use of which has already been sanctioned by custom being considered as properly belonging to the language. When admitted into Teloogoo, such verbs

assume either the termination ించు or ిల్లు ; in the former case, they are conjugated like దీవించు and other regular దేశ్యము verbs in చు of the 3d conjugation ; in the latter case, like కొట్టు, or any other verb of the 1st conjugation. With this general rule, it will be sufficient to shew how the Teloogoo root is formed from the Sanscrit root.

Sanscrit roots are adopted into Teloogoo in five different ways. 370

1st, by changing the final syllable of the Sanscrit verbal noun into ించు; for instance, the Sanscrit root పుష్ *to protect*, makes it's verbal noun in Sanscrit పోష, this by changing the final syllable into ించు makes the Teloogoo root పోషించు, which is conjugated precisely in the same manner as దీవించు.

A few other examples are subjoined. 371

Sanscrit Root.	Sanscrit verbal noun.	Teloogoo Root.	
ను	నుతి	నుతించు	*to praise.*
ధ్యై	ధ్యాన	ధ్యానించు	*to contemplate, to meditate.*
స్తు	స్తుతి	స్తుతించు	*to praise.*
క్రుధ్	క్రోధ	క్రోధించు	*to be angry.*
కుప్	కోప	కోపించు	*to be angry.*
గమ్	గతి	గతించు	*to pass, to go.*
కప్	కంప	కంపించు	*to tremble, to shake, &c.*
స్తభ్	స్తంభ	స్తంభించు	*to stand without motion.*

2dly, by changing final ి or ీ of Sanscrit roots into యించు, final ు or ూ, into వించు, and final ృ or ౄ into రించు.

జి	జయించు	*to conquer.*
క్షి	క్షయించు	*to be exhausted.*
ద్రు	ద్రవించు	*to damp.*
భృ	భరించు	*to bear.*
హృ	హరించు	*to take.*
స్మృ	స్మరించు	*to think, to reflect.*
ధృ	ధరించు	*to bear.*
వృ	వరించు	*to select.*

3dly, by affixing ఇంచు to the Sanscrit root; thus,

Sanscrit Root.	Teloogoo Root.	
త్యజ్	త్యజించు	*to renounce, to quit.*
నశ్	నశించు	*to be destroyed.*
శప్	శపించు	*to curse.*
తప్	తపించు	*to perform penance.*
శబ్ద్	శబ్దించు	*to sound.*
భ్రమ్	భ్రమించు	*to be confused.*
భజ్	భజించు	*to praise, or meditate on God.*
రచ్	రచించు	*to compose.*
లిఖ్	లిఖించు	*to write.*
నట్	నటించు	*to dance.*
గణ్	గణించు	*to calculate.*
వస్	వసించు	*to dwell.*

4thly, by changing the final syllable of crude Sanscrit substantives or adjectives into ఇంచు; thus,

Sanscrit nouns.		Teloogoo root.	
మూర్ఖ	*obstinate*	మూర్ఖించు	*to insist obstinately.*
స్వతంత్ర	*independent*	స్వతంత్రించు	*to make one's self independent.*
సమీప	*vicinity*	సమీపించు	*to approach.*
శుష్క	*lean*	శుష్కించు	*to become lean.*
గర్వ	*pride*	గర్వించు	*to be proud.*
శృంగార	*ornament*	శృంగారించు	*to adorn.*

5thly, a few neuter verbs are formed by adding to certain Sanscrit words the affix ఇల్లు, sometimes also converted into ఇంచు.

Sanscrit Root.	Teloogoo Root.	
ఖిద్	ఖేదిల్లు	*to be afflicted.*
శుభ్	శోభిల్లు	*to shine.*
చిత్	చింతిల్లు or చింతించు	*to reflect, to study.*

PASSIVE VERBS.

Neuter verbs, from their nature, do not admit of a passive signification; but all active verbs in Teloogoo, of whatever description, may become passive, by adding to the infinitive the different tenses of the verb పడు *to fall*, meaning in composition, *to suffer*. 372

The verb which is made passive continues invariably in the infinitive, the auxiliary పడు only being conjugated through all its persons, numbers, and tenses. The infinitive being a ద్రుతప్రకృతిక, the ప of పడు is generally changed, in composition, into బ; and in the superior dialect ఁ is placed before that letter. 373

The following is an example of a passive verb. 374

Root......................కొట్టఁబడు

		common.	common.
Present verbal participle	కొట్టఁబడుచున్న....	కొట్టఁబడుచు......	కొట్టబడుతున్న
			[కొట్టబడుతు......*being beaten.*
Past..........*do*..........	కొట్టఁబడి..........		*having been beaten.*
Infinitive..................	కొట్టఁబడ..........		*to be beaten.*

AFFIRMATIVE VERB.

INDICATIVE MOOD.

PRESENT.

				common.	
Singular.	1st.		కొట్టఁబడుచున్నాను....	కొట్టబడుచాను........	*I am beaten.*
	2d.		కొట్టఁబడుచున్నావు....	కొట్టబడుచావు........	*Thou art beaten.*
	3d.	*M.*	కొట్టఁబడుచున్నాఁడు ..	కొట్టబడుచాడు.......	*He is beaten.*
		F.&N.	కొట్టఁబడుచున్నది......	కొట్టబడుచున్నది. or కొట్టబడుచుంది...	*She, or it is beaten.*
Plural.	1st.		కొట్టఁబడుచున్నాము....	కొట్టబడుచాము.....	*We are beaten.*
	2d.		కొట్టఁబడుచున్నారు.....	కొట్టబడుచారు......	*You are beaten.*
	3d.	*N.F.&M.*	కొట్టఁబడుచున్నారు.....	కొట్టబడుచారు....	*They are beaten.*
			కొట్టఁబడుచున్నవి........	కొట్టబడుచున్నవి.	

common. *common.*

Singular. 1st. కొట్టబడుతున్నాను……కొట్టబడుతాను…*I am beaten.*

2d. కొట్టబడుతున్నావు……కొట్టబడుతావు…*Thou art beaten.*

3d. M. కొట్టబడుతున్నాడు……కొట్టబడుతాడు…*He is beaten.*

F. & N. కొట్టబడుతున్నది……కొట్టబడుతున్నది. or కొట్టబడుతుంది……కొట్టబడుతుంది… } *She, or it is beaten.*

Plural. 1st. కొట్టబడుతున్నాము……కొట్టబడుతాము…*We are beaten.*

2d. కొట్టబడుతున్నారు……కొట్టబడుతారు….*You are beaten.*

3d. N. F. & M. కొట్టబడుతున్నారు……కొట్టబడుతారు… / కొట్టబడుతున్నవి……కొట్టబడుతున్నవి } *They are beaten.*

PAST.

Singular. 1st. కొట్టఁబడితిని…కొట్టఁబడినాను…కొట్టఁబడ్డాను.*I was beaten.*

2d. కొట్టఁబడితివి…కొట్టఁబడినావు…కొట్టఁబడ్డావు..*Thou wast beaten.*

3d. M. కొట్టఁబడెను…కొట్టఁబడినాఁడు.కొట్టఁబడ్డాఁడు.*He was beaten.*

F. & N. కొట్టఁబడెను { కొట్టఁబడినది. *common.* కొట్టబడింది… } కొట్టఁబడ్డది……*She, or it was beaten.*

Plural. 1st. కొట్టఁబడితిమి..కొట్టఁబడినాము.కొట్టఁబడ్డాము..*We were beaten.*

2d. కొట్టఁబడితిరి…కొట్టఁబడినారు.కొట్టఁబడ్డారు…*You were beaten.*

3d. N. F. & M. కొట్టఁబడిరి….కొట్టఁబడినారు…కొట్టఁబడ్డారు. / కొట్టఁబడెను…కొట్టఁబడినవి….కొట్టఁబడ్డవి… } *They were beaten.*

FUTURE.

common.

Singular. 1st. కొట్టఁబడెదను…కొట్టబడేను………*I shall be beaten.*

2d. కొట్టఁబడెదవు..కొట్టబడేవు………*Thou wilt be beaten.*

3d. M. F. & N. కొట్టఁబడెడిని { కొట్టబడేని…… / కొట్టబడీని…… } *He, she, or it will be beaten.*

Plural. 1st. కొట్టఁబడెదము..కొట్టబడేము………*We shall be beaten.*

2d. కొట్టఁబడెదరు…కొట్టబడేరు…….*You will be beaten.*

3d. N. M. & F. కొట్టఁబడెదరు…కొట్టబడేరు…. / కొట్టఁబడెడిని. { కొట్టబడేని…. / కొట్టబడీని…. } *They will be beaten.*

AORIST.

Singular.	1st.	కొట్టఁబడుదును	I am, was, or shall be beaten.
	2d.	కొట్టఁబడుదువు	Thou art, wast, or wilt be beaten.
	3d. M.F.&N.	కొట్టఁబడును	He, she, or it is, was, or will be beaten.
Plural.	1st.	కొట్టఁబడుదుము	We are, were, or shall be beaten.
	2d.	కొట్టఁబడుదురు	You are, were, or will be beaten.
	3d. N.M.&F.	కొట్టఁబడుదురు / కొట్టఁబడును	They are, were, or will be beaten.

IMPERATIVE MOOD.

common.

కొట్టఁబడుము. ..కొట్టఁబడుమీ......కొట్టబడు....................*be thou beaten.*

కొట్టఁబడుదము........................కొట్టబడుదాము..............*let us be beaten.*

కొట్టఁబడుఁడు .. కొట్టఁబడుఁడి........కొట్టబడండి....................*be ye beaten.*

RELATIVE PARTICIPLES.

PRESENT.

common.

కొట్టఁబడుచున్న........................కొట్టబడుతున్న..............*that is beaten.*

PAST.

కొట్టఁబడిన..............................కొట్టఁబడ్డ....................*that was beaten.*

INDEFINITE.

కొట్టఁబడు { కొట్టఁబడెడు ....కొట్టఁబడెడి / *common.* *common.* / కొట్టబడే.......కొట్టబడేటి } .. *that is, was, or will be beaten.*

VERBAL NOUN.

common.

కొట్టఁబడుట.........................కొట్టబడడము..................*the being beaten.*

NEGATIVE VERB.

INDICATIVE MOOD.

AORIST.

Singular.	1st.	కొట్టఁబడను	I am not, was not, or shall not be beaten.
	2d.	కొట్టఁబడవు	Thou art not, wast not, or wilt not be beaten.
	3d. M.	కొట్టఁబడఁడు	He is not, was not, or will not be beaten.
	3d. F.&N.	కొట్టఁబడదు	She or it, is not, was not, or will not be beaten.

Plural.

1st. కొట్టఁబడము.........*We are not, were not, or will not be beaten.*

2d. కొట్టఁబడరు..........*You are not, were not, or will not be beaten.*

3d. { N.M.&F. } కొట్టఁబడరు...... / కొట్టఁబడవు...... } *They are not, were not, or will not be beaten.*

IMPERATIVE MOOD.

common.

కొట్టఁబడకుము.....కొట్టఁబడకుమీ.....కొట్టఁబడక..........*be not thou beaten.*

కొట్టఁబడకుఁడు....కొట్టఁబడకుఁడీ.....కొట్టఁబడకండి.........*be not ye beaten.*

VERBAL PARTICIPLE.

కొట్టఁబడక.................*without being, or without having been, beaten.*

RELATIVE PARTICIPLE.

కొట్టఁబడని.................*that is not, was not, or will not be beaten.*

VERBAL NOUN.

కొట్టఁబడమి..................*the not being beaten.*

OF CAUSAL VERBS.

375 All verbs in Teloogoo admit of being converted into causals. It is however to be observed that neuter verbs, in this language, when they assume the causal form, become in fact active verbs: the Teloogoo root లేచు *to rise* is a neuter verb, లేపు *to cause to rise* is it's causal, which corresponds precisely with the English active verb to *raise.*

376 Except verbs in చు of the 3d conjugation, and a few others hereafter noticed, all roots, by changing the final ు into ించు, convert active verbs into causals, and neuter verbs into actives; thus,

మ్రొక్కు......*to salute* *makes*..........మ్రొక్కించు ....*to cause to salute.*

కక్కు.......*to vomit* do.............కక్కించు............*to cause to vomit.*

పొంగు......*to bubble* do............పొంగించు.............*to cause to bubble.*

మింగు........*to swallow* do.............మింగించు.............*to cause to swallow.*

పొడుగు......*to be raised* do.............పొడిగించు.............*to heighten.*

రాజు.........*to flame up* do.............రాజించు..............*to enflame.*

అంటు........*to touch* do.............అంటించు...........*to cause to touch.*

మొట్టు.....*to sting* do..........మొట్టించు...........*to cause to sting.*

పండు......*to ripen*........makes............పండించు...........*to cause to ripen.*
మండు.......*to burn* v. n. do..................మండించు..........*to burn* v. a.
ఎత్తు.........*to raise up*....do.................ఎత్తించు...........*to cause to raise.*
విత్తు.........*to sow*.........do.................విత్తించు............*to cause to sow.*
ఈఁదు.......*to swim*........do.................ఈఁదించు............*to cause to swim.*
దున్ను.......*to plough* v. n. as applied.....దున్నించు.............*to plough* v. a. as
[to oxen &c. [applied to men.
కప్పు.........*to cover*.......do.................కప్పించు............*to cause to cover.*
ఉబ్బు.......*to swell*........do.................ఉబ్బించు............*to cause to swell.*
అమ్ము........*to sell*..........do..............అమ్మించు..............*to cause to sell.*
చేయు........*to make*........do.................చేయించు.........*to cause to make.*
మూయు.....*to shut*.........do.................మూయించు........*to cause to shut.*
కోయు.........*to cut*..........do.................కోయించు.........*to cause to cut.*
వ్రాయు....*to write*.........do...........వ్రాయించు......*to cause to write.*
వేయు........*to throw, or put*..do..............వేయించు..........*to cause to throw, or put.*
నేయు........*to weave*.......do.................నేయించు...........*to cause to weave.*
పోయు........*to pour*........do.................పోయించు.........*to cause to pour.*
ఎగురు.........*to fly*...........do.................ఎగిరించు............*to cause to fly.*
అల్లు..........*to plait*.......do.................అల్లించు..............*to cause to plait.*
మళ్లు.........*to return*......do.................మళ్లించు.............*to cause to return.*
తొవ్వు......*to dig*.........do..................తొవ్వించు..........*to cause to dig.*

EXCEPTIONS.

చిదుకు.......*to burst* v. n. applied to soft...చిదుపు or చిదుము..*to burst* v. a.
[substances such as fruit &c.
కాఁగు.......*to boil* v. n......................కాఁచు.............*to boil* v. a.
దాఁగు.......*to conceal one's self, to*.........దాఁచు.......... *to hide* v. a.
[*abscond* v. n.
తూఁగు ... *to be weighed*...do........ తూఁచు......... *to weigh.*
కుంగు......*to fall, to sink, to be humbled.* కుంచు ....*to cause to fall, or sink,*
[*to humble.*
వంగు.....*to bend* v. n..... .... do.....వంచు.......... *to bend* v. a.
ఊఁగు.... *to be rocked* (as a child in.... ఊఁచు .... *to rock.*
a cradle.)

మణఁగు.... or మడఁగు.... *to be folded*..... makes.. మణఁచు ... మడఁచు *to fold.*

విరుగు ..... *to be broken*. .... do... విరుచు .... *to break.*

వేఁగు ..... *to be fryed* .... do... వేఁచు or వేయించు *to fry.*

వాఁగు ..... *to sound* v. n. .... do... వాఁచు or వాయించు *to sound* v. a.

మునుఁగు or మణుఁగు or ముడుఁగు ...*to be drowned, to sink*... ముంచు.......... *to drown, to sink* v. a.

పెరుగు..... *to grow*. .... makes పెంచు.......... *to cause to grow, to nourish.*

సాఁగు...... *to be stretched*. .... do { సాఁచు... సాఁపు / చాఁచు... చాఁపు. } *to stretch.*

సాఁగు .... { *to pass, to go*; added to the infinitive of another verb, it signifies *to continue*...do. } సాఁగించు .... *to cause to pass &c.*

దంగు .... *to be beaten in a mortar* do. దంచు or దంపు. ... *to beat in a mortar.*

నలుగు.... *to be crushed* .... do... నలుచు or నలుపు... *to crush.*

చినుఁగు or చిరుఁగు *to be torn* .... do... చించు or చింపు. ... *to tear.*

తునుఁగు... *to be broken*. .... do... తుంచు or తుంపు... *to break.*

తెగు.... *to be broken or cut*. .... do... తెంచు or తెంపు.... *to break, to cut.*

దిగు / డిగు / డిగ్గు ......*to descend*........... do... { దించు-దింపు or డించు-డింపు } ...*to put or pull down.*

మెదుగు ..... { *to be beaten in a mortar, to be inured* ...do } మెదుపు. .... *to beat, to inure.*

మలుగు.... *to be extinguished* ...... do... మలుపు. .... *to extinguish.*

మరఁగు.... *to be habituated* .... do.... మరపు .... *to habituate.*

త్రాగు.... *to drink* .... do... త్రాపు. త్రాగించు *to cause to drink.*

ఉడుగు.... *to cease*. .... do.... ఉడుపు. ఉడిగించు.... *to cause to cease.*

జరుగు.... *to creep, to slide, to pass*, do. జరుపు. జరిగించు.... *to cause to creep, slide, or pass.*

తిరుగు......*to wander*............makes త్రిప్పు-తిప్పు......... *to turn.*

పూడు......*to be buried* ....do...పూడుచు...............*to bury.*

వాడు......*to fade*................do.... వాడుచు.................*to cause to fade.*

మాడు......*to be roasted*.........do...మాడుచు...............*to roast.*

పడు.........*to fall*..............do....పఱచు ....*to spread.*

చెడు.........*to become bad*.........do... చెఱుచు... చెఱుపు......*to corrupt.*

విడు.........*to be disunited*......do...విడుచు- విచ్చు- విప్పు..*to leave.*

నిండు.......*to be filled*............do...నించు-నింపు-నిండించు··*to fill.*

మాను.......*to be healed, to cease*do...మానుచు or మానుపు..*to heal, &c.*

నాను.......*to be soaked*...........do... నానుచు or నానుపు.....*to soak, to steep.*

తిను.........*to eat* ....do...తినిపించు ....*to cause to eat.*

అను.........*to say*.................do...అనిపించు..................*to cause to say.*

విను ....*to hear*...............do...వినుచు or వినిపించు.....*to cause to hear.*

కను.........*to see, to produce, to bring forth*......do. కనిపించు.................*to shew, or to deliver in child birth.*

మేల్కొను..*to awake* v. n........do... మేలుకొలుపు............*to awake* v. a.

మేయు......*to graze*..................do... మేపు..........................*to feed cattle.*

మాయు.....*to be tarnished*........do...మాపు...............................*to tarnish.*

జడియు......*to be afraid*.........do...జడిపించు........................*to frighten.*

కురియు.....*to rain*...............do...కురిపించుorకురియించు *to cause to rain.*

మెఱయు...*to shine*.............do... మెఱపించు...... ....*to cause to shine.*

కారు.......*to leak*. ....do... కారుచు ....*to cause to leak.*

చేరు........*to arrive*.............do.. చేరుచు................. ...*to cause to arrive.*

ఆఱు.........*to be extinguished*..do...ఆఱుచుorఆఱుపు .... *to extinguish.*

మాఱు.......*to change* v. n.........do...మాఱుచుorమాఱుపు)....*to change* v. a.

కాలు......*to burn* v. n..........do...కాలుచు.................*to burn* v. a.

కూలు.......*to fall down*.........do...కూలుచు.. ....*to cause to fall down.*

రాలు......*to drop down*.......do...రాలుచు or రాలుపు ...*to cause to drop down.*

తేలు........*to float*...............do... తేలుచు or తేలించు.....*to cause to float.*

కదలు......*to move, to shake* v. n. do.కదలుచుor కదలించు....*to move, &c.* v. a.

పోవు.....*to go*............do. { పంపు అంపు / పంపించు.అంపించు } *to send.*

377 తత్సమము neuter verbs in ిల్లు become active by changing ిల్లు into ించు; thus రంజిల్లు *to be pleased* makes రంజించు *to please*; ఖేదిల్లు to *be afflicted* makes ఖేదించు *to afflict.*

378 Roots in చు of the third conjugation by changing చు into పించు, and చ్చు into ప్పించు, convert actives into causals, and neuter into active verbs, thus,

పిలుచు.......*to call*...............makes పిలిపించు.......... *to send for.*

తెఱచు......*to open*...............do... తెఱపించు .... *to cause to open.*

దీవించు......*to bless*...............do...దీవింపించు ....*to cause to bless.*

ఇచ్చు ......*to give* .... do...ఇప్పించు ....*to cause to give.*

తెచ్చు.......*to bring*. . ... do... తెప్పించు...........*to cause to bring.*

EXCEPTIONS.

లేచు..........*to rise*...............makes లేపు.................*to raise.*

నిలుచు......*to stand*...............do....నిలుపు...................*to stop.*

మోచు......*to bear a burden*.....do....మోపు.....................*to load.*

చూచు......*to see*...................do.....చూపు or చూపించు....*to shew.*

వచ్చు......*to come*.................do....రప్పించు or రావించు *to cause to come.*

ఎచ్చు.........*to increase*..........do. .ఎచ్చించు. ....*to cause to increase.*

చచ్చు.....*to die*. ....do......చంపు. ....*to kill.*

379 The following is an example of a causal verb.

Root.................... కొట్టించు

Present verbal participle......కొట్టించుచున్న or కొట్టింపుచున్న ..కొట్టించుచు
common. *common.*

[కొట్టించుతున్న...కొట్టించుతు..*causing to beat.*

Past.........do...................కొట్టించి..............*having caused to beat.*

Infinitive..................... కొట్టించ or కొట్టింప. ....*to cause to beat.*

Causal verbs do not derive any form of the present tense from the participle in చుచు.

AFFIRMATIVE VERB.

INDICATIVE MOOD.

PRESENT.

Singular.	1st.		కొట్టించుచున్నాను	కొట్టింపుచున్నాను	I cause to beat.
	2d.		కొట్టించుచున్నావు	కొట్టింపుచున్నావు	Thou causest to beat.
	3d.	N.M.	కొట్టించుచున్నాఁడు	కొట్టింపుచున్నాఁడు	He causes to beat.
		F.&	కొట్టించుచున్నది	కొట్టింపుచున్నది	She, or it causes to beat.
Plural.	1st.		కొట్టించుచున్నాము	కొట్టింపుచున్నాము	We cause to beat.
	2d.		కొట్టించుచున్నారు	కొట్టింపుచున్నారు	You cause to beat.
	3d.	M.&F.	కొట్టించుచున్నారు	కొట్టింపుచున్నారు	They cause to beat.
		N.	కొట్టించుచున్నవి	కొట్టింపుచున్నవి	

Number	Person		*common.*	*common.*	
Singular.	1st.		కొట్టించుతున్నాను	కొట్టించుతాను	I cause to beat.
	2d.		కొట్టించుతున్నావు	కొట్టించుతావు	Thou causest to beat.
	3d.	M.	కొట్టించుతున్నాడు	కొట్టించుతాడు	He causes to beat.
		F. & N.	కొట్టించుతున్నది or కొట్టించుతుంది	కొట్టించుతున్నది, or కొట్టించుతుంది	She, or it causes to beat.
Plural.	1st.		కొట్టించుతున్నాము	కొట్టించుతాము	We cause to beat.
	2d.		కొట్టించుతున్నారు	కొట్టించుతారు	You cause to beat.
	3d.	M. & F.	కొట్టించుతున్నారు	కొట్టించుతారు	They cause to beat.
		N.	కొట్టించుతున్నవి	కొట్టించుతున్నవి	

PAST.

Singular.	1st.		కొట్టించితిని	కొట్టించినాను	I caused to beat.
	2d.		కొట్టించితివి	కొట్టించినావు	Thou causedst to beat.
	3d.	M.	కొట్టించెను	కొట్టించినాఁడు	He caused to beat.
		F. & N.	కొట్టించెను	కొట్టించినది or *common.* కొట్టించింది	She or it caused to beat.
Plural.	1st.		కొట్టించితిమి	కొట్టించినాము	We caused to beat.
	2d.		కొట్టించితిరి	కొట్టించినారు	You caused to beat.
	3d.	M.&F.	కొట్టించిరి	కొట్టించినారు	They caused to beat.
		N.	కొట్టించెను	కొట్టించినవి	

FUTURE.

common.

Singular. 1st. కొట్టించెదను.................కొట్టించేను......*I shall cause to beat.*

2d. కొట్టించెదవు.................కొట్టించేవు.......*Thou wilt cause to beat.*

3d. M.F.&N. కొట్టించెడిని...............{ కొట్టించేని...... / కొట్టించీని...... } *He, she, or it, will cause to beat.*

Plural. 1st. కొట్టించెదము.................కొట్టించేము.......*We shall cause to beat.*

2d. కొట్టించెదరు.................కొట్టించేరు.........*You will cause to beat.*

3d. N.M.&F. కొట్టించెదరు.................కొట్టించేరు......

కొట్టించెడిని { కొట్టించేని...... or కొట్టించీని...... } *They will cause to beat.*

AORIST.

Singular. 1st. కొట్టించుదును...కొట్టింపుదును..కొట్టింతును..*I cause, caused, or shall cause to beat.*

2d. కొట్టించుదువు...కొట్టింపుదువు..కొట్టింతువు...*Thou causest, causedst, or wilt cause to beat.*

3d. N.M.&F. కొట్టించును......కొట్టించును......కొట్టించును...*He, she, or it causes, caused, or will cause to beat.*

Plural. 1st. కొట్టించుదుము...కొట్టింపుదుము...కొట్టింతుము...*We cause, caused, or shall cause to beat.*

2d. కొట్టించుదురు...కొట్టింపుదురు....కొట్టింతురు.. *You cause, caused, or will cause to beat.*

3d. M.F.&N. { కొట్టించుదురు....కొట్టింపుదురు....కొట్టింతురు.. / కొట్టించును......కొట్టించును......కొట్టించును.. } *They cause, caused, or will cause to beat.*

IMPERATIVE MOOD.

Singular. 2d. { కొట్టించుము....కొట్టింపుము,......కొట్టించుమీ / కొట్టింపుమీ......కొట్టించు (*common.*)..........కొట్టింపు (*common.*)...... } *cause thou to beat.*

Plural. 1st. { కొట్టించుదము...కొట్టింపుదము....కొట్టింతము... / కొట్టించుదాము (*common.*).కొట్టింపుదాము (*common.*)..కొట్టింతాము (*common.*) } *let us cause to beat.*

2d. { కొట్టించుఁడు....కొట్టింపుఁడు.....కొట్టించుఁడీ / కొట్టింపుఁడీ......కొట్టించండి (*common.*)......కొట్టింపండి (*common.*).. } *cause ye to beat.*

RELATIVE PARTICIPLES.

PRESENT.

కొట్టించుచున్న ....కొట్టింపుచున్న ....కొట్టించుతున్న (*common.*) ...*that causes to beat.*

PAST.

కొట్టించిన ....*that caused to beat.*

INDEFINITE.

కొట్టించు....కొట్టించెడు (*common.*)...కొట్టించెడి ...కొట్టించే (*common.*)....కొట్టించేటి *that causes, caused, or [will cause to beat.*

VERBAL NOUN.

కొట్టించుట....కొట్టించడము (*common.*)...కొట్టింపడము (*common.*)........................*the causing to beat.*

NAGATIVE VERB.

INDICATIVE MOOD.

AORIST.

Singular.

1st. కొట్టించను..కొట్టింపను..*I do not, did not, or shall not cause to beat.*

2d. కొట్టించవు..కొట్టింపవు..*Thou dost not, didst not, or wilt not cause to [beat.*

3d. *F. & N. M.* కొట్టించఁడు.కొట్టింపఁడు *He does not, did not, or will not, cause to beat.*

కొట్టించదు..కొట్టింపదు *She, or it does not, did not, or will not cause [to beat.*

Plural.

1st. కొట్టించము.కొట్టింపము *We do not, did not, or shall not cause to beat.*

2d. కొట్టించరు...కొట్టింపరు *You do not, did not, or will not cause to beat.*

3d. *N. M. & F.* కొట్టించరు..కొట్టింపరు / కొట్టించవు..కొట్టింపవు } *They do not, did not, or will not cause to beat.*

IMPERATIVE MOOD.

Sing. 2d. { కొట్టించకుము...కొట్టింపకుము...కొట్టించకుమీ / కొట్టింపకుమీ...కొట్టించక (*common.*)......కొట్టింపక (*common.*)........ } *cause not thou to beat.*

Plu. 2d. { కొట్టించకుఁడు..కొట్టింపకుఁడు...కొట్టించకుఁడీ / కొట్టింపకుఁడీ....కొట్టించకండి (*common.*)........................ } *cause not ye to beat.*

VERBAL PARTICIPLE.

కొట్టించక......కొట్టింపక......*without causing to beat.*

RELATIVE PARTICIPLE.

కొట్టించని......కొట్టింపని......*that does not, did not, or will not cause to beat.*

VERBAL NOUN.

కొట్టించమి......కొట్టింపమి......*the not causing to beat.*

CHAPTER SIXTH.

SYNTAX.

An extensive command of words, a knowledge of their various inflexions, and the choice of such as are most fit to convey our ideas, are necessary to the correct use of every language. But these alone are not sufficient: the force, the elegance, and even the meaning of our expressions, must still depend, in a great degree, on an idiomatical arrangement of the terms which we employ. To illustrate the particular disposition of words which is most consonant to the genius of the Teloogoo language, is the object of the present chapter, and as immediately connected with this subject, I shall here take occasion to treat of the adverbs, conjunctions, interjections, and other indeclinable words, unnoticed in the preceding part of this work.

A strict adherence to the rules which have been laid down regarding the permutation and elision of letters, might possibly distract the reader's attention from the main subject of the present chapter. I shall therefore purposely neglect them, in the examples adduced in support of the following remarks, except where the observance of them may be necessary for the elucidation of any particular part of the syntax; and in order to render the study of the Teloogoo more easy to those who have acquired a knowledge of the Tamil tongue, and to shew in what respects the two sister languages coincide, I shall endeavour as much as possible, in this part of my work, to follow the Jesuit Beschi, an author of established authority in the Tamil language.

OF THE CASES OF SUBSTANTIVES, AND THE USE OF THE POSTPOSITIONS.

380 The reader has been already informed, that in nouns denoting inanimate things, the nominative is constantly used for the accusative. This will be explained more fully when we treat of the government of nouns by verbs.

381 The genitive, possessive, or inflected case, seldom affixes the postposition యొక్క. We constantly find రామునియిల్లు, used for రామునియొక్కయిల్లు *Rama's house;* ఇంద్రునిసభ for ఇంద్రునియొక్కసభ, *the court of Indra;* మన్మథునిబాణము for మన్మథునియొక్కబాణము, *the arrow of Cupid;* and కుబేరునిధనము for కుబేరునియొక్కధనము, *the wealth of Koobéra* (the God of riches) &c. Deprived of this affix, the genitive in Teloogoo has frequently, as in English, the power of an adjective, అడవిమృగము means *a beast of the forest* that is, a wild beast, యెండకాలము *the season of sun shine,* or the sultry season; యేటియిసుక *the sand of the river,* or river sand; చెరువునీళ్లు *the water of the lake,* or lake water.

382 Two or more substantives relating to the same object agree in case; but if they refer to different objects, the one governs the other in the genitive; thus, దేవుని or దేవునియొక్కదయ *the favour of the deity,* మనుష్యుల or మనుష్యులయొక్కపాపములు *the sins of men &c.*

383 The inflected or genitive cases of substantive nouns or pronouns, with the terminations of the neuter demonstrative pronouns affixed to them, viz. ది in the singular, and వి in the plural number, are constantly used, without any verb, to denote the affirmation of possession; as ఆసొమ్మునాది *that property is mine,* యీగుఱ్ఱములువారివి *these horses are theirs,* అదిరామునిది *that is Ráma's,* యిదిబ్రాహ్మణునిది *this belongs to the Bramin,* యీతోటరాజుది *this garden is the King's;* ఆపుస్తకముమాతండ్రిది *that book belongs to my father,* యీయిల్లువకకోమిటివానిది *this house belongs to a Bramin.*

384 The dative case has generally the same force as the prepositions *to, for* in English; thus, స్త్రీలకుఅణుకువమంచిది *modesty is essential to women,* మొగవాండ్లకుధైర్యముగత్యము *courage is requisite for men.* It sometimes represents the English genitive; as, మాటకుప్రాణముసత్యము *the soul of a promise*

is truth, బోటికిప్రాణముమానము *the soul of a woman is her honor.* Soomutee Shutukum, literally, *truth is life to a promise, honor is life to a woman.*

The dative is also often used, without a verb, to denote actual possession, 385
as expressed by our verb *to have*; అతనికినిండారూకలు *he has much money;* literally, *to him, much money*; రాజుకుపదిమందికొమాళ్లు *the King has ten sons,* literally, *to the King, ten sons.* This coincides with the latin rule "*Est pro habeo regit dativum,*" only that in Teloogoo the *est* is not expressed but understood.

The dative case, used with the positive degree of an adjective, gives the 386
adjective the force of the comparative degree; and the sign of the dative case serves to represent the English *than;* thus, వానికివీఁడుసమర్థుఁడు *this man is more clever than that person,* literally *to that person, this man is clever.*

In stating the distance of two places from each other, either one or both of 387
the names of these places may be in the dative case; thus, కాశీకిన్నికంచికిన్నిమున్నూరామడదూరము or కాశీకికంచిమున్నూరామడదూరము *Benares and Conjeveram are* 300 *amadas distant*; *or Conjeveram is* 300 *amadas from Benares.*

అవతల *beyond,* యివతల *on this side,* పైన *above,* కింద *below,* ముందర 388
before, వెనక *behind,* and other words denoting relation of place, govern the preceding noun in the dative case; as దీనికిపైన *above this,* దానికికింద *below that,* దీనికిముందర *before this,* దానికివెనక *beyond that* &c.

When we speak of motion towards any place, the name of the place must 389
be in the dative; as, తోటకుపోయెను *he, she, or it went to the garden,* గ్రామానికివచ్చెను *he, she, or it went to the village.* It is to be observed however, that if the object towards which motion is directed be of such a nature as not to admit of entrance, the postposition వద్ద or దగ్గిర (*near*) must be inserted between the noun and the sign of the dative; as, చెట్టువద్దికిపోయెను *he, she, or it went to the tree,* రాజుదగ్గిరికివచ్చెను *he, she, or it came to the King.*

Nouns of time are generally placed in the dative; thus, అదిరేపటికియిస్తున్నా 390

ను *I will give it to-morrow,* యెల్లుండికివస్తాను *I shall come the day after to-morrow.*

391 When any end, purpose, or intention is to be expressed, we may either place the noun denoting it in the dative case, or use the postposition కొరకు or కై, corresponding with the English phrases *in order to, with a view that, for the purpose of,* &c. &c. thus, స్వర్గముపొందుటకు or కొరకు or కైయీశ్వరుని యందుభక్తివుండవలెను *in order to obtain bliss, we must put our trust in God.*

392 Words expressing the different degrees of consanguinity or affinity, or denoting any connection or dependence, govern the noun, to which they refer in the dative case. Thus, if we ask మీకువాడేమికావలెను, *In what relation does that man stand to you?* the answer will be అతడునాకుభావ-నాకుమామ-నాకుమనమడు-నాకుభృత్యుడు-నాకుమిత్రుడు *he is my brother in law, father-in law, grand son, servant, or friend;* literally, he is *to* me a brother in law, &c. &c. In Teloogoo, we may ask, as in English మీపేరేమి, *what is your name?* మీవయసేమి *what is your age?* or we may use the dative, and say మీకుపేరేమి-మీకువయసేమి *To you, what name? what age?*

393 The postpositions కోసరము-కొరకు or కై (composed of the noun ఓసరము *a side,* ఒరకు the dative case of ఒర, from ఓర *a side,* and అయి the past verbal participle of the affirmative mood of అవు *to become,* all added to the sign of the dative case) are used nearly in the same sense as the dative itself; thus, వర్తకముకోసరము or కొరకు or కైరూకలుపంపించినాడు *he sent money for merchandize,* or *on account of trade.*

394 Of the use of the accusative, we shall treat under the head "General Rules."

395 The vocative is used precisely as in English; but, in prefixing to nouns the vocative participles ఓరి-ఓసి and ఓయి, particular attention should be paid to the rank and sex of the person addressed, as explained in rule 157; thus, ఓరిబోయీ *O Palanqueen bearer!* ఓసిపాపాత్మురాలా *O Wicked woman!* ఓయిబ్రాహ్మణుడా *O Bramin!*

The *local* ablative, formed by the postposition లో, corresponds with our 396 prepositions *in, on, upon, among* &c. It points out the place where any thing is ; for example, దేవతలుస్వర్గములోవున్నారు *The Gods reside in Paradise,* పరమాత్మప్రతిహృదయములోవున్నాడు *the Supreme Being in every heart* ; లో likewise expresses descent on any object ; thus, భూమిలోపడేవర్షము *the rain that falls on the earth.* When it affixes the particle నుంచి, derived from ఉంచి, the past verbal participle of ఉంచు, *to place,* it expresses motion *out of* a place ; as కావేరిలోనుంచిప్రవాహమువస్తున్నది *the flood comes flowing out of the Cavery,* నేనుశ్రీరంగపట్నములోనుంచివస్తిని *I came out of Seringapatam.*

లో is also used in comparison, and makes the comparative or superlative 397 degree, according as the objects spoken of are two, or more ; thus, రామలక్ష్మణులలోరాముడధికుడు *Rama is superior to Lutchmana* ; literally *among Rama and Lutchmana ; Rama is superior* ; మనుష్యులలోరాజులుబలవంతులు *among men, kings are the most powerful* ; literally, *the powerful.* The particle కి, or the drootuprucrootica affixesను&c. may somtimes be added to లో, which, in this state, is often attached to nouns, in comparison ; and the same noun twice repeated, either with, or without this addition, has the force of a superlative ; thus, పేదలలోను or లోకిపేద *the poorest of the poor,* మూర్ఖులలోను or లోకిమూర్ఖుడు *the most obstinate of the obstinate.* Like the English *in,* లో is also used with nouns denoting time ; పూర్వకాలములో *in former times,* వెనకటికాలములో *in after times.*

From లో is derived the word లోపలి, the inflexon of an irregular దేశ్య 398 ము noun which wants the nominative. It is generally used in the dative or ablative case ; thus, in the dative, లోపలికిఅవుషధముయిచ్చినాడు *he has given medicine internally.* In the ablative, it has the same meaning as the English prepositions *within, inside,* &c. as యింటిలోపల *within the house,* పెట్టెలోపల *inside the box.*

లోగా is an adverb of the same meaning as లోపల, formed by adding గా, 399

the infinitive of the root, అవు *to become*, to the postposition లో; as లోగా వచ్చినాడు *he came inside.*

400 లో is often prefixed to the verbs పడు *to fall*, or అవు *to become*, which then signify *to submit, to yield* &c. corresponding to the English phrase *to give in.* లోపడినాడు *he has submitted.*

401 The postposition చేత, or it's contraction చే, the sign of the ablative termed *instrumental*, is itself the inflected ablative case of the irregular దేశ్యము noun చెయ్యి *the hand.* It represents the cause or agency by which any effect is produced, and may generally be translated by the English preposition *by*; thus, లోకముయీశ్వరునిచేతసృజింపబడ్డది *the world was created by God,* వర్షముచేతభూమిచల్లబడుతున్నది *the earth is cooled by rain.* To the postposition చేత, as well as to వలన or వల్ల, which are synonymous with it, the drootuprucrootica affixes ను &c. are often added; as, సూర్యునివల్లనుకాక *heat is produced by the sun,* యాగమువల్లను or చేతనుమోక్షముగలదు *bliss is attainable by sacrifice*: literally *by the sun, heat-by sacrifice, bliss.*

402 తో, the sign of what we have named the *social* ablative, is equivalent to the English preposition *with*; తండ్రితనకొమారునితోవచ్చెను *the father came with his son,* రామునినేత్రంబులతోచూడనామనంబుతృప్తిబొందెను *viewing Rama with my eyes, my mind was satiated*; కూడ, the infinitive of the verb కూడు *to join*, generally written by the vulgar కూడా, is often added to తో to strengthen the connection; thus, వానినాతోగూడారమ్మనిచెప్పు *tell him to come along with me.* తోడ and తోడుత are not so much in use as తో.

403 The postposition న, affixed only to nouns denoting inanimate objects ending in ు, has occasionally the power of each of the three ablatives above mentioned; thus, చెట్టునపండుబండెను *the fruit ripened on the tree,* రాజుసింహాసనమునగూర్చుండెను *the king sat upon the throne,* సంతోషమునగృహంబుననుండెను *he staid at home from joy,* బలమునతనపగవారినిజయించెను *he vanquished his enemies by his prowess.*

404 The inflected ablative, peculiar to the irregular దేశ్యము nouns, has the

same power with respect to these nouns, as the postposition న has with regard to nouns in ు denoting inanimate objects; thus, ముంగిటవున్నాడు *he is in the court yard,* వాని నోటవున్నది *it is in his mouth,* పడమట *in the west,* గోట *in the nail,* పంటకరిచినాడు *he bit with his teeth,* (literally, with the tooth) నాకంటచూస్తిని *I saw with my eyes,* (literally, with the eye) చేతధనుస్సు పట్టెను *he held the bow with his hand,* వింటచంపెను *he killed with a bow,* నన్ను చేతపట్టిపిలుచుకపోయెను *taking me by the hand, he conducted me.*

నిమిత్తము and విషయము are nominatives of two తత్సమము nouns, frequently used as postpositions; నిమిత్తము denotes some cause, reason, &c. and విషయము corresponds precisely with our word *respecting,* or *respect* in such phrases as "in this respect," "in one respect." The use of these words as postpositions will be best understood by the following examples. యీయిల్లుమీనిమిత్తముకొంటిని *I purchased this house for you, or on your account,* పెండ్లివిషయముమాట్లాడెను *he spoke respecting the marriage,* రాచకార్యవిషయము (వ్రా) సెను *he wrote respecting affairs of state*: కోసము or కోసరము, mentioned in rule 393, has often the same meaning as నిమిత్తము; thus, we say మిమ్ము చూచేటందుకోసరము or కోసమునేనువస్తిని, *I came on purpose to see you.* 405

అందు is nearly synonymous with the postposition లో. The differenco between them will be best defined by examples; thus, వనములో and వనమునందు both mean *in the garden or forest,* but the former refers more strongly than the latter to the *inside;* రామునిలోభక్తి and రామునియందుభక్తి both mean *faith in Rama,* but the former expression denotes the faith that exists *within* Rama, the faith that he possesses in others; the latter phrase denotes the faith which others have in him. 406

వలె is derived from the root పోలు which signifies to *resemble*; it denotes similitude, likeness &c. thus, వైకుంఠమువలె *like Vycoontha,* (the residence of Vishtnoo) నావలె *like me:* the word పోలె whence వలె is immediately derived, is used, in books, instead of వలె; but being part of an active verb, it always governs the accusative, instead of the inflexion, and the ప of పోలె is, in this case, changed into బ, the accusative preceding it being included in the 407 class of drootuprukrootooloo; thus నన్నుబోలె *like me,* వైకుంఠంబునుంబోలె *like Vycoontha.*

408 నుండి-నుంచి are used to denote motion *from* a place; as శానావాడలుకలకత్తానుంచి or నుండివచ్చినవి *a great number of vessels have arrived from Calcutta,* చెన్నపట్నమునుంచిమచిలీపట్ణమునకు యెంతదూరము *how far is it from Madras to Masulipatam?*

409 The following are a few examples shewing the mode in which most of the other common postpositions are used, యిండ్ల or యిండ్లకు-సందున or మధ్య *between the houses,* వాని or వానికివెంబడి or వెనకవచ్చినాడు *he came behind or after him,* రెండుగడియలవెనక యిస్తున్నాను *I will give it in (or after) two hours;* in this last example, వెంబడి cannot be used, because it refers exclusively to situation, not to time. యింటికి or యింటియెదుట *opposite the house,* తోటకుయెదురుగా *opposite the garden.*

410 కూర్చి governs the accusative, thus; శివునిగూర్చి or గురించితపస్సుచేశెను *he performed penance to (or on account of) Shiva,* అతడుపట్టణముగూర్చిపోయినాడు *he went towards the city.*

411 The very useful and common postposition మీద *on, upon,* has been omitted, by mistake, from the list of the postpositions given in rule 130; it denotes rest on a place, and governs the noun preceding it in the oblique case; as భూమిమీద *on the earth* &c.

412 The postpositions of which the following are examples are found only in books: విశ్వామిత్రునఱుత or అఱురాముఁడేఁగెను *Rama went with Viswamitra,* శివునిపొంతపార్వతియేఁగెను *Parvatee departed with Shiva,* ధనముపేరుఁడిగర్వించెను *he was elated by riches,* భక్తిమెయి or మెయిఁబ్రార్థించితిని *I prayed with faith,* విద్యబట్టుఁడికీర్తి *through learning, fame accrues,* నీవువచ్చుటంజేసిజనులుసంతోషించిరి *the people are pleased by your coming,* బలముఁబట్టిజయము *victory is attainable by prowess.*

413 With the exception of యొక్క, all cases of substantive nouns or pronouns formed by postpositions ending in ˇ, such as చేత *by,* తోడ *with,* బైట *outside,*

పైన *above, upon,* కింద *down, below,* వద్ద *near* &c. &c. when immediatly followed by other substantives with which they agree, change the final ు of these postpositions into ి; thus, మీతోడిచెలిమి *the friendship with you,* గానిబైటితోటలు *the gardens without the gate,* మిద్దెపయినియిండ్లు *the houses above the terrace,* కొండకిందినేలలు *the lands below the mountain,* పట్టణమువద్దివనములు *the gardens near the city,* కుబేరునివద్దిసంపత్తు *the wealth of the god of riches,* literally the wealth *near* the god of riches. In such constructions, the ు of the postposition అందు is changed into లి; thus, నాయందలికరుణ *the regard towards me.*

OF THE FORMATION OF VARIOUS CLASSES OF NOUNS.

Nouns denoting the agent are often formed by adding to the inflexion of a noun substantive the pronoun వాఁడు for the masculine, and అది for the feminine; thus, from ఇంటి, the inflexion of ఇల్లు *a house,* is formed యింటివాఁడు *a house owner,* from పండ్ల, the inflexion of పండ్లు *fruits,* పండ్లవాఁడు *a fruiterer,* from గుడి *a temple,* గుడివాఁడు *an officer of the temple,* and from అంగడి *a shop,* అంగడివాఁడు *a shopkeeper* &c. &c. Nouns in ము, however, in this construction, are not placed in the inflexion, but change the final ము into పు, thus; గుఱ్ఱము *a horse,* makes గుఱ్ఱపువాఁడు *a horsekeeper.* 414

When the agent to be denoted is familiar, or contemptible, కాఁడు is sometimes used instead of వాఁడు, and కత్తె instead of అది; thus, from చెలిమి *friendship,* comes చెలిమికత్తె *a female friend*; thus, also, we say విటకాఁడు *a rake,* సొగసుకాఁడు *a coxcomb, a good looking fellow,* సొగసుకత్తె *an affected female, a fine girl.* 415

Nouns denoting the agent are also formed from తత్సమము nouns in ము, by changing that termination into ి; thus, from కోపము *anger,* comes కోపి *an angry person,* from పాపము *sin,* పాపి *a sinner,* from బలము *strength,* బలి *a strong person,* from లోభము *covetousness,* లోభి *a miser.* 416

Besides the verbal noun denoting the action itself which the verb signifies, there are many abstract nouns derived from verbs: some of these abstract nouns are the same as the roots themselves; thus, from 417 the root మ్రొక్కు ...to salute..............comes... మ్రొక్కు ...salutation.

do.........పలుకు.......to speak................do......పలుకు.......a word.

do.........దుముకు.....to leap...................do.......దుముకు......a leap.

do..........తూఁగు......to sleep...................do......తూఁగు......sleep.

do..........వెలుఁగు......to shine...................do......వెలుఁగు......light.

do..........పొడుఁగు.......to heighten..............do.......పొడుగు......height.

do..........తిట్టు..........to abuse, to call names..do.......తిట్టు........abuse.

do..........కొట్టు..........to flog......................do......కొట్టు.......a lash, a blow.

do..........తన్ను..........to kick......................do......తన్ను.........a kick.

do..........నవ్వు.........to laugh....................do......నవ్వు.........laughter.

418 Others are formed from roots in యు or చు, by changing these syllables into పు, and if ి precede యు, it is changed into ు.

జడియు........to fear..........................జడుపు..........fear.

మెఱియు.......to glare.........................మెఱుపు.........lightning.

పొడుచు.........to stab...........................పొడుపు.........a stab.

ఏడుచు.........to cry.............................ఏడుపు.........weeping.

మఱచు..........to forget.........................మఱపు..........forgetfulness.

నేరుచు.........to learn..........................నేరుపు.........skill.

గెలుచు.........to vanquish.....................గెలుపు.........victory, success.

ఓరుచు.........to suffer patiently..........ఓరుపు..........patience.

తలఁచు.........to think.........................తలఁపు.........thought.

మోచు..........to bear a burden.......మోపు..........a load or burden.

చూచు..........to see...........................చూపు............sight.

మెచ్చు........to cpprove.....................మెప్పు...........approbation.

419 Some are formed from roots in యు by changing that syllable into పు, and if ి precede యు it is changed in ు.

బిగియు.........to tighten.....................బిగుపు............tightness.

ఎగియు..........to fly............................ఎగుపు.............flight.

Others are formed from roots in యు or చు by changing the final యు or చు to ఁత or త. 420

నేయు.........*to weave*.....................నేఁత.................*texture.*

మోయు......*to sound, to roar*..........మోఁత.............*a roaring.*

వ్రాయు.....*to write*........................వ్రాఁత..............*writing.*

గీయు.........*to draw a line*...............గీత..................*a line.*

మూయు......*to shut*..........................మూత.................*a lid.*

అప్పగించు / వప్పగించు } *to deliver*............... { అప్పగింత... / వప్పగింత... } ......*deliverance.*

కలవరించు....*to dream*.......................కలవరింత..............*dreaming.*

Some are formed by changing the final ు of the root into ిక. 421

నమ్ము..........*to trust*.......................నమ్మిక...................*trust.*

తేలు...........*to float*..........................తేలిక...................*lightness.*

బడలు..........*to be fatigued*...............బడలిక...................*tiresomeness.*

ఏలు............*to govern*.......................ఏలిక.....................*a governor.*

కోరు...........*to hope*...........................కోరిక...................*hope.*

Some abstract nouns are formed from roots in డు and ను by changing డు to ట, and ను to ంట. 422

మండు........*to burn*...........................మంట...................*a flame.*

వండు..........*to cook*...........................వంట...................*cooking.*

పాడు..........*to sing*............................పాట...................*a song.*

అను.............*to say*............................అంట...................*a saying.*

కొను...........*to buy*.............................కొంట...................*purchase.*

The following abstract nouns are irregularly formed from their respective roots. 423

అలయు...*to be tired*...............అలఁత-అలపు-అలయిక-అలసట...*tiresomeness.*

మేయు...*to graze*..................మేఁపు-మేఁత............................*grazing.*

కూయు...*to make a noise*.........కూఁత-కూఁక............................*a noise, a cry.*

మొలుచు *to shoot, or sprout*......మొలక-మొక్క-మోక...............*a sprout.*

కలంచు...*to disturb*..............కలంత-కలంక................*a disturbance.*

మడుచు...*to fold*..................మడుపు-మడత..................*a fold.*

అమ్ము......*to sell*....................అమ్మడు-అమ్మకము..........*a sale.*

మిగులు...*to remain*..................మిగులు-మిగత.................*remainder.*

ఉండు.....*to be or reside*...........ఉంట-ఉనికి.......................*residence.*

తిను.......*to eat*........................తింట-తిండి.........................*eating.*

విను.......*to hear*......................వినికి-వినికిడి...................*hearsay, information.*

పోలు.......*to resemble*.................పోలిక-పోల్కి.......................*resemblance.*

విత్తు......*to sow*........................విత్తు-విత్తనము....................*seed.*

తప్పు......*to miss*.......................తప్పు-తప్పితము.....................*a mistake.*

పుట్టు......*to be born*....................పుట్టు-పుట్టువు-పుట్టుక..........*birth.*

చచ్చు......*to die*............................చావు..................................*death.*

చొచ్చు....*to enter*..........................చోటు..................................*a place.*

నొచ్చు....*to pain*..........................నొప్పి...................................*pain.*

కలుగు......*to have*.........................కలిమి..................................*riches.*

దున్ను......*to plough*.....................దుక్కి...................................*a plough.*

కొలుచు { when it means *to serve* makes...... } కొలువు..............................*service.*
{ when it means *to measure* makes..... } కొలత.................................*a measure.*

పండు *to ripen* makes పంట *a product of the earth* and పండు *fruit.*

424 A great number of abstract nouns are formed by adding the termination తనము to దేశ్యము adjectives, and sometimes to దేశ్యము nouns, or even occasionally to the relative participles of దేశ్యము verbs; thus, from

the adjective.....మంచి......*good*.........comes......మంచితనము.....*goodness.*

do..........గొప్ప......*great*.........do.........గొప్పతనము....*greatness.*

do..........మడ్డి.........*dull*..........do..........మడ్డితనము......*dullness.*

do..........చక్కని.......*beautifull*...do.......చక్కనితనము.....*beauty.*

do..........చిన్న......*small*..........do..........చిన్నతనము......*smallness.*

thus, also, from the
substantive......పిల్ల.........*a child*......do.........పిల్లతనము........*childhood.*

and from the relative participle తెలియని......... {*that is, was, or will not be known*} తెలియనితనము *ignorance.*

తనము is never added to any except pure దేశ్యము words.

తత్సమము adjectives or substantives of any termination become abstract nouns by affixing త్వము or త; as, 425

గురు......*great, heavy* makes...గురుత్వము...or...గురుత...*greatness, weight.*

లఘు.......*small, light*....do.......లఘుత్వము...or....లఘుత....*smallness, lightnees.*

దృఢ.....*hard*...........do.......దృఢత్వము...or....దృఢత....*hardness.*

ప్రభు....*a master*.......do.......ప్రభుత్వముor....ప్రభుత..*mastership.*

వీర.........*a hero*...........do.......వీరత్వము...or....వీరత......*heroism.*

శూర......*valiant*..........do......శూరత్వము.or....శూరత....*valour.*

OF ADJECTIVES.

In the fourth chapter of this work, we have so fully explained the mode in which adjectives agree with substantives, that little remains to be added respecting that part of syntax. 426

The adjective is generally placed before the substantive noun or pronoun with which it agrees; as మంచి బ్రాహ్మణుఁడు *a good bramin,* మంచి స్త్రీ *a good woman,* చెడ్డగుఱ్ఱము *a bad horse,* చక్కనిమనిషి *a beautiful person.* 427

In English, when the verb *to be,* in any of it's variations, comes between a substantive and an adjective, the sense may be well expressed in Teloogoo by placing the adjective after the substantive; but, in this case, the verb *to be* is not expressed, but only understood in Teloogoo. A దేశ్యము adjective has no gender or number, except what it receives from the word to which it is prefixed; it is therefore necessary, when it thus follows it's substantive, to add to it the pronouns వాఁడు or అది, or వారు or అవి, according to the gender and number of the substantive with which it agrees, thus, in the phrases *that bramin is good* ఆబ్రాహ్మణుఁడుమంచివాఁడు, *those bramins are good* ఆబ్రాహ్మణులుమంచివారు, *that woman is good* ఆస్త్రీమంచిది, *these women are good* ఈస్త్రీలుమంచివారు, *that horse is good* ఆగుఱ్ఱముమంచిది, *these horses are* 428 *good* ఈగుఱ్ఱములుమంచివి, no verb is used, the adjective merely follows it's substantive, the pronouns in question being at the same time affixed to the adjective, because it belongs to the దేశ్యము class. But తత్సమము adjectives do not admit of the addition of these pronouns, because they possess within themselves the distinction of gender and number; thus, using a తత్సమము adjective, instead of a దేశ్యము one, we should say *that bramin is good* ఆబ్రాహ్మణుఁడు శ్రేష్ఠుఁడు, *that woman is good* ఆ స్త్రీ శ్రేష్ఠురాలు, *that horse is good* ఆగుఱ్ఱము శ్రేష్ఠము see rule 289, &c.

429 Many substantives are converted into adjectives, by affixing the word కల *possessing,* from the root కలుగు; thus, బలముకల *possessing strength, strong,* బుద్ధికల *wise,* that is *possessing wisdom,* సుఖముకల *happy, possessing happiness,* ధనముకల *wealthy, possessing wealth,* &c. &c.

430 In Teloogoo, the degrees of comparison are formed, not by any change in the adjective itself, but by the use of certain particles. In treating of the postpositions, the manner in which కి-లో - లోకి and లోను are employed in com parison, has been fully explained; and it only remains here to observe that the words కన్న and కంటె are often affixed, in a similar manner, to the inflexions of substantive nouns or pronouns, to express the comparative degree. It is generally thought that కన్న is the past relative participle of the root కను *to see,* signifying *that has seen,* and that కంటె is the subjunctive of the same verb signifying *if any one see*; thus, దీనికన్నమంచిదిలేదు *there is nothing better than this* signifies, literally, *to those that regard this, there is nothing better*; and దీనికంటెమంచిదిలేదు *there is nothing better than this,* literally translated, means, *if you look at this, there is nothing better.* But it seems more probable that these particles are derived from the corresponding parts of the root అను *to say,* added to the dative case, and that కన్న is formed of కు or కి and అన్న, and కంటె of కు or కి and అంటె; for if these particles were derived from the active verb కను *to see* they would govern the accusative, instead of the inflexion; but we say నాకంటె never నన్నుకంటె *than me:* in this sense, the abovementioned

expressions, literally translated, would mean *to those that speak of this, nothing is better ; and if you speak of this, nothing is better.*

The superlative degree is generally formed by prefixing to the adjective the words బహు *very,* నిండా *much,* &c. thus, బహుబుద్ధిమంతుడు *a very wise man,* నిండాగొప్పయిల్లు *a very large house.* To express *the wisest, the greatest,* &c. the phrase అందరికంటె *than all* is used for the masculine and feminine, and అన్నిటికంటె *than all things* for the neuter. If we would express *the wisest man* we must say in Teloogoo అందరికంటెబుద్ధిమంతుడు that is, *the man wiser than all.* If we would express *the largest tree* we must say అన్నిటికంటెగొప్పవృక్షము, or *the tree larger than all,* అందరికంటెగొప్పవాడు *the greatest of men,* అందరికంటెసొగసుకత్తె *the most beautiful of women.* 431

OF THE USE OF THE SIMPLE TENSES OF VERBS.

Nothing will at first be more perplexing to the Teloogoo Student than the use of one tense of the verb for another. After studying the different conjugations, he will be surprized to find what I have termed the *present* tense constantly used, even by his teacher, in a *future* signification. I hope, however, that he will not, on this account, too hastily question the correctness of the principles I have endeavoured to inculcate, and recommend the following observations on this subject to his particular attention. 432

In rule 329, it was explained that the particular form of the present tense terminating in చాను is peculiar to the religious Bramins of the Northern districts ; and the reader was requested to bear in mind that those terminating in తాను and తున్నాను are the only forms to be employed in the colloquial use of the language ; that in చున్నాను is seldom found except in books, and to distinguish the other three from it, the word *common* has been always prefixed to them, in the conjugation of the verbs. These rules cannot be too strongly impressed on the memory of the student. 433

The two forms of the present tense, derived from the verbal participles ending inన్న, spring originally, like those participles themselves, from the auxi- 434 liary verb ఉండు *to be.* They consist in fact of the participles in చు or తు with that tense of ఉండు which commences with ఉ న్నాను affixed to them, thus, దీవించుచు or దీవించుతు, with ఉన్నాను affixed, by the rules for sund,hi given in the second chapter, become respectively దీవించుచున్నాను or దీవించుతున్నాను. The verb ఉండు, therefore, cannot, in any of it's forms, be affixed to the verbal participles in న్న, because it has already been added to them: but, in the common dialect, when we wish to mark more strongly the present time, we lengthen the final ు of the verbal participles in చు or తు, and, without sund,hi, add to them the abovementioned tense of ఉండు, which is commonly written వున్నాను; thus, కొట్టుచూవున్నాను or కొట్టుతూవున్నాను denotes that I am *now* beating, వ్రాస్తూవున్నాను that I am *now* writing, &c. &c.

435 The perfect tense is used to denote past time, precisely in the same manner as the corresponding tense in English. It does not therefore here require any elucidation.

436 The first form of the future tense scarcely ever occurs, except in studied compositions; and the use of the second form is not common. In lieu of this tense, the present is constantly used; thus, నేటిదినంచెన్నపట్టణమువిడిచివచ్చేనెల ౧౫ తేదిలోగాశ్రీరంగపట్టణముచేరుతాను *having left Madras to-day, I shall arrive at Seringapatam within the 15th of next month,* literally *I arrive;* రేపుమీయింటికివస్తాను *I shall come to your house to-morrow,* literally *I come,* వెల్లుండిజాబువ్రాస్తాను *I shall write the letter the day after to-morrow,* literally *I write:* a thousand other examples might be added. The use of the aorist for the future is explained in the following rule.

437 The affirmative and negative aorists express, according to the context, the present, the past, or the future; but I beg the reader will bear in mind that, in the common dialect, they are most generally used in a future sense. The following examples will best shew the nature of this tense (Past) కలికిమునుపు జనులుసరిగానూరేండ్లుబ్రతుకుదురు. *Before the commencement of the Caleyoogum men lived exactly a hundred years,* (Present) యిప్పుడుసరాసరియాభై యైదుసంవత్సరములుబ్రతుకుదురు *at present they live on an average*

55 *years,* (Future) యికనురాఁగాఁరాఁగాఁ కేవలమాయుస్సుక్షీణమవును *and by degrees the length of human life will be greatly shortened,* (Past) దేవదత్తునికినాకుమునుపునిండా స్నేహముకద్దు *There existed formerly a very intimate friendship between Davadatta and me,* (Past) మాయింటికిప్రతిదినంవచ్చును నేనున్నువాడియింటికిపోదును *he came to my house frequently, and I went to his,* (Present) ఇప్పుడు వానికినాకు ద్వేషముగనక నేను వాని యింటికి పోను, వాడు మాయింటికిరాడు *at present, as enmity exists between us, I never go to his house, and he never comes to mine.* In the common dialect, we constantly say అట్లాచేతును *I shall do so,* మీరువత్తురా *will you come?* నేనురాను *I shall not come* &c. In fact, the student can seldom err in translating the English future by the Teloogoo aorist. In explaining the Teloogoo aorist in English, he must be guided chiefly by the context.

OF THE FORMATION OF COMPOUND TENSES OF VERBS.

The present, the past, the future, and the aorist, are the only tenses mentioned in the conjugation of the verb. The compound tenses, formed by auxiliary verbs, were reserved for consideration in this place. 438

Tenses corresponding with the imperfect and pluperfect in English are formed by prefixing the present and past verbal participles of any verb to the perfect tense of ఉండు *to be*; thus, 439

IMPERFECT.

Singular. 1st.	పాడుతూవుంటిని	*I was singing.*
2d.	పాడుతూవుంటివి	*Thou wast singing.*
3d. M.F.&N.	పాడుతూవుండెను	*He, she, or it was singing.*
Plural. 1st.	పాడుతూవుంటిమి	*We were singing.*
2d.	పాడుతూవుంటిరి	*You were singing.*
3d. M.&F.	పాడుతూ వుండిరి	*They were singing.*
3d. N.	పాడుతూవుండెను	*They were singing.*

PLUPERFECT.

Singular.	1st.	పాడివుంటిని	*I had sung.*
	2d.	పాడివుంటివి	*Thou hadst sung.*
	3d. M.F.&N.	పాడివుండెను	*He, she, or it had sung.*
Plural.	1st.	పాడివుంటిమి	*We had sung.*
	2d.	పాడివుంటిరి	*You had sung.*
	3d. N.M.&F.	పాడివుండిరి	*They had sung.*
		పాడివుండెను	

440 For example, if we say భరతుడుఅయోధ్యకువచ్చినప్పుడుఅతనిఅన్నరాముడువనమునకుపోతూవుండెను *when Bharata came to Oude, his eldest brother Rama was going to the forest.* As far as regards the present time, Bharata's arrival is past, as well as Rama's departure, but the two actions were simultaneous, and this is represented by adding the *past* tense of ఉండు *to be* to the *present* verbal participle of పోవు *to go*; but if the actions denoted by both verbs are not only past as regards the present time, but the action denoted by one verb is antecedent to the action denoted by the other, then the *past* verbal participle is prefixed to the *past* tense of ఉండు, to form the pluperfect; thus, రాజుయుద్ధరంగమునుంచిపట్టణమునకువచ్చేటందుకుమునుపే అతనికిఒకకొమారుడుపుట్టివుండెను *before the King returned to the city, from the field of battle, a son had been born to him.* The return of the King and the birth of his son are both past, but the birth was antecedent to the King's return.

441 Certain other tenses are formed by affixing to the infinitive of any verb particular tenses of the verbs పోవు *to go,* కలుగు *to possess, to be able,* నేర్చు *to learn,* చాలు *to suffice,* and ఓపు *to be able,* used as auxiliaries. The original verb remains in the infinitive, whilst these auxiliaries are conjugated through all the persons of the tenses thus used.

పోవు *to go.*

The present, perfect and aorists of this verb may be affixed, as in English, to the infinitive of any verb, *to denote a future signification;* but the infinitive being a ద్రుతప్రకృతిక, the ప of పోవు is, in the superior dialect, changed into బ, according to rule 115; thus,

పాడఁ-బోచున్నాను..........................*I am going to sing.*
చేయఁ-బోచున్నావు..........................*Thou art going to do.*

M. *F. & N.*
చూడఁ-బోచున్నాఁడు-బోచు-న్నది or ంది...*He, she, or it is going to see.*
వ్రాయఁ-బోచున్నాము......................*We are going to write.*
పంపించఁ-బోచున్నారు.....................*You are going to send.*

M. & F. *N.*
చెప్పఁ-బోచున్నారు-బోచున్నవి..............*They are going to say &c. &c.*

కలుగు *to be able.*

కలుగుదును or కలను the affirmative, and లేను the negative aorist, together with కలిగితిని the perfect tense of this verb, added to the infinitive of any other verb, imply *the possession, or want, of power or ability*: the క of కలుగు, however, is changed into గ when preceded by an infinitive, or any other word of the class named ద్రుతప్రకృతిక.

పాడఁ-గలుగుదును-గలను..................*I can sing.*
చెయ్యఁ-గలుగుదువు-గలవు.................*Thou canst do.*

M.F.&N. *M.* *F.&N.*
చూడఁ-గలుగును-గలఁడు-గలదు.............*He, she, or it can see.*
వ్రాయఁ-గలుగుదుము-గలము..............*We can write.*
పంపించఁ-గలుగుదురు-గలరు...............*You can send.*

M.&F. *M.&F.* *N.*
చెప్పఁ-గలుగుదురు-గలరు-గలవు............*They can tell.*
పాడలేను......................................*I cannot sing.*
చెయ్యలేవు....................................*Thou canst not do.*

M. *F.&N.*
చూడలేఁడు-లేదు..............................*He, she, or it cannot see.*
వ్రాయలేము...................................*We cannot write.*
పంపించలేరు..................................*You cannot send.*

M. &F. N.
చెప్పలేరు-లేవు...............................*They cannot tell.*
పాడఁగలిగితిని................................*I could sing.*
చెయ్యఁగలిగితివి..............................*Thou couldst do.*

M. F. & N.

చూడఁగలిగెను.................................*He, she, or it could see.*

వ్రాయఁగలిగితిమి.................................*We could write.*

పంపించఁగలిగితిరి.................................*You could send.*

M. & F. *N.*

చెప్పఁగలిగిరి-గలిగెను.................................*They could tell.*

గలను &c. is a contraction of గలుగుదును &c.; the former sometimes implying *futurity*, but the latter *ability only*; చేయఁగలను may mean either *I will or I can do*, but చేయఁగలుగుదును means only *I can do*: the relative participle గల is often used, after an infinitive, in a future sense; the phrase చేయఁగలవిన్నపములు *the requests which I am about to make*, occurs at the commencement of almost every Teloogoo letter addressed by an inferior to a person in a superior station.

నేర్చు *to learn.*

The affirmative and negative aorists, and the perfect tense of this root, added to the infinitive of any verb, have the same power as the corresponding tenses of కలుగు.

పాడనేర్తును.................................*I can sing.*

చేయనేర్తువు.................................*Thou canst do.*

చూడనేర్చును.................................*He, she, or it can see.*

వ్రాయనేర్తుము.................................*We can write.*

పంపించనేర్తురు.................................*You can send.*

M. & F. *N.*

చెప్పనేర్తురు - నేర్చును.................................*They can tell.*

పాడనేరను.................................*I cannot sing.*

చెయ్యనేరవు.................................*Thou canst not do.*

M. *F. & N.*

చూడనేరఁడు - నేరదు.................................*He, she, or it cannot see.*

వ్రాయనేరము.................................*We cannot write.*

పంపించనేరరు.................................*You cannot send.*

M. & F. *N.*

చెప్పనేరరు - నేరవు.................................*They cannot tell.*

పాడనేర్చితిని..*I could sing.*
చెయ్యనేర్చితివి..*Thou couldst do.*
చూడనేర్చెను..*He, she, or it could see.*
వ్రాయనేర్చితిమి..*We could write.*
పంపించనేర్చితిరి..*You could send.*

M. & F. *N.*

చెప్పనేర్చిరి-నేర్చెను..*They could tell.*

చాలు *to suffice,* ఓపు *to be able.*

The affirmative and negative aorists of these verbs are used, after infinitives, in the same manner as the corresponding tenses of కలుగు and నేర్చు; but the infinitive being included in the ద్రుతప్రకృతికలు the చా of చాలు is changed into జా and the ఓ of ఓపు into నో in conformity to rules 115 and 92.

పాడఁజాలుదును..*I can sing.*
చెయ్యఁజాలుదువు..*Thou canst do.*
చూడఁజాలును..*He, she, or it can see.*
వ్రాయఁజాలుదుము..*We can write.*
పంపించఁజాలుదురు..*You can send.*

M.&F. *N.*

చెప్పఁజాలుదురు-జాలును..*They can tell.*
పాడఁజాలను..*I cannot sing.*
చెయ్యఁజాలవు..*Thou canst not do.*

M. *F.&N.*

చూడఁజాలఁడు-జాలదు..*He, she, or it cannot see.*
వ్రాయఁజాలము..*We cannot write.*
పంపించఁజాలరు..*You cannot send.*

M. & F. *N.*

చెప్పఁజాలరు-జాలవు..*They cannot tell.*

పాడనోపుదును..*I can sing.*
చెయ్యనోపుదువు..*Thou canst do.*
చూడనోపును..*He, she, or it can see.*
వ్రాయనోపుదుము..*We can write.*
పంపించనోపుదురు..*You can send.*

M. & F. N.	
చెప్ప నోపుదురు- నోపును	They can tell.
పాడ నోపను	I cannot sing.
చెయ్య నోపవు	Thou canst not do.
M. F. & N.	
చూడ నోపఁడు- నోపదు	He, she, or it cannot see.
వ్రాయ నోపము	We cannot write.
పంపించ నోపరు	You cannot send.
M. & F. N.	
చెప్ప నోపరు- నోపవు	They cannot tell.

The affirmative and negative aorists of కూడు *to join* are sometimes placed after an infinitive, and conjugated through all the persons, in the same manner as the corresponding tenses of చాలు: they denote *expediency* rather than *ability*; but the use of the third person neuter only of these tenses is more correct, as explained hereafter.

442 Some other tenses are formed by affixing to infinitives the third person neuter only of certain tenses of a few verbs, used as auxiliaries. In this case the nominative only undergoes a change; the original verb remains in the infinitive, and the auxiliary in the 3d person neuter of the singular number.

వలెను or వలసినది the third person of the past tense, and వలయును the third person of the affirmative aorist of the root వలయు, when affixed to the infinitive of a verb, imply *obligation or neecssity* without reference to any particular time. They may be translated by the English auxiliary *must*, and are governed by any of the three persons in the nominative case; thus, నేను చెయ్యవలెను *I must do*, నీవువిచారించవలెను *you must enquire*, వాఁడు రావలెను *he must come*.

The third person neuter of the negative aorist of this verb is irregular, namely వలవదు or వలదు, more commonly contracted into వద్దు. It is used negatively, in the same manner as the affirmative tenses above mentioned; but, when affixed to infinitives, it has rather an imperative than an indicative meaning, and is therefore applied more frequently to the second and third persons than to the first; as, నీవు రావద్దు *dont come*, వారు పోవద్దు *let them not go*. Interrogatively, however, it is sometimes used with the first person, నేను రావద్దా *must I not come?*

These tenses of the verb వలయు are also occasionally added, in the same indeclinable state, to nouns in the nominative case, to denote *want or desire.* In this construction, the affirmatives వలెను-వలసినది and వలయును invariably take before them the infinitive కా, but the negative వద్దు does not require it; thus, గుఱ్ఱము నాకు కావలెను *I want a horse,* గుఱ్ఱము నాకు వద్దు *I do not want a horse.* The noun denoting that which is wanted is placed in the nominative case, but the noun or pronoun denoting the person who desires or wants is placed in the dative.

తగినది or తగ్గది the third person neuter of the past tense, and తగదు the third person neuter of the negative aorist of the root తగు *to be becoming, decent, fit, proper,* &c. are respectively used, after infinitives, to express *propriety or impropriety,* without reference to any particular time, and may be considered to represent the English auxiliary *ought* : the త may be changed into ద after an infinitive, see rule 115.

నేను చేయఁదగ్గది.............................*I ought to do.*
నీవు వ్రాయఁదగ్గది.............................*Thou oughtest to write.*
వాఁడు or అది చదవఁదగ్గది ....*He, she, or it ought to read.*
మేము అక్కడవుండఁదగ్గది.........................*We ought to be there.*
మీరు నిలవఁదగ్గది.............................*You ought to stand.*
వారు పంపించఁదగ్గది.............................*They ought to send.*
నేను చేయఁదగదు.............................*I ought not to do, &c. &c.*

వచ్చును and రాదు, the third persons neuter of the affirmative and negative aorists of the root వచ్చు *to come,* are respectively added to infinitives to denote *liberty or want of liberty* ; thus,

నేను చేయవచ్చును.............................*I may do.*
నీవు వ్రాయవచ్చును.............................*Thou mayst write.*
వాఁడు or అది-చదవవచ్చును.........................*He, she, or it may read.*
మేము అక్కడవుండవచ్చును.........................*We may be there.*
మీరు నిలవవచ్చును.............................*You may stand.*
వారు పంపించవచ్చును.............................*They may send.*

నేను చేయరాదు............................*I may not do.*

నీవు వ్రాయరాదు............................*Thou mayst not write.*

వాఁడు or అది-చదవరాదు....................*He, she, or it may not read.*

మేముఅక్కడవుండరాదు......................*We may not be there.*

మీరునిలవరాదు............................*You may not stand.*

వారుపంపించరాదు..........................*They may not send.*

కూడును and కూడదు, the third persons neuter of the affirmative and negative aorists of the root కూడు *to join* are added to infinitives to denote, *possibility or impossibility*; the క being changed to గ according to rule 115, thus,

నేనుచేయఁగూడును..........................*I can do.*

నీవు వ్రాయఁగూడును..........................*Thou canst write.*

వాఁడు or అదిచదవఁగూడును...................*He, she, or it can read.*

మేముఅక్కడవుండఁగూడును....................*We can be there.*

మీరునిలవఁగూడును..........................*You can stand.*

వారుపంపించఁగూడును........................*They can send.*

నేను చేయఁగూడదు...........................*I cannot do.*

నీవు వ్రాయఁగూడదు..........................*Thou canst not write.*

వాఁడు or అదిచదవఁగూడదు....................*He, she, or it cannot read.*

మేముఅక్కడవుండఁగూడదు.....................*We cannot be there.*

మీరునిలవఁగూడదు...........................*You cannot stand.*

వారుపంపించఁగూడదు.........................*They cannot send.*

443 Various negative compound tenses may be formed by affixing the several tenses of the verb పోవు *to go,* to the negative verbal participle of any verb: the original verb remains in the negative verbal participle, whilst the auxiliary tsnses of పోవు are conjugated through all the persons; thus,

నేను వ్రాయకపోతిని..........................*I did not write.*

నీవుచదవకపోదువు...........................*Thou wilt not read.*

నేనుపంపించకపోను..........................*I will not fail to send.*

We have already explained, under rule 441, that లేను - లేవు - లేఁడు - లేదు- 441
లేము - లేరు - లేవు, the negative aorist of the root కలుగు, when added to infinitives as an auxiliary, denotes *want of ability, as I cannot* &c. But it is often used alone as an original defective verb, representing the negative of the perfect tense of ఉండు *to be*; thus,

అక్కడవున్నాను....*I was there*...........అక్కడ లేను..*I was not there.*

అక్కడవున్నావు....*Thou wast there*.....అక్కడ లేవు..*Thou wast not there.*

అక్కడవున్నాఁడు...*He was there*.........అక్కడ లేఁడు. *He was not there.*

అక్కడవున్నది or ఉంది *She, or it was there.* అక్కడ లేదు . *She, or it was not there.*

అక్కడవున్నాము...*We were there*.........అక్కడ లేము...*We were not there.*

అక్కడవున్నారు.....*You were there*.........అక్కడ లేరు...*You were not there.*

M. & F. *M. & F.*

అక్కడవున్నారు.....*They were there*.......అక్కడ లేరు...*They were not there.*

N. *N.*

అక్కడవున్నవి......*They were there*......అక్కడ లేవు...*They were not there.*

In these two senses లేను agrees with it's nominative in gender and number.

లేదు, the neuter of the third person singular, is used indeclinably, in two other senses, as explained under the head "Particles."

Condition or contingency, is expressed, in the superior dialect of the Teloo- 445
goo, by changing the final vowel of each of the different persons in the first forms of the several affirmative tenses into ేని; and in the common dialect, by merely changing the termination తిని of the first person in the first form of the past tense into తే; thus, in the superior dialect, from

కొట్టుచున్నాను......*I beat*...........comes. కొట్టుచున్నానేని.....*if I beat.*

కొట్టితిని..............*I have beaten*...........కొట్టితి నేని...........*if I beat.*

కొట్టెదను.............*I shall beat*................కొట్టెద నేని.........*if I beat.*

కొట్టుదును.........{*I beat, did beat, or shall beat.*}......కొట్టుదు నేని........*if I beat.*

చేయుచున్నాను.......*I do*..................... చేయుచున్నానేని...*if I do.*

చేసితిని..................*I did*..................... చేసితి నేని...........*if I do.*

చేసెదను...............*I shall do*............... చేసెద నేని........*if I do.*

చేయుదను ....*I do, did, or shall do*.... చేయుదు నేని.....*if I do.*

దీవించుచున్నాను... *I bless*.................... దీవించుచున్నానేని... *if I bless.*

దీవించితిని.......... *I blessed*.................... దీవించితినేని.......... *if I bless.*

దీవించెదను.......... *I shall bless*............... దీవించెదనేని.......... *if I bless.*

దీవించుదును...... { *I bless, blessed, or shall bless* } .... దీవించుదునేని........ *if I bless.*

and in the inferior dialect, from

కొట్టితిని.............. *I have beaten*.....comes... కొట్టితే.............. *if I beat.*

చేసితిని.............. *I did*.................... చేసితే.... { *if I do*, contracted by rule 354 to చేస్తే }

దీవించితిని.......... *I blessed*................ దీవించితే { *if I bless*, do. do. 364 to దీవిస్తే }

446 The word ending in ేని varies with the numbers and persons, thus;

Sing........
- 1................ చేసితినేని.............. *if I do.*
- 2................ చేసితివేని.............. *if thou do.*
- 3 *M. F. & N.*.... చేసెనేని................ *if he, she, or it do.*

Plu..........
- 1................ చేసితిమేని.............. *if we do.*
- 2................ చేసితిరేని.............. *if you do.*
- 3 { *M. & F.*..... చేసిరేని.............. / *N.*.......... చేసెనేని.............. } *if they do.*

but the word terminating in స్తే is used for every person and number, చేస్తే means *if I, thou, he, she, it, we, you, or they do.*

447 Although the above examples are translated in English by the present tense of the subjunctive mood, it is to be observed that, in the superior dialect, the present tense with ేని is seldom used, the past tense with ేని often occurs in a past, or future, as well as in a present conditional meaning; the future tense with ేని is used in a future conditional sense only, and the aorist with ేని in a conditional sense, indefinite as to time; thus,

Present.... { వాఁడుపోవుచున్నాఁడేని / వీఁడెదురుపడును...... } *If he goes, he will meet him.*

Past.......	రాజు లెస్సగా రాజ్యము పాలించె నేని ప్రజలు సుఖముగా నుందురు............ in a present sense.........	*If the king governs the kingdom well, his subjects will be happy.*
....	రేపు నేను వచ్చితి నేని వానితో మాట్లాడుదును......... in a future sense.........	*If I should come to-morrow, I will speak with him.*
....	నేను నిన్న వానిఁ జూచితి నేని మాట్లాడుదును.......... in a past sense...........	*If I had seen him yesterday, I would have spoken to him.*
Future.......	రేపు వచ్చెద వేని నేనిచ్చెదను...	*If you come to-morrow, I will give.*
Aorist.......	రాజు లెస్సగాఁ బాలించు నేని ప్రజలు సుఖముగా నుందురు..................	*If the king govern well, his subjects will be happy.*
....	వాఁడు రేపు వచ్చు నేని నేనిత్తును.........................	*If he come to-morrow, I will give.*

In the common dialect, this form of the verb is not restricted to any time; but, according to the context, represents a present, past, or future conditional meaning.

నేను యిచ్చి*తే వాఁడు వచ్చును.............*If I give, he will come.*

రేపు నేను యిచ్చితే వాఁడు వచ్చును......*If I give to-morrow, he will come.*

నిన్న నేను యిచ్చితే వాఁడు వచ్చును.......*If I had given yesterday, he would have [come.*

By using the conditional form of the verb ఉండు *to be*, commonly written 448 వుంటే, with the present or past *verbal* participle of any other verb, we give that verb a present or past conditional meaning; thus, దేవదత్తుఁడు యిప్పుడు ముత్యాలసలాపమునకు పోతూవుంటే ఇతరులకంటే ముందుగా వచ్చును *if Devadutlu be now going to the pearl fishery, he will arrive before all the rest,* శీమ వాడలు ముందరనే వచ్చి వుంటే యీసరుకులు యింత గిరాకీ కాబొయ్యేది లేదు *If Europe ships had arrived before this period, these articles would not have become so dear.*

---

* by rule 364, యిచ్చితే may be contracted into యిస్తే.

449 In the superior dialect, each of these conditional forms of the verb, by affixing యు, represents the English subjunctive with the words *although, notwithstanding* prefixed to it; thus, వచ్చితినేనియు *although I come, came, or should come.* The same meaning is expressed by the past *relative* participle of the verb, with the addition of the indeclinable particle ను in the superior dialect, and ప్పటికిన్ని or గానిన్ని in the common dialect; thus వాఁడు, వచ్చినను. వచ్చినప్పటికిన్ని or వచ్చినాగానిన్ని *although he come, came, or should come,* వాఁడుయిచ్చినప్పటికిన్ని *although he give, gave, or should give*; వాఁడు వ్రాశినప్పటికిన్ని *although he write, wrote, or should write*; when గానిన్ని is added, the final ˇ of the past relative participle is lengthened; thus, వచ్చినాగానిన్ని never వచ్చినగానిన్ని; and the past relative participle itself, with the final ˇ thus lengthened, is often used in this sense; as, వాఁడువచ్చినా *although he come, came, or should come.*

450 The conditional form of any verb may also be expressed in the common dialect by adding to it's past *relative* participle the particles ట్టయితే and ట్టాయెనా; as చేసినట్టయితే - చేసనట్టాయెనా *if I, thou, he, she, it, we, you, or they do.* ట్టయితే is composed of the particle అట్టు meaning *so as, as if*, and అయితే the conditional form of the root అవు *to become*; ట్టాయెనా is composed of the same particle అట్టు, and ఆయెను the third person singular in the first form of the past tense of అవు, with it's final ు changed into ా.

451 When the *condition or contingency* is of a *negative* nature, it is expressed in the superior dialect by adding ేని to the respective persons of the negative aorist, and in the common dialect by affixing to the negative verbal participle the common conditional form of పోవు *to go* or ఉండు *to be*; thus, in the superior dialect we say

కొట్టనేని.................*if I do not beat, have not beaten, or shall not beat.*
చేయవేని.................*if thou dost not do, hast not done, or wilt not do.*
దీవించఁడేని............*if he does not bless, has not blessed, or will not bless.*

and in the inferior dialect.

కొట్టకపోతే or కొట్టకుంటే - చేయకపోతే or చేయకుంటే - దీవించకపోతే or దీవించకుంటే *If I, thou, he, she, it, we, you, or they beat, do, or bless-have beaten, done, or blessed - or shall beat, do, or bless.*

CONSTRUCTION OF THE PARTICIPLES

VERBAL PARTICIPLES.

There is no part of the verb of more frequent occurrence in Teloogoo than the *verbal* participles, with the proper use of which, therefore, it is of great importance that the student should be well acquainted: they can never, like the English participles, be used as adjectives, but must invariably be governed by some tense of a verb.

The verbal participles are used in Teloogoo when we wish to express any minor actions of the person who performs the chief action mentioned in the sentence. The verbal participles, denoting the minor actions performed, or placed first in the sentence, and are governed by the verb denoting the main action, with which the sentence elegantly terminates. 452

The peculiarity in these participles, therefore, is that they always refer to some subordinate action, performed by that particular agent only which is the nominative to the final governing verb, and never can express actions performed by others. 453

If the minor action be simultaneous with the main action in the sentence, the *present* verbal participle is used; if antecedent in point of time to it, we use the *past* verbal participle; and if it be of a negative nature, the *negative* verbal participle is used. 454

The following examples are subjoined in illustration of these rules.

PRESENT.

శత్రుబాణంబులను పొడిసేయుచుతనబాణంబులుశత్రువులదేహంబులనా 455
టంజేయుచుశత్రుబలంబులమనంబునకుభీతియుతనబలంబులమనంబునకును
త్సాహంబునుగలుగజేయుచుఅర్జునుండురణంబుసలిపెను *Reducing to dust the arrows of his foes, piercing the bodies of his enemies with his own arrows, exciting a panic in the minds of the opponent's forces, and animating the spirits of his own soldiers, Arjoona ruled the battle.* ప్రజలనుపాలించుచుపేదలనురక్షించుచుపెద్దలనుసమ్మానించుచుధర్మరాజు దొరతనముచేశెను. *Fostering his subjects, protecting the poor, and honoring the great, Dhurmarajah conducted the government.* కృష్ణుఁడుగోపాలులతోడనాడుచుపాడుచునవ్వుచుయమునా

తటంబుప్రవేశించెను *Playing, singing, and laughing, with those who attended kine, Krishna arrived on the banks of the river Jumna.*

PAST.

456 విక్రమార్కుఁడువేటపోవలెననితలచిసారథినిపిలిపించిరథముతెమ్మనితనస్నేహితులతోఁగూడిఅడవికిపోయెను *Vikramarka, having resolved to proceed to the chase, having sent for his charioteer, and having ordered his car, accompanied by his friends, proceeded to the forest.* రాముఁడులంకలోఁప్రవేశించిరాక్షసులనుచంపివిభీషణునికిపట్టాభిషేకము చేశి దివ్య పుష్పకవిమానమెక్కి అయోధ్యకువచ్చెను. *Rama, having entered Ceylon, having killed the giants, having installed Vib,hishana, and having mounted the divine car, named Pooshpuku, returned to Oude.*

NEGATIVE.

457 పరిజనులను పిలవక ధనుర్బాణములను ధరించక కవచము తొడుగుకొనక వొంటిగాశత్రువులతోఁఅతఁడుయుద్ధముచేశెను. *Without calling his retinue, without taking his bow and arrows, and without putting on his armour, he singly fought with his enemies.*

458 It will be observed that, in each of these examples, the verbal participles are placed first in the sentence, and invariably denote actions subordinate to that expressed by the verb at the conclusion of the period, by which they are governed; thus, in the three examples given of the present verbal participle, *ruled*, *conducted* and *arrived*, are the main actions expressed; and the participles *reducing, piercing &c. fostering, protecting &c. playing, singing &c.* are all minor actions subordinate thereto. It will further be perceived that the minor actions in question were all performed by that agent only which is the nominative to the governing verb. *Arjoona ruled*, and it was he also that *reduced* and *pierced*; *Dhurmarojah conducted*, and it was he also that *fostered* and *protected*; *Krishna arrived*, and it was he also that *played* and *sung*. Had any one else performed these minor actions, the verbal participles could not have been used.

As the minor actions of *reducing* and *piercing* were simultaneous with the main action of *ruling*, the *fostering* and *protecting* with that of *conducting*, and the *playing* and *singivg* with that of *arriving*, the *present* verbal participles are used, in these cases: but, in the examples given of the past verbal participle, it will be perceived that the resolution of Vikramarka to proceed to the chase, his sending for his charioteer, and his ordering his car, were all, in point of time, antecedent to the main action of his proceeding to the forest; so also Rama's entering Ceylon, killing the giants, &c. were actions performed by him previously to his return to Oude; hence, in these instances, the *past* verbal participle is used; and in the last example, because the minor actions are of a negative nature, we use the *negative* verbal participle.

As an exception to the foregoing rules, it is to be observed that when we 459
speak of the time that has elapsed since any particular event occurred, the past verbal participle may be used absolutely, and then has a nominative of it's own, independent of that of the final governing verb; thus, నేనువచ్చిపదిదినాలుఆయెను *it is ten days since I came,* literally, *I having come, ten days have passed;* here దినాలు *days* is the nominative to the final governing verb ఆయెను *passed;* but నేను *I* is the nominative to the verbal participle వచ్చి *having come,* which is used absolutely.

The verbal participles always govern the same case as the verb to which they 460
belong; thus, వానికొట్టివచ్చి నాడు *having beaten him he came;* వాని being governed by the active verbal participle కొట్టి in the accusative case.

The foregoing remarks will give the student some idea of the importance of the verbal participles in the construction of the Teloogoo; they are peculiarly well adapted to a language that abounds in descriptive passages, and the Student will occasionally find them carrying on and connecting the sense for pages together, but suspending the full meaning until the conclusion of the period. Hence, in some degree, the rare occurrence of conjunctions in Teloogoo; for the connexion between the subordinate and chief action in a sentence, which is implied by the verbal participles, often supersedes the use of them.

RELATIVE PARTICIPLES.

Separate relative pronouns are rendered unnecessary in Teloogoo, by certain 461
participles of the verb which have the power of the relative inherent in them,

and which, like the దేశ్యము adjectives, must always be followed by some noun or pronoun.

462 The relative participles also denote the action of the verb to which they belong; and the present, the past, the indefinite, or negative participle is used, according to the sense intended to be expressed.

463 The peculiarity of these participles consists in the relative inherent in them invariably referring to the noun or pronoun which immediately follows them, and which is also the agent to the action denoted by them, unless the relative participle stands between two nouns or pronouns; thus, వచ్చుచున్నమనుష్యులు *the persons that are coming,* కాఁగుచున్నపాలు *the milk that boils,* కొట్టినమనిషి *the person that beat,* చంపినపులి *the tiger that killed,* మాటలాడేచిలుక *the parrot that talks, talked, or will talk,* వ్రాసేవాఁడు *the man that writes, wrote, or will write,* చూడనిదేశము *the county that is, was, or will not be to be seen,* రాజులేనిభూమి *the country in which there is not, was not, or will not be a king.*

464 If the relative participle of an *active* verb stands between two nouns or pronouns, and the first be in the nominative case, it is the agent to the action denoted by the participle, and the noun following, in whatever case it may be, is the object affected by that action; thus, వారుచంపినపులి *the tiger that they killed,* మీరుచూచినవాఁడు *the man that you saw,* వాడుపిలిచినమనిషి *the person that he called;* but if the first noun or pronoun be in the accusative, it is the object affected by the action which the active participle denotes, and the following noun, in whatever case it may be, is the agent thereto; వానిచంపినపులి *the tiger that killed him,* మిమ్మునచూచినవాఁడు *the man that saw you,* వానిపిలిచినమనిషి *the person that called him.* If, independently of the agent and object, the relative inherent in an active participle, refers to the instrument, place, or other subordinate correlative to the action which it denotes, the agent is placed first in the nominative case, then the object in the accusative, next the relative participle, and finally the instrument, place, or other correlative to which it refers; thus నేనుపులినిచంపినకత్తి or చోటు *the sword with*

which, or *the place in which, I killed the tiger;* రాజుగోవునిచ్చినబ్రాహ్మ ణుఁడు *the bramin to whom the king gave the cow.* In those examples *I* and *the king* are the agents, and therefore in the nominative case, *the tiger* and *the cow* are the objects, and therefore in the accusative, and *the sword, the place,* and *the bramin* are the subordinate correlatives referred to, and therefore placed immediately after the participle.

If the relative participle of a *neuter* verb stands between two nouns or 465
pronouns, the first must always be in the nominative case, because neuter verbs cannot govern the accusative; and it is also always the agent to the action denoted by the participle, the noun following being merely the subordinate correlative thereto; thus, నేనువుండినయిల్లు *the house in which I was,* మీరునడుస్తు న్నదోవ *the road in which you walk,* వాఁడుకూచుండినస్థళము *the place on which he sat,* మీరుపడుకొన్నయిల్లు *the house in which you slept.*

The foregoing and following examples will best explain the manner in which 466
these participles supply, in construction, the cases of the relative pronouns, and the mode in which they must be translated in English by corresponding prepositions.

N. వారినిచంపినపులి............*The tiger which killed them.*
మిమ్మునచూచినవాఁడు......*The man who saw you.*
వాణ్ణిపిలిచినమనిషి.........*The person who called him.*

G. బట్టచినిగినమనిషి.............*The man whose clothes are torn.*
పూలువాడినచెట్టు..........*The tree of which the flowers are faded.*
గోడవ్రేరిగినయిల్లు...........*The house of which the wall is inclined.*
పంటపండినచేను.............*The field of which the produce is ripe.*

D. నేనువచ్చినపని.............*The business for which I came.*
వాఁడువచ్చినయిల్లు.........*The house to which he came.*

Ac. వారుచంపినపులి............*The tiger which they killed.*
మీరుచూచినవాఁడు........*The man whom you saw.*
వాఁడుపిలిచినమనిషి........*The person whom he called.*

Ab. పూలుగోసినచెట్టు..........*The tree from which flowers were gathered.*

నేను పండుకొన్నయిల్లు......*The house in which I slept.*

పండుకోశినకత్తి.......... *The knife with which the fruit was cut.*

వానకురిశినయిల్లు..........*The house on which it rained.*

467 It is not easy, by any general rule, to define on what the case of the relative depends; in rule 464 the mere substitution of the word చోటు *a place,* for కత్తి *a sword,* changed the relative *with which,* into *for which;* and in rule 466 the substitution of యిల్లు *a house,* for పని *business,* changed the relative *for which* into *to which.* In the examples given in 466 the relative participle constantly stands between two nouns in the nominative case, yet the relative itself, which in Teloogoo is inherent in the participle, is in the genitive, dative, or ablative; and it is curious that in Teloogoo when an active participle is placed between two nominatives, the relative in English must be in the objective case (see examples of the accusative); while if the objective case in Teloogoo precede an active participle, the relative in English must be in the nominative case (see examples of the nominative). In rule 464, the correlative బ్రాహ్మణుడు *a bramin* is in the nominative, yet from the nature of the verb *to give,* the relative *to whom,* which is inherent in the Teloogoo participle, is in the dative case; thus, therefore, the case of the relative would seem to depend in some instances on the nature, rather than the case of the following word; in others, on the case of the preceding word; and in some, on the nature of the verb itself.

468 The common indefinite relative participle, by affixing అది, has often the same signification as an abstract noun; thus, using the abstract noun, we may say కొలువుమంచిది *service is excellent,* or we may use the common relative participle with అది, and say కొలిచేదిమంచిది; but, while the abstract nouns are declined and construed as substantives, the relative participles as well as the verbal nouns (such as కొలుచుట and కొలవడము) being integral parts of the verb, although declined like nouns, are invariably construed like verbs, and govern the same case as the verb from which they are derived; thus, using the abstract noun కొలువు, we say మీకొలువుమంచిది *your service is excellent,* మీ being placed in the possessive case; but when we use కొలిచేది - కొలుచుట or

కొలవడము, we must place the pronoun in the accusative case and say మిమ్ముల కొలిచేదిమంచిది - మిమ్ములకొలుచుట or మిమ్ముల కొలవడముమంచిది *to serve you*, or *the serving you is excellent*.

Nouns denoting the agent may be formed from every verb, by adding to the relative participles, either affirmative or negative, the pronoun వాడు for the masculine, and అది for the feminine and neuter, in the singular number; and వారు for the masculine and feminine, and అవి for the neuter, in the plural; thus, కొట్టేవాడు *the man who beats, the beater*, కొట్టేది *the woman or the thing that beats*, చంపేవారు *the men or women that kill, the killers*, చంపేది *the woman or the thing that kills*, కొట్టనివాడు *the man who does not beat, has not beaten*, or *will not beat*, కొట్టనిది *the woman or the thing that does not beat, has not beaten, or will not beat.* 469

కొట్టేది - చంపేది &c. have, by some, been called infinitives; but they are no more infinitives than కొట్టేవాడు or చంపేవాడు. They are merely, as above stated, relative participles, with the pronouns వాడు and అది added to them; thus, చంపేవాడు is composed of చంపే the common indefinite relative participle of the root చంపు *to kill*, with the pronoun వాడు added to it; and చంపేది is composed of the same word చంపే with the pronoun అది added to it; such compound words may be declined through all the cases of the pronoun వాడు and అది in the following manner. 470

SINGULAR.

	M.	*N. & F.*
N.	చదివేవాడు	చదివేది
G.	చదివే-వాని-వానియొక్క	చదివే-దాని-దానియొక్క
D.	చదివేవానికి	చదివేదానికి
Acc.	చదివేవాని	చదివేదాని
Ab.	చదివేవాని-లో-చేత-తో	చదివేదాని-లో-చేత-తో

PLURAL.

	M. & F.	*N.*
N.	చదివేవారు	చదివేవి
G.	చదివే-వారి-వారియొక్క	చదివే-వాటి-వాటియొక్క

D. చదివేవారికి......................చదివేవాటికి

Acc. చదివేవారిని......................చదివేవాటిని

Ab. చదివేవారి-లో-చేత-తో......చదివేవాటి-లో-చేత-తో

So, also may we decline చంపుచున్నవాఁడు and చంపుచున్నది-చంపినవాఁడు and చంపినది-చంపనివాఁడు and చంపనిది.

GENERAL RULES.

471 In Teloogoo, the word agreeing with the verb is always in the nominative case, and has generally the first place in the sentence, then follows the word denoting the object governed by the verb, next any intermediate explanatory clause, and the verb itself closes the period.

472 A verb agrees with it's nominative in gender, number, and person; but when two or more nominatives agree with the same verb, it is placed in the plural number, and agrees in gender with the masculine or feminine nominative, in preference to the neuter; thus, తామరయు నెలయుఁ బ్రకాశించిరి *the moon and the lotus shone,* గొల్లలుపశువులువచ్చిరి *the cowherds and cows came*: but such forms of expression are very uncommon, it would be more elegant to say గొల్లలుపశువులతోవచ్చిరి *the cowherds came with the cows*; and to express in Teloogoo that the king, the minister, their horses, and elephants, all entered into the city, we never should say రాజుమంత్రియుగజతురంగంబులునగరముప్రవేశించిరి but వారుగజతురంగంబులతోప్రవేశించిరి *they arrived with thier elephants and horses.*

473 If two or more nouns and pronouns, of different persons, connected by a copulative conjunction are nominatives to the same verb, the verb is placed in the plural number, but agrees with the second person in preference to the third, and with the first in preference to both; as నేనుమీరువాడువస్తిమి *I, you, and he came.*

474 Neuter verbs, from their nature, never can govern a noun or pronoun; when made causal they are construed in the same manner as active verbs. Active verbs govern substantives in the accusative case; thus, we say రాముఁడురావ

ణునిసంహరించెను *Rama killed Ravana;* but all nouns denoting inanimate objects, when governed by active verbs, may be placed in the nominative, instead of the accusative case; and, unless the use of the nominative would render the meaning obscure, this is the more correct and elegant construction; thus, రథమునెక్కెను or రథమెక్కెను *he mounted the car,* చదరంగమును or చదరంగముఆడితిని *I played at chess,* నేనుకొండను or కొండచూస్తిని, *I saw the mountain,* తోటవాడుచెట్లను or చెట్లునాటినాడు *the gardener has planted trees.*

The verbs పితుకు *to milk,* అడుగు *to ask,* దండగతీయు *to amerce,* గెల్చు *to* 475
win, దోచు *to rob,* with a few others, may govern two accusatives; but if one of these accusatives denote an inanimate object, it may be placed in the nominative instead of the accusative case, గొల్లవాడావునుపాలను or పాలుపితికెను *the cowherd milked the cow,* దొరనునూరువరాలను or నూరువరాలుఅడిగెను *he asked his master for one hundred pagodas,* న్యాయాధిపతినేరస్థులనునూరువరాలను or వరాలుదండగతీసెను *the magistrate amerced the guilty one hundred pagodas,* నేనువాణ్నినూరువరాలను or వరాలుగెల్చినాను *I won from him one hundred pagodas,* దొంగలుభాటసార్లనుసొమ్ములను or సొమ్ములుదోచిరి *the thieves robbed the travellers of their jewels.*

Active verbs, when converted into causals, govern the noun which would 476
have been the agent in their active form in the instrumental ablative; the noun which would have been the object in their active form continues in the accusative, or, if it denote something inanimate, in the nominative case; thus, వాడు యిల్లుకట్టినాడు *he built a house,* నేనువానిచేతయిల్లుకట్టిస్తిని *I caused him to build a house,* నాకొమారుడుపుస్తకమువ్రాసెను *my son wrote the book,* నేను నాకొమారునిచేతపుస్తకమువ్రాయిస్తిని *I caused my son to write the book,* పులిమేకనుచంపెను *the tiger killed the goat,* నేనుపులిచేతమేకనుచంపిస్తిని *I caused the tiger to kill the goat,* మీరుయీవర్తమానముచెప్పితిరి *you mentioned this news,* మీచేతయీవర్తమానముచెప్పిస్తిని *I caused you to mention this news.*

But verbs denoting to read, to sing, or to eat, with perhaps a few others, 477
when converted into causals, govern the noun which would have been the agent

in their simple form either in the ablative or accusative case; గురువుతనశిష్యులను or శిష్యులచేతపుస్తకములుచదివించెను *the master caused his pupils to read books,* గాయకులను or గాయకులచేతసంగీతముపాడించిరి *they caused the songsters to sing,* బిడ్డలను or బిడ్డలచేతఅన్నముతినిపించెను *he caused children to eat boiled rice.*

478 When a verb directly affects two nouns, the one denoting a whole, and the other a part of that whole, the noun denoting the part stands in the nominative, but the principal noun is placed in the genitive case; thus, గుఱ్ఱములయొక్క తోకలుకోస్తారు *they are cutting off the tails of horses.* The principal noun may also stand in the dative; thus గుఱ్ఱములకుతోకలుకోస్తారు, or the principal noun may stand in the accusative; thus, గుఱ్ఱాలనుతోకలుకోస్తారు and this, in Teloogoo, is considered the most elegant mode of expression.

479 The verb *to be*, which so often occurs in the English language, is generally omitted in Teloogoo: it may occasionally be used, but it is thought more elegant to dispense with the use of it. The mode in which it is omitted in Teloogoo when it is placed between an adjective and a substantive noun or pronoun, has been already explained (see rule 428), where it would intervene in English between a substantive pronoun and a substantive noun, it is also omitted in Teloogoo. Indeed, as the personal terminations of the verb are derived from the substantive pronouns, it does not seem strange that these pronouns themselves should partake in some degree of the essence of the verb.

In Teloogoo, when a substantive pronoun immediately precedes a substantive noun, the latter has the force of the present tense of the verb *to be* inherent in it; and if the pronoun be of the 1st or 2d person, the noun assumes certain affixes.

If the pronoun be of the 1st person, the affix to the noun is in the singular, ని for nouns in ి or ీ, ఁను for nouns in ు, and ను for nouns of any other termination; and in the plural, ఁము for all nouns.

If the pronoun be of the 2d person, the affix to the noun is in the singular, వి for nouns in ి or ీ, ఁవు for nouns in ు, and వు for nouns in any other termination; and in the plural ఁరు for all nouns.

If the pronoun be of the third person, the noun takes no affix.

The following examples will more fully explain this construction.

నేనుకవిని.. *I am a poet.*

నీవుకవివి.. *Thou art a poet.*

వాఁడుకవి.. *He is a poet.*

నేనుబ్రాహ్మణుఁడను.. *I am a bramin.*

నీవుబ్రాహ్మణుఁడవు.. *Thou art a bramin.*

వాఁడుబ్రాహ్మణుఁడు.. *He is a bramin.*

ఇదిగుఱ్ఱము.. *This is a horse.*

ఇదిఆవు.. *This is a cow.*

నేనుబిడ్డను.. *I am a child.*

నీవుబిడ్డవు.. *Thou art a child.*

వాఁడుబిడ్డ.. *He is a child.*

మేము or మనముకవులము.. *We are poets.*

మీరుకవులరు.. *Ye are poets.*

వారుకవులు.. *They are poets.*

మేము or మనముబ్రాహ్మణులము.. *We are bramins.*

మీరుబ్రాహ్మణులరు.. *Ye are bramins.*

వారుబ్రాహ్మణులు.. *They are bramins.*

ఇవిగుఱ్ఱములు.. *These are horses.*

ఇవిఆవులు.. *These are cows.*

మేము or మనముబిడ్డలము.. *We are children.*

మీరుబిడ్డలరు.. *Ye are children.*

వారుబిడ్డలు.. *They are children.*

It will be observed that కవి *a poet,* with the singular pronouns of the 1st and 2d persons prefixed to it, in the one case affixes ని, and in the other వి, because it terminates in ి; but బ్రాహ్మణుఁడు *a bramin* ends in ు, and therefore affixes ను and వు, or rather changes the final ు into these terminations; and బిడ్డ *a child* ending neither in ి or ీ, nor in ు, takes simply ను and వు.

Each of these nouns, viz. కవి - బ్రాహ్మణుడు and బిడ్డ, with the pronouns of the 1st and 2d persons plural prefixed to it, takes ˘ము and ˘రు ; and none of them, when preceded by the pronouns of the third person, take any affix whatever.

480 One verb governs another that refers to it, or depends on it, in the infinitive; but the infinitive invariably precedes the governing verb, instead of following it as in English; thus, *I wish to conquer my foes* శత్రువులనుజయించనిచ్ఛయిస్తున్నాను, *I hoped to adore Shiva* శివునిపూజించకోరితిని.

481 When the speaker states what another has said, he does not, as in English, use the infinitive mood; he repeats the words of the original speaker, adding the particle అని *having said;* thus, he told me to write, would in the Teloogoo idiom be rendered వ్రాయమనిచెప్పెను namely వ్రాయుము *write thou,* అని *having said,* చెప్పెను *he told*; thus also, the sentence వాడుపామునుచంపమనివానికివుత్తరువుయిచ్చెను *he ordered him to kill the snake,* consists of the words వాడు *he* పామును *the snake,* చంపుము *kill thou,* అని *having said,* వానికి *to him,* వుత్తరువు *order,* యిచ్చెను *gave*; చేయుము and చెప్పుము preceding అని are changed, by the rules for Sund,hi, to చేయమని and చెప్పమని respectively, for in the common dialect the ు before the ము of the imperative is generally dropped in this construction, for the sake of alliteration ; thus, also, we say *I heard that Devadutta went* దేవదత్తుడుపోయెననివింటిని &c. In this sense, the relative participles, with అది either in the nominative or accusative case, are sometimes elegantly used in Teloogoo ; as, దేవదత్తుడుపోయినది or పోయినదాన్నివింటిని, or the particle కా, hereafter mentioned, may be added to the participles joined with అది in the nominative case ; thus, దేవదత్తుడు పోయినదిగావింటిని *I heard that Devadutta went* ; thus also, we say విష్ణువుఅవతరించపోతున్నాడనిచెప్పుచున్నారు or అవతరించపోయ్యేదిచెప్పుచున్నారు or అవతరించపొయ్యేదిగాచెప్పుచున్నారు *they affirm that an incarnation of the God Vishnoo is about to take place.*

482 అని is used, in the same manner, when we address to a second person orders to be delivered to a third, *tell him to send* పంపించమనిచెప్పు, literally పంపిం

పుము *send thou,* అని *having said,* చెప్పు *tell;* వ్రాయమనిచెప్పు *tell him to write,* చదవమనిఆజ్ఞాపించు *direct him to read,* &c.

When we wish to represent various minor actions *performed by others* as contemporaneous with the chief action performed by a particular person mentioned in the sentence, a number of infinitives, denoting these minor actions, are placed together in the sentence, which terminates, in an elegant manner, with the verb denoting the main action placed in it's appropriate tense; thus, మిథిలాపురములోఛప్పన్న దేశాధిపతులువచ్చి సవింప - వరాంగనలునాట్యమాడ - గాయకులుసంగీతముచేయ - భేరిమొదలుగాఁగలవాద్యములువాయించ - దేవతలుపుష్పవర్షముగురియింప - వందిమాగధులుస్తోత్రముచేయ - పట్టణములోనుండేజనులుప్రమోదముబొంద - దశరథుండుతనపుత్రుండగురామునికివివాహంబుచేసినవాఁడాయెను. *While the rulers of fifty-six countries, having arrived at the city of Mid,hila, were in attendance, while fair damsels sported in the dance, while choristers chaunted songs, while they sounded the great drum and other musical instruments, while the gods showered flowers, while the bards and genealogists proclaimed panegyrics, while the people of the city were filled with joy, the king Dasarad,ha celebrated the nuptials of his son Rama.* Even in familiar conversation this mode of expression is sometimes used. 483

If the infinitive of a verb with the particle గా added to it, be twice repeated, it denotes progression; thus, అక్షరాలువ్రాయగావ్రాయగాకుదురును *writing improves gradually as we write,* చదవగాచదవగాతెలుసును *it will be understood gradually by reading,* నడవగానడవగాదోవజరుగును *as we walk the road gradually shortens,* వర్షముకురియగాకురియగాచెరువులు నిండును *as it rains the lakes will be gradually filled.* 484

The root కొను *to buy,* conjugated through all its moods, tenses, and persons, is frequently added to the past verbal participle of another verb, when it is intended to restrict the action denoted by that verb exclusively to the benefit of the agent; and often in the superior, but always in the inferior dialect, final ి of the past verbal participle is changed to ు when కొను is thus added; as చేసి

కొను or చేసుకొను *to do for one's own benefit,* వ్రాసికొను or వ్రాసుకొను *to write for one's own benefit*; thus we say వ్రాసినాను *I wrote,* వ్రాసికొన్నాను or వ్రాసుకొన్నాను *I wrote for my own benefit*; చేస్తాను *I do,* చేసికొంటాను - చేసుకొంటాను *I do for my own benefit;* చెప్పినాడు *he told,* చెప్పికొన్నాడు or చెప్పుకొన్నాడు *he told for his own benefit.* Sometimes, however కొను is added merely for the sake of elegance; thus we may say either జాబుచూస్తిని or జాబుచూచుకొంటిని *I saw the letter*; at other times, it alters the signification of the verb to which it is added in a manner scarcely to be defined వాడుచక్కగానడుస్తాడు *he walks well,* వాడుచక్కగానడుచుకొంటాడు *he behaves well*; it occasionally makes a neuter verb active నాకుతెలిసినది *it was understood to me,* నేనుతెలుసుకొంటిని *I understood,* తీయు *to draw, to pull,* తీసుకొను *to bring,* మ్రొక్కు *to prostrate,* మ్రొక్కుకొను *to invoke* &c.

485 The present verbal participle of a verb prefixed to any tense of the verb వచ్చు *to come* denotes that the action expressed by the participle is habitual or of long continuance; thus, అతడుమాయింటికివస్తూవచ్చెను *he was in the habit of coming to my house,* వాడుచక్కగానడుచుకొంటూవచ్చెను *he continued to behave himself well,* యీభూమిలోమునుపుధాన్యముపండుతూవచ్చెను *grain formerly used to be produced in this land,* రాజుధర్మముగారాజ్యపరిపాలనచేస్తూవచ్చెను *the king continued to govern the kingdom in a just manner,* మీరుజాబులుపంపిస్తూరావలెను *you must continue sending letters.*

486 It has already been stated that active verbs become passive by adding to the infinitive the verb పడు *to fall, to suffer.* By affixing this verb to the nominative case of neuter nouns, particularly to such as denote any bodily suffering or mental affection, a compound verb is formed of a neuter signification; and if the noun end in ము, this termination may be changed into ం, or may be dropped altogether; the latter is the more common form; thus, from భయము *fear* is formed భయముపడు or భయంపడు or భయపడు *to fear;* from దెబ్బ *a blow* comes దెబ్బపడు *to be beaten* &c. But if instead of the neuter form పడు, the active form పరుచు be added to the substantive, it makes an active

verb; thus, from భయము *fear* comes భయపరుచు *to frighten,* and from సంతోషము *gladness* comes సంతోషపడు *to be pleased,* and సంతోషపరుచు *to please.*

The verb ఇచ్చు which properly signifies to deliver any thing from one's 487
own possession into that of another, although it may be translated in English by the verb *to give,* is not in Teloogoo synonymous with that English verb. It cannot be used unless the thing delivered is taken by the receiver; for example, if a bramin invites another to dine with him, we cannot in Teloogoo say with propriety that he *gave* him boiled rice అన్నమిచ్చెను; because the boiled rice is not delivered into the hands of the bramin invited, but only placed on a leaf before him. We must therefore say అన్నముపెట్టెను *he placed rice before him.* But if he were to give the food to his palanqueen bearer, who, being of an inferior cast, is not allowed to pollute the house of a bramin by eating in it, he does not place the boiled rice before him, but delivers it into his hands, and in this case therefore we might say ఆబ్రాహ్మడుతనబోయీకిఅన్నమిచ్చెను *that bramin gave rice to his palanqueen bearer.* In the same manner, if you give grass to a horse, you cannot say in Teloogoo గుఱ్ఱానికికసువుయిస్తిని *I gave grass to the horse,* but నేనుగుఱ్ఱానికికసువువేస్తిని *I threw grass to the horse.*

OF PARTICLES OR INDECLINABLE WORDS.

కా

There are scarcely any proper adverbs in Teloogoo, యిప్పుడు *now,* అప్పుడు 488
then, ఎప్పుడు *when,* నేడు *to-day,* నిన్న *yesterday,* రేపు *to-morrow,* &c. are not adverbs, but substantive nouns which are declined; adverbs however are easily made, or rather their want is supplied, by adding to any noun substantive or adjective the infinitive కా, from the verb అవు *to become,* which, following a nominative, is changed into గా, according to the rules given in Chapter Second; thus,

from సుఖము......*happiness*...is derived,....సుఖముగా....*happily.*

.......అందము...*beauty*.........................అందముగా....*beautifully.*

.........గొప్ప......*great*...........................గొప్పగా.....*greatly.*

from త్వర..............*quickness*...is derived...త్వరగా......*quickly.*
......చల్ల................*cold*....................చల్లగా........*coldly.*
......తిన్న...............*soft, slow*..................తిన్నగా......*softly, slowly.*
......తియ్య.............*sweet*.......................తియ్యగా.....*sweetly.*
......చేదు..........*bitter*......................చేదుగా......*bitterly.*

గాలిచల్లగాకొట్టుతున్నది *the wind blows coldly,* గుఱ్ఱముతిన్నగానడుస్తున్నది *the horse goes slowly.*

489 It is to be remarked that గా can never be added to the nominative with which the verb agrees, but only to an adjective or substantive qualifying that nominative. If I would express that the water of the sea is salt, to the word denoting *salt* I may add గా, and say సముద్రపునీళ్లువుప్పుగావున్నవి ; because *salt* is not the nominative to the verb, it only qualifies *the water of the sea* which is the nominative. But if I wish to state that there is salt water in the sea, the sentence refers not to the essence or quality of the water, but to it's existence ; therefore without adding గా I should say సముద్రములోవుప్పునీళ్లువున్నవి : we say ఆపుష్పములువాసనగావున్నవి *those flowers are fragrant,* but when we merely assert that there is fragrance in flowers we say పుష్పములయందు వాసనవున్నది.

490 Besides converting substantives and adjectives into adverbs, గా when added to them may denote resemblance, similitude, &c. దూరములోనుంచిచూస్తే పర్వతములుధూమముగాఅగుపడుతున్నవి *if mountains be viewed from a distance, they appear like smoke.*

491 The infinitive గా, added to the pronoun తాను, also represents the English expressions *spontaneously, of his own accord* ; for example, supposing a person to die voluntarily by eating poison, if I wish to ascertain whether he died of any disease, or of his own accord, I should say in Teloogoo అతడురోగముచేతచచ్చెనా లేకతనకుతానే or తానుగానేచచ్చెనా, I might also say తానేచచ్చెనా, but తానే is liable to equivocation, for besides meaning *spontaneously* in contradistinction to *forcibly,* it may likewise signify that he *himself* died in contradistinction to *any other person.*

Sometimes the past verbal participle or infinitive of a verb is used as an adverb ; thus, 492

from.....*the root* తిరుగు......*to turn*......comes.....తిరుగ......or తిరిగి.....*again.*
..................మళ్లు.........*to return*..................మళ్ల......or మళ్లి.....*again.*
..................నిండు.........*to fill*..................నిండా....or నిండి.....*much.*

The following Sanscrit particles cannot properly be termed adverbs, but they 493
enter so frequently into the composition of తత్సమము words that some notice of them seems to be necessary ; and I know not that I can offer the few observations which I have to make respecting them in a more appropriate place. They are prefixes compounded with substantives, adjectives, or verbs of Sanscrit derivation.

ప్ర denotes *excess* ; as హర్షః *joy*, ప్రహర్షః *excess of joy*, ధనము *wealth*, ప్రధనము *great wealth.*

పరా is a privative implying *opposition, reverse ;* as జయము *victory*, పరాజయము *defeat.*

అప is also a privative ; as కీర్తిః *fame*, అపకీర్తిః *infamy*, జయము *victory*, అపజయము *defeat*, ధనము *money*, అపధనుఁడు *a poor man.*

సమ్ is an incrementive denoting also *goodness*, or *connexion* ; as అర్చితుఁడు *adored*, సమర్చితుఁడు *well adored*, వాదము *declamation*, సంవాదము *an argumental dispute.*

అను signifies *after*, *near*, *each*, *every* ; as సరణము *going*, అనుసరణము *following*, వనము *a garden*, అనువనము *near a garden*, దినము *a day*, అనుదినము *every day.*

అవ is a privative, meaning also *below* ; as తరణము *going*, అవతరణము *descending* ; నతము *bent*, అవనతము *bent down* ; మానము *honor*, అవమానము *dishonor.*

నిర్ - నిస్ are privatives, meaning also *going through, the whole* ; as, రసము *juice*, నీరసము *juiceless* ; గ్రామము *a village*, నిర్గ్రాముఁడు *a man who went through a village* ; దత్తము *given*, నిర్దత్తము *given altogether.*

దుర్ - దుస్ *ill, bad, reverse*; as, కర్మము *business*, దుష్కర్మము *bad business*; గమ్యము *passable*, దుర్గమము *impassable*.

వి signifies *excess, variety, badness*; it also denotes *opposition*; as జయము *victory*, విజయము *a great victory*; విధము *manner or method*, వివిధము *various methods*; రూపము *form*, విరూపము *deformity*; వాదము *talking*, వివాదము *a quarrel*; మలము *filth*, విమలము *purity*.

ఆఙ్ signifies *as far as, from, every where*; as, అంతము *the end*, ఆంతము *as far as the end*; మూలము *the root*, ఆమూలము *from the root*.

ని *excess, within*; as హననము *torturing*, నిహననము *killing*.

అధి means *above, excess*; as, ఆసీనుడు *sitting*, అధ్యాసీనుడు *sitting upon any thing*; పాదము *a foot*, అధిపాదము *a foot over*.

అపి in most Sanscrit words adopted into Teloogoo is a mere expletive.

అతి means *much, beyond moderation*; as, మధురము *sweet*, అతిమధురము *very sweet*; వేల *a limit*, అతివేలము *beyond the limit*; భోజనము *eating*, అతిభోజనము *eating immoderately*.

సు *good, well*; as, పథము *a road*, సుపథము *a good road*; గుణము *the disposition*, సుగుణము *a good disposition or temper*.

ఉద్ denotes *up, beyond*; as ధృతము *held*, ఉద్ధృతము *held up*; స్థానము *not moving*, ఉత్థానము *rising*; వేల *limit*, ఉద్వేలము *beyond the limit*.

అభి *before*; as ముఖము *a face*, అభిముఖము *before the face*; సూర్యుడు *the sun*, అభిసూర్యము *before the sun*.

ప్రతి *again, in return, back, each, opposite, in exchange, towards*; as వనము *a garden*, ప్రతివనము *each garden*; ఉపకారము *kindness*, ప్రత్యుపకారము *a return of kindness*; వాది *a complainant*, ప్రతివాది *a defendant*; సూర్యుడు *the sun*, ప్రతిసూర్యము *towards the sun*; విష్ణువు *Vishnoo*, ప్రతివిష్ణువు *a second Vishnoo*.

పరి signifies *well*; as, ఆలోచన *consideration*, పర్యాలోచన *considering well, deep reflexion*; శోధన *a trial*, పరిశోధన *well tried*.

ఉప *near*; as గ్రామము *a country*, ఉపగ్రామము *environs*.

494 Conjunctions are seldom used in Teloogoo; they are necessary chiefly in works on science, where a chain of reasoning is required for the elucidation of

some position, but in short detached maxims regarding moral conduct, and in poetical compositions, which form the principal part of Teloogoo literature, the frequent use of conjunctions would destroy that simplicity and elegant conciseness of phrase, which is the great characteristic of the language.

In the superior dialect, యు is equivalent to the English conjunction *and*, 495
but it is added only to words ending in ు ూ ృ ౄ or ై. This particle being included in the class of words termed *drootuprucrootica*, is liable to all the changes mentioned in the second chapter of this work as peculiar to words of that description. If the word end in any other vowel than those abovementioned, the drootuprucrootica affix ను is added to it, instead of యు, to express the conjunction *and*; thus, గాడీయు - ఎద్దునుగొఱ్ఱెయు *a carriage, a bullock, and a sheep.*

In the common dialect ని - న్ని, or నిన్ని are added to words ending in ి ీ or 496
ై; and ను - న్ను or నున్ను to words in any other terminations, to express our conjunction *and*; న్ను however is seldom affixed to any nouns except to those in ం; న్ని if affixed to a word ending in long ీ requires it to be shortened into ి; and ని-నిన్ని as well as ను-నున్ను always lengthen the final vowel of the word to which they are affixed; thus, కోయ్యానున్ను కొరడానున్ను - కఱ్ఱనున్ను *a staff, a whip, and a stick*; బండిన్ని గాడిన్ని బాగావున్నవి *the cart and the carriage are in good order*; రాముడున్ను లక్ష్మణుడున్ను యుద్ధము చేశిరి *Rama and Lutchmana fought.* A terminational emphasis, or the lengthening of the final vowel, is also equivalent to the conjunction; as కొయ్య కొరడా కఱ్ఱ *a staff, a whip, and a stick*; సేనలో యేనుగు లూ గుఱ్ఱములూ ఒంటెలూ రథములూ అన్ని వున్న వి *elephants, horses, camels, and cars are all in the army*, యిండ్లూ తోటలూ దొడ్లూ నేలలు యేలం బడ్డవి *houses, gardens, godowns, and lands, are sold by auction.*

The abovementioned particles which are equivalent to the conjunction *and* 497
may be affixed to all, to any, or to none of the objects enumerated; but in the case last mentioned, the final vowel must be lengthened, or pronounced with emphasis; thus నేనున్ను నా స్నేహితుడున్ను తిరువట్టూరికి పోతిమి or నేనునా

స్నేహితుడున్నుతిరువట్టూరికిపోతిమి or నేనూనా స్నేహితుడూ తిరువట్టూరికి పోతిమి *I and my friend went to Trevatoor.*

498 When we wish particularly to mark the nature, rather than the number of the objects enumerated, not saying, for example, *two* hills, but these are *both* hills; then, some of the participles abovementioned must be added to the word denoting the number, or the emphasis must be laid on the last syllable of it; thus, అవుగో పొగవలెఅగుపడుతున్నవేఅవి రెండున్నూ or రెండూ-కొండలు *those are both mountains that appear yonder like smoke;* if we said రెండు కొండలు it would mean that there are *two* mountains, not that *both* are mountains.

499 When we allude to the whole of any number of objects, some of the participles abovementioned must be added to the word expressing the object, not to the word expressing the number; thus, if I were to say I am wounded in one of my hands, one is not here a complete number, because I have two hands; therefore, without adding the particles abovementioned, I must say నాకుఒకచేతిలోగాయము తగిలినది; but if both my hands were wounded, then I must add some of those particles to the Teloogoo word denoting *hands;* thus, నా రెండు చేతులలోనున్ను గాయముతగిలినది; for if I did not add న్ను here, it would be understood that I had more than two: thus also, if I say నాతబేలాలోనాలుగుగుఱ్ఱములుపరిగెత్తిపోయినవి *four horses ran out of my stable,* as న్ను is not added, it is understood that I have yet more horses; for if these four were all that belonged to me, then I should have added న్ను, and said నాతబేలాలోనాలుగుగుఱ్ఱములున్నుపరిగెత్తిపోయినవి.

600 న్ను and its synonymous particles abovementioned often represent the English words *also, even* &c; thus, యిదిన్నినాది *this also is mine.* Hence, if న్ని be added to the word వొకటి *one thing,* and a negation follow, it expresses the English word *nothing;* thus వొకటిన్నిచేయను *I will do nothing;* in other words I will not do *even one thing.* These particles followed by a negation, are likewise equivalent to our negatives *neither, nor* &c.; thus, మంచిదిన్నికాదు చెడ్డదిన్నికాదు *it is neither good, nor bad.* If these particles are added to any interrogative pronoun or adverb beginning with the letter ఎ, more

commonly written ను, they denote universality; thus, ఎక్కడ *where ?* ఎక్కడనున్ను *every where* ; ఎవరు *who ?* ఎవరున్ను *all* ; ఎట్లు *how ?* ఎట్లానున్ను *any how, at any rate* ; ఎప్పుడు *when ?* ఎప్పుడున్ను *always* &c. This is also the case when these particles are added to the past relative participles of verbs, with an interrogative pronoun prefixed; thus, వాడుఎక్కడవుండినానున్ను *wheresoever he may be,* వాడుఎట్లావ్రాశినానున్ను *howsoever he may write,* &c. It will be observed that in this construction the final న of the past relative participle is lengthened to నా.

The following is a list of the most common interjections in Teloogoo. 501

అయ్యో అయ్యయ్యో అయ్యవో కటకటా అకటా		express *pain, grief, or compassion*	as అయ్యో &c. ఆయనకొమారుడు నష్టమైనాడు *alas! his son is dead.*
ఓహో ఓహోహో		*astonishment*	*as* ఓహో or ఓహోహోతమదర్శనముచేతధన్యుడనైతిని *ah! how fortunate have I been to meet you.*
ఛీ ఛీఛీ		*aversion*	as ఛీ or ఛీఛీఅవతలపో *pshaw! go along,* ఛీ or ఛీఛీవాడుదుర్మార్గుడు *pshaw! the fellow is a rascal.*
శాబాసు భళి భళా మఝా అద్దిర		*praise, excellence*	as శాబాసుయితడుయెంతసమర్థుడుయెంతగట్టివాడు *bravo! how clever and expert he is.*
సద్దు		*hush! silence!*	సద్దుచెయ్యకండి *hush! do not make such a noise.*
అహహా		*admiration*	as అహహాయెంత వేడుక *how delightful! how charming!*

In Teloogoo there are three final significant letters, which may be added to all words; namely ా to denote interrogation, ో to express doubt or ignorance, and ే to mark emphasis. 502

ా is purely interrogative, and should always be affixed to the word denoting the object respecting which the question is asked. For example, 503 in crossquestioning a witness, a person may wish to ascertain whether he did, or did not go to the house of the complainant on a certain day: in this case he would ask, నీవుపోయినఆదివారమునాడువాదియింటికిపోయినావా did you go *last Sunday to the house of the complainant?* but if he knew that he went to some place, and wished to ascertain particularly whether it was to the complainant' s house or not, in this case he would ask నీవుపోయినఆదివారము నాడువాదియింటికాపోయినావు *Was it* to the house *of the complainant that you went last Sunday?* Supposing he is aware that the witness went to the house of the complainant, but wishes to ascertain the precise day, he would in that case ask, నీవుపోయినఆదివారమునాడా వాదియింటికిపోయినావు *Was it* on Sunday last, *that you went to the comqlainant' s house?* Again he might have learned that some one went to the house in question, but might be desirous to ascertain whether it was the witness or not, he should then ask నీవాపోయినఆదివారమునాడు వాదియింటికిపోయినావు *was it* you *that went to the complainant' s house last Sunday?* It is however to be observed that to words which are already of an interrogative nature, such as the pronouns beginning with the letter ఎ, more commonly written యె, the significant letter ా is never added.

504 ో denotes ignorance or doubt, and must be added to the particular word expressing that of which we are ignorant, or of which doubt is entertained: for instance, supposing I am in doubt whether you have, or have not given me money; to the affirmation *you have given* I add the particle ో and say నీవునా కురూకలుయిచ్చినావో: but if I am certain of having received some money from you, and am in doubt respecting the quantity, not recollecting whether it was Fanams, or Pagodas that you gave me, then the ో must not be added to the verb, because I have no doubt but you gave something; it must be added both to the word expressing *Fanams* and to that denoting *Pagodas*, because I stand in doubt respecting both, నీవునాకురూకలోవరాలోయిచ్చినావు ;again, if I am aware both of the payment, and of the amount, and only doubt whether you gave it to me, or to some one else, then I add the ో to the word denoting *to me* నీవునాకోరూకలుయిచ్చినావు; lastly, if I am certain that I myself received

the money, but am in doubt whether I received it from you, or from another, then the ో is added to the word *thou* నీవ్వోనాకురూకలుయిచ్చినావు. In this manner, the peculiar object of doubt or interrogation is at once clearly defined in Teloogoo.

The particle ో added to the common conditional form of the verb ending 505
in తే, with the drootuprucrootica affix న్ becomes నో and represents our phrases *but if, on the contrary, should it* &c. &c. thus, వర్షముకురియకపోతే జనులునశింతురు - వర్షముకురిస్తేనో జనులుసుఖమునుపొందుదురు *If it does not rain the people will suffer severely; but if it rains they will be happy.*

In Teloogoo there are many interrogatives, especially among the pronouns, 506
which commence with the letter ఎ, or as it is commonly written యె; thus, ఎవరు *who?* ఎట్లా *how?* ఎక్కడ *where?* &c. if ో be added to these words the interrogation is converted into an affirmation of ignorance or doubt. A person asks another అక్కడయెవరు *who is there?* the answer may be ఎవరో *I do not know, or am in doubt who he is.* In the same manner, we say వాడుయెక్కడనో *I do not know, or am in doubt where he is,* ఇక్కడయెవరోనిద్రపోచున్నారు *some people whom I do not know are sleeping here.*

ే is used to express emphasis, and is added to any word on which particular 507
stress is intended to be laid, nearly in the same manner as the significant letters ా and ో; thus, నాడుమనతోకూడాతోటకువచ్చినాడేవాణ్ని పిలువు *call the very man who came with us that day to the garden;* వాఁడుమహాయోగ్యుఁడే యేలకొట్టితిరి *he is indeed a worthy man, wherefore did you strike him?* నీవు నిండావోర్పుగలవాడవే వానితోయేలజగడమాడితివి *thou in particular art a patient man, why didst thou quarrel with him?* మీరుకోటకుపోతి రేఅప్పుడు నేనువచ్చితిని *at the very time you went to the fort I came here.* This particle is also used when we wish to select one out of many objects; for instance, supposing that there are many ripe mangoes upon a tree from which the gardener is plucking them, and that I ask for one, but that he throws down another which I did not want, I reject it, and pointing with my finger to the particular mangoe

which I wanted, say దీన్నేకోశివెయ్యి *cut and throw me this very one.* I could not say this if there were only one mangoe on the tree.

508 The final significant affix ే in the latter part of a sentence, preceded by the final significant letter ో in the former part of it, have the correspondence of the English *as* and *so*; thus, మీరుయేప్రకారముఆజ్ఞాపించితిరోఆప్రకారమేచేసినాను *as you directed, so have I done*; మీరుయెట్లాచెప్పినారో నేనుఅట్లాగేవ్రాస్తిని *as you said, so have I written.*

509 లేక the negative verbal participle derived from లేను the negative aorist of the root కలుగు signifies *without*; and కాక the negative verbal participle derived from కాను the negative aorist of the root అవు signifies *besides*; thus, ఆయుధములులేకశత్రువులనుజయించగూడదు *without arms it is impossible to conquer enemies*; ఇండ్లుతోటలుకాకరొక్కముయెంతవున్నది *besides houses and gardens how much is there in ready cash?* Both లేక and కాక by the addition of ఉండ the infinitive of the root ఉండు *to be* frequently become లేకుండ or కాకుండ without any alteration in their meaning.

510 యేల means *why?* It may be placed either before or after a verb: if placed first the verb agrees in person, number, and gender with it's nominative; thus, యేలచూస్తిని *why did I look?* యేలచూచినాఁడు *why did he look?* యేలచూచినారు *why did they look?* But if this particle follows the verb it is placed in the infinitive, which, being a drootuprucrootica, takes న *n* before the ఏ of ఏల, and it is thus used promiscuously for every person, number, or gender; thus, నేనువాఁడు or వారుచూడనేల *why did I, he, or they look?* నేనునీవువారుఅది &c. రానేలపోనేల &c. *why did I, thou, they, she, or it &c. come, go, &c.?*

511 ఐనను or ఐనప్పటికిన్ని, the forms of the root అవు denoting *although I, thou, he, &c. become,* if placed at the commencement of a sentence, represent the English word *nevertheless*; ఐనప్పటికిన్నివాడుసమర్థుఁడు *nevertheless he is a clever man.* But if either of these phrases is placed after two or more words in the same sentence, it will have the effect of the disjunctive conjunctions

either, or ; thus, we say సరకులైనప్పటికిన్ని రొక్కపు రూకలయినప్పటికిన్ని *either goods or ready money.* The same particles if not repeated, but following one word only in a sentence signify *at least ;* thus, పదివరాలయినప్పటికిన్ని యిప్పించు *give me at least ten Pagodas.* Lastly, if any of these phrases are added to interrogatives beginning with the letters ఎ or ఏ, more commonly written యె or యే, they give such words a peculiar signification which will be best understood by the following examples ; ఏవిధము *in what manner ?* ఏవిధమైనప్పటికిన్ని *in what manner soever ;* ఎట్లు *how ?* ఎట్లైనప్పటికిన్ని *how soever ;* ఎప్పుడు *when ?* ఎప్పుడైనను *when soever :* the power of these phrases differs essentially from the power of న్ను &c. added to similar words ; both imply universality, but these phrases restrict the meaning to *one of all,* న్ను &c. include *all collectively ;* thus, ఎప్పుడున్ను *always, at every time ;* ఎప్పుడైనప్పటికిన్ని *at what time soever ;* ఎక్కడనున్ను *every where,* ఎక్కడనైనప్పటికిన్ని *where soever ;* ఎవ్వడున్ను *every one,* ఎవ్వడైనప్పటికిన్ని *whosoever.*

అవును - కాదు - లేదు.

Besides the two senses in which లేను - లేవు - లేఁడు - లేదు - లేము - లేరు, 512
లేరు the aorist of the root కలుగు is used, as explained in rules 441 and 444, లేదు the neuter of the third person singular is used in two other senses.

1st, placed after a nominative of any of the three persons and the infinative of a verb, it is a simple negative participle denying *the action of the verb,* with reference to the past time only ; thus, నేను &c. చేయలేదు *I &c. did not do :* this use of the third person neuter must be distinguished from that of the whole tense before mentioned ; thus,

నేను చేయలేను ....*I cannot do*.................నేను చేయలేదు....*I did not do.*

నీవు చేయలేవు......*Thou canst not do*..........నీవు చేయలేదు....*Thou didst not do.*

వాఁడు చేయలేఁడు *He cannot do*...............వాఁడు చేయలేదు *He did not do.*

మేము చేయలేము..*We cannot do*...............మేము చేయలేదు..*We did not do.*

మీరు చేయలేరు...*You cannot do*................మీరు చేయలేదు *You did not do.*

వారు చేయలేరు...*They cannot do*.............వారు చేయలేదు *They did not do.*

in the one case the auxiliary లేను &c. agrees with it's nominative in gender, number, and person; in the other లేదు is indeclinable.

2ndly. లేదు is used independently by itself as a simple negative particle denying *existence*, applicable to all persons, without reference to any time, and opposed to కాదు which denies *essence, quality* &c: the contrary of the first is కద్దు, the irregular third person singular of the affirmative aorist of the root కలుగు; the contrary of the second is the word అవును, the third person singular of the affirmative aorist of అవు *to become*. If I ask *is there a house here?* I enquire respecting existence, and the answer, if there is one, is కద్దు; if not లేదు. But if I see something at a distance, and, doubtful not of its existence but of its essence or quality, ask, *is that a house*, the answer, if it is not, is కాదు; if it is, అవును.

513 అవును indeed may be considered to represent the English word *yes*, being constantly used as an affirmative reply to questions of all kinds, and not restricted like its negative కాదు to a denial of essence or quality; for example, అవును *yes* may be used in reply to any of the following interrogations. వాఁడు వూరినుంచివచ్చినాఁడా *has he returned from the country?* ఈకాలంవానలుకురిస్తేమంచిదా *would rain be seasonable at this time?* ఈరాజుధర్మాత్ముఁడా *is this King virtuous?* మీకువిద్యచదువుకోవలెననిఅపేక్షవున్నదా *do you desire to learn science?* మీదేశమందువర్షముసమృద్ధిగాకురిశినదా *have you had abundance of rain in your country?* దక్షిణదేశమందుకావేరీప్రవాహమువచ్చినదా *have the freshes of the Cauvery reached the southern districts?* ఇతఁడుమీకొమారుఁడా *is he your son?*

514 Notwithstanding అవును may thus be used as a general affirmative, its use is properly confined to affirmations respecting quality or essence only; thus, if I ask, *is there rice in the house?* I enquire about the existence of something, not respecting its quality; therefore, if there is, although we may say అవును *yes*, it will be more correct to answer కద్దు, or వున్నది, *there is*: but if, seeing a basket with something in it, I ask, *is that rice in the basket?* I enquire respecting the essence or quality of something, not regarding its existence, and if it is rice, అవును *yes* is the only proper answer; if it is not, కాదు.

Such is the use of these words when used independently by themselves, but when అవును follows a noun in the common dialect, it does not signify *yes* or *it is,* but *it will or may be:* and if used in speaking of the present time, it also implies doubt; thus if to my question, *what is there?* they answer బియ్యమవును *it may be rice*; this is the same as saying, I cannot speak with certainty, but I think, or have understood, that it is rice. The particle అట *it is said* or *they say*, is often used in this sense; thus, if I ask, *is Gooroomoorty here?* and the answer is యింటికిపోయినాడట this means, *I do not know, but they say that he is gone home.* When used in speaking of any future event, the word అవును may imply either doubt or certainty; for example, should I ask వాడు కష్టపడిచదువుకొంటే తెలుగులో సమర్థుఁడవునా *if he take pains and read, will he become well versed in Teloogoo,* and am answered సమర్థుఁడవును it means either that *he will certainly become well versed in Teloogoo,* or that *he may perhaps become well versed in Teloogoo*: a prevaricating witness may often attempt to shelter himself under the equivocal meaning of this word. 515

లేకపోతే.

This phrase represents the English word *otherwise*; మీరుదాన్నియిస్తేసరి *if you give it, 'tis well,* లేకపోతే నేనుబలవంతముగాతీసుకొంటున్నాను *otherwise, I will take it forcibly.* It consists of the negative verbal participle లేక, derived from లేను the negative aorist of కలుగు, prefixed to the conditional form of the verb పోవు *to go,* used here merely as an expletive. 516

వర - మట్టు.

These words imply *a term,* or *limit,* they are generally used in the dative case, and often with the conjunction న్ను; thus, వరకు or వరకున్ను and మట్టుకు or మట్టుకున్ను signify *until*; as ఈగడియవరకు or వరకున్ను - మట్టుకు or మట్టుకున్ను *until this hour, hitherto*; వర may also be used in the local ablative; thus, ఈవరలో వాణ్ని చూడలేను *I never saw him till this time;* we say also ఇంతమట్టుకు *this much, thus far*; అంతమట్టుకు *that much, as far as that*; ఎంతమట్టుకు *how much? how far*; &c. 517

మాత్రము.

This word applies to all computation, whether by number, weight, or 518 measure; thus, యీపొలములోపండేధాన్యముయెంతమాత్రము *what quantity of grain is produced in this field?* యీబంగారుయెంతమాత్రము *what is the weight of this gold?* యీబియ్యముయెంతమాత్రము *how much is this rice?* నిడుపుయెంతమాత్రము *how long?* వెడల్పుయెంతమాత్రము *how broad?* పొడుగుయెంతమాత్రము *how high?* లోతుయెంతమాత్రము *how deep?* The word యెంత alone is also used in the same sense; thus, యీబంగారుయెంత- యీధాన్యముయెంత - నిడుపుయెంత &c. but so far as regards number, the collective pronouns often represent యెంత &c.; thus, మనుష్యులుయెందరు *how many persons?* రూకలుయెన్ని *how many fanams?* సంవత్సరములుయెన్ని *how many years?*

కాని.

519 The participle కాని from the root అవు *to become,* according to circumstances represents the English words *either, or, unless, only, except, although*; as తాటాకుమీదగానీకాగిదముమీదగానీవ్రాయి *write either on cadjans, or on paper*; వాడుయిక్కడికివస్తేనేకానియీపనికానేరదు *this business cannot be effected, unless he come here*; యీపుస్తకమునీకేకానివానికివ్వను *I will give this book to you only, not to him*; వానివల్లగానియీపనిచక్కబడదు *this business cannot be well done except by him*; మెడబట్టితోసినాగానీవాడుపోడు *although you push him by the neck, he will not go.* It will here be observed that when కాని follows words belonging to the class *drootuprucrootica* it is changed into గాని; and when it means *either, or,* or *although,* the final ి is lengthened into ీ.

APPENDIX.

OF NUMBERS.

1st. CARDINAL NUMBERS.

The cardinal numbers in Teloogoo, may, like adjectives, be prefixed to substantives, or like nouns, be used independently by themselves: in either state, each of them, except the first, has two forms; of which one is applicable to masculine or feminine, the other to neuter objects. I shall give the neuter cardinals first, as the others are derived from them.

English Figure.	*Teloogoo Figure.*	*Neuter Name.*
1	౧	ఒకటి
2	౨	రెండు
3	౩	మూడు
4	౪	నాలుగు
5	౫	అయిదు
6	౬	ఆఱు
7	౭	ఏడు
8	౮	ఎనిమిది
9	౯	తొమ్మిది
10	౧౦	పది
11	౧౧	పదకొండు
12	౧౨	పన్నెండు
13	౧౩	పదమూడు
14	౧౪	పధ్నాలుగు
15	౧౫	పదిహేను

English Figure.	*Teloogoo Figure.*	*Neuter Name.*
16	౧౬	పదహారు
17	౧౭	పదిహేడు
18	౧౮	పద్దెనిమిది
19	౧౯	పందొమ్మిది
20	౨౦	ఇరువై
30	౩౦	ముప్పై
40	౪౦	నలుభై
50	౫౦	ఏభై
60	౬౦	అరువై
70	౭౦	డెబ్భై
80	౮౦	ఎనభై
90	౯౦	తొంభై
100	౧౦౦	నూఱు
200	౨౦౦	ఇన్నూఱు
300	౩౦౦	మున్నూఱు
400	౪౦౦	నన్నూఱు
500	౫౦౦	ఏనూఱు
600	౬౦౦	ఆఱ్నూఱు
700	౭౦౦	ఏళ్నూఱు
800	౮౦౦	యెనమన్నూఱు
900	౯౦౦	తొమ్మన్నూఱు
1,000	౧౦౦౦	వెయ్యి
10,000	౧౦౦౦౦	పదివేలు
100,000	౧౦౦౦౦౦	లక్ష
10,000,000	౧౦౦౦౦౦౦౦	కోటి

The forms common to the masculine and feminine genders are derived from the foregoing neuters in the following manner.

The numeral ఒక *one*, when used as an adjective, is the same for all genders: when used as a substantive, it has a separate form for each gender; viz. ఒకటి

for the neuter, ఒకడు for the masculine, and ఒకతె for the feminine. The neuter రెండు *two*, whether used as an adjective, or as a substantive, becomes ఇద్దరు in the masculine and feminine; the neuter మూడు *three* becomes ముగ్గురు, నాలుగు *four* becomes నలుగురు, and all the other neuters, whether used substantively or adjectively, become masculine or feminine by affixing the particle మంది; thus, అయిదుమంది *five*, ఆరుమంది *six*, ఏడుమంది *seven* &c. &c. &c.

In addition to these forms, the neuter numbers noted below admit, in the masculine and feminine gender, of some irregular forms.

ఆరు.......... *six* may in the masculine and feminine form become.. ఆరువురు or ఆరుగురు

ఏడు.............*seven*...ఏడువురు or ఏడుగురు

ఎనిమిది...........*eight*..ఎనమండ్రు

తొమ్మిది.........*nine*...తొమ్మండ్రు

పది...............*ten*...పదుగురు

పన్నెండు.........*twelve*..పన్నిద్దరు

పదమూడు.......*thirteen*...పదముగ్గురు

పద్నాలుగు......*fourteen*..పద్నలుగురు

The neuter cardinals రెండు *two*, మూడు *three*, and నూరు *a hundred*, when used as substantives, make in the singular inflexion రెంటి - మూంటి - నూటి respectively, and are declined in the same manner as the irregular దేశ్యము noun: the masculine ఒక్కడు *one* is declined like the regular దేశ్యము nouns of the 1st declension, the feminine ఒక్కతె and the neuter ఒక్కటి *one*, with all other cardinal numbers, when used as substantives are declined according to the rules for the third declension; except masculines and feminines ending in గురు, which in the singular inflexion change that termination into గురి; thus, nominative నలుగురు *four*, inflexion నలుగురి, dative నలుగురికి *to four* &c. &c.

2d. ORDINAL NUMBERS.

The ordinals are formed by changing the final vowel of the neuter cardinal numbers into వ in the superior dialect, and into ో in the common dialect, the first cardinal number excepted, which in the cardinal form, becomes మొదటి in both dialects, as shewn below.

Neuter cardinal number.	Ordinal number. superior dialect.	common dialect.	
ఒకటి.	మొదటి		first.
రెండు.	రెండవ	రెండో.	second.
మూడు.	మూడవ	మూడో.	third.
నాలుగు.	నాలుగవ.	నాలుగో	fourth.
అయిదు.	అయిదవ	అయిదో	fifth.
ఆఱు.	ఆఱవ	ఆఱో.	sixth.
ఏడు.	ఏడవ	ఏడో.	seventh.
ఎనిమిది.	ఎనిమిదవ.	ఎనిమిదో.	eighth.
తొమ్మి ది.	తొమ్మిదవ	తొమ్మిదో.	ninth.
పది.	పదియవ.	పదో.	tenth.

3d. FRACTIONS.

The subdivision of unity is carried to a great extent, in common practice, among the people of Telingana. Their fractions descend by fours; in the same manner that our decimal fractions descend by tens, and the four thousand and ninety sixth part of an integer often occurs in a common Teloogoo account.

The following table exhibits the subdivisions of an unit.

English Figure.	*Teloogoo Figure.*	*Name.*
1	౧	ఒకటి
$\frac{3}{4}$	౻	ముక్కాలు
$\frac{2}{4}$ or $\frac{1}{2}$	౺	అర
$\frac{1}{4}$	౹	కాలు
$\frac{3}{16}$	వి ౾	మువ్వీసము
$\frac{2}{16}$ or $\frac{1}{8}$	వి ౽	పరక
$\frac{1}{16}$	వి ౼	వీసము
$\frac{3}{16}$	కా ౻	ముక్కాని
$\frac{2}{64}$ or $\frac{1}{32}$	కా ౺	అరవీసము

$\frac{}{64}$ .... కా౹ .... కాని

$\frac{3}{256}$ .... ప్రి౾ .... ముప్ప్రియ

$\frac{2}{256}$ or $\frac{1}{128}$ .... ప్రి౽ .... అరకాని

$\frac{1}{256}$ .... ప్రి౼ .... ప్రియ

$\frac{3}{1024}$ .... సు౻ .... మూడుసురలు

$\frac{2}{1024}$ or $\frac{1}{512}$ .... సు౺ .... రెండుసురలు

$\frac{1}{1024}$ .... సు౹ .... సుర

$\frac{3}{4096}$ .... గో౾ .... మూడుగోకరకానులు

$\frac{2}{4096}$ or $\frac{1}{2048}$ .... గో౽ .... రెండుగోకరకానులు

$\frac{1}{4096}$ .... గో౼ .... గోకరకాని

It will be perceived that the subdivision of an unit into fourths is marked by perpendicular lines, and that into sixteenths by horizontal lines: in either case, the number of these lines corresponds with the number of fractional parts intended to be represented. Thus, ౹ is $\frac{1}{4}$, ౺ is $\frac{2}{4}$ (or $\frac{1}{2}$) and ౻ $\frac{3}{4}$; ౼ is $\frac{1}{16}$, ౽ $\frac{2}{16}$, (or $\frac{1}{8}$); and ౾ $\frac{3}{16}$; and in the further subdivision of unity, the number of fractional parts (which in English vulgar fractions we term *the numerator*) is denoted, in the same manner, by a corresponding number of lines, alternately perpendicular and horizontal.

The particular kind of parts into which the integer itself is divided, which in our vulgar fractions is called *the denominator*, is marked in Teloogoo, much in the same way as in our decimal fractions; namely, by the distance of the perpendicular and horizontal lines from the integer number; thus, ౧౻౽ ౹ ౾౺౼ 1 $\frac{3}{4}$ $\frac{2}{16}$ $\frac{1}{64}$ $\frac{3}{256}$ $\frac{2}{1024}$ and $\frac{1}{4096}$. It will here be observed that the lines next the integer are fourths, those a degree further to the right, sixteenths, then follow sixty fourths, next, two hundred and fifty sixths, and so on. But when fractions are written separately from the integer number, *the denominator* is marked by prefixing to all the lines, except those of the first subdivision, a contraction of the Teloogoo word which expresses the particular subdivision to which the fraction belongs:

as ఏ for వీసము before the second subdivision, కా for కాని before those of the third subdivision, as specified in the foregoing table.

In accounts, if the whole of one subdivision be wanting, the deficiency is marked by substituting for the perpendicular lines the mark 9 called హళ్ళి, and for the horizontal lines o, or a cypher; Thus, ∩9౽9o౺| $\frac{2}{16}$ $\frac{2}{1024}$ the first 9 shews that fourths are wanting, the second 9 denotes that sixty fourths are wanting, and the o shews the deficiency of two hundred and fifty sixths.

Accounts of money are kept in Pagodas or Rupees, and Fanams: the fractions of these are represented in the same manner as the fractions of any other unit, but those of a Pagoda as far as sixty fourths, those of a Rupee as far as a sixteenth, and those of a Fanam as far as quarters, have names different from the general fractions of an unit before specified.

The fractions of a Pagoda as far as sixty fourths are respectively named.

$\frac{3}{4}$*ths* of a Pagoda.........X౻.........................ముప్పావు
$\frac{2}{4}$ or $\frac{1}{2}$.......do...............X౺.........................మాడ
$\frac{1}{4}$.........do.................X౹.........................పావు
$\frac{3}{16}$.........do...............X9౾.........................ముద్దుగలము
$\frac{2}{16}$...or $\frac{1}{8}$.....do...............X9౽.........................చవలము
$\frac{1}{16}$.........do...............X9౼.........................దుగలము
$\frac{3}{64}$.........do...............X9o౻.........................ముప్పాతిక
$\frac{2}{64}$ or $\frac{1}{32}$......do...............X9o౺.........................బేడ
$\frac{1}{64}$.........do...............X9o౹.........................పాతిక

those of a Rupee as far as a sixteenth are called,

$\frac{3}{4}$*ths* of a Rupee...........రూ౻.........................ముప్పావులా
$\frac{2}{4}$ or $\frac{1}{2}$.....do..........రూ౺.........................అర్ధరూపాయీ
$\frac{1}{4}$.........do..........రూ౹.........................పావులా
$\frac{1}{16}$......do..........రూ9౼.........................అణా

and those of a Fanam as far as quarters are termed,

¾ths of a fanam	ఽ ɰ	ముప్పాతిక
2/4 or ½ ... do	ఽ ч	అర్ధగ
¼ ... do	ఽ |	పాతిక

In English accounts, Pounds, Shillings and Pence are marked by the letters £ S D; in Teloogoo, Pagodas are distinguished by the letter గ; Rupees by the syllables రు or రూ, and Fanams by ఽ prefixed to the integer number.

OF MEASURES.

Measures, in Teloogoo called మానము, are divided into three sorts; viz. పరిమాణము - ఉన్మానము and ప్రమాణము. The first is that by which the quantity of grain and the like articles is ascertained, and may be termed the measure of *capacity;* the second, that which relates to *weight;* and the third refers to the measurement of *extent,* or to the length, breadth, or width of any thing.

1st. *OF* పరిమాణము OR *THE MEASURES OF CAPACITY.*

The chief measure of this kind is that by which grain is usually measured, the largest of which is called పుట్టి, and is marked thus ఖ. If there be one, two, three, or more such measures, the numeral figures, ౧ - ౨ - ౩ &c. are affixed to the ఖ, and written thus, ఖ ౧ - ఖ ౨ - ఖ ౩ &c. The పుట్టి is divided into twenty smaller measures, called తూములు, which are named and marked as follows:

తూము	ల ౧	పదకొండుతూము	ఖ ౦ч౧
ఇద్దుము	ల ౨	పన్నిద్దుము	ఖ౦ч౨
ముత్తుము	ల ౩	పదముత్తుము	ఖ౦ч౩
నల్తుము	ల ౪	పధ్నల్తుము	ఖ౦ч౪
పదుము	ఖ ౦|౦	పదిహేదుము	ఖ౦ɰ౦
ఆర్దుము	ఖ ౦|౧	పదహార్దుము	ఖ౦ɰ౧
పడ్డుము	ఖ ౦|౨	పదిహేడ్డుము	ఖ౦ɰ౨
ఎనమందుము	ఖ ౦|౩	పద్ధెనమందుము	ఖ౦ɰ౩
తొమ్మందుము	ఖ ౦|౪	పంధొమ్మందుము	ఖ ౦ɰ|౪
పందుము	ఖ ౦ч౦	పుట్టి	ఖ ౧

The తూము again is divided into four కుంచములు which are named and marked in the following manner.

కుంచము............................౹ | ముక్కుస ....౻
ఇరస...............................౺ | తూము...............................౧

The కుంచము is divided into four మానికలు ; thus,

మానిక..............................మా౧ | మూడుమానికలు......................మా౩
అడ్డ...............................మా ౨ | కుంచము.............................౹

The మానిక is subdivided into four సోలలు , thus,

సోల................................సో౹ | మూడుసోలలు........................సో౻
తవ్వ...............................సో౺ | మానిక..............................మా ౧

The సోల is divided into four గిద్దలు ; thus,

గిద్ద...............................గి ౼ | మూడుగిద్దలు........................గి ౾
అరసోల.............................గి ౽ | సోల...............................సో 1

2d. *OF* ఉన్మానము OR *WEIGHT.*

The greatest Teloogoo weight is a బారువ or a *Candy* which is equivalent to twenty మణుగులు or *maunds.*

Every మణుగు contains eight వీశెలు.

Every వీశె five శేరులు or *seers.*

Each శేరు *seer* is divided into quarters, which are marked thus,

శేరు................................శే ౧ | అద్ద శేరు...............................శే౦౺
ముప్పావు శేరు.......................శే౦౻ | పావు శేరు...............................శే ౦ ౹

Every పావు శేరు contains two నవటాకులు or పలములు, and each నవటాకు is equivalent to three తులాలు.

3d. *OF* ప్రమాణము OR *EXTENT.*

The greatest measurement of extent is a యోజనము, more commonly termed ఆమడ, which consists of four పరుగులు or కోసులు, termed by us *cosses.*

Each కోసు or పరుగు is equivalent to 1,000 దండములు.

do. . . .దండము . . . . . . .do . . . . . .to . . . .2 . . . .బారలు. . . . .*or fathoms.*
do. . . బార . . . . .do . . . . . . .to . . . .2. . . .గజములు . . . . . . *or yards.*

Each...గజము.........is equivalent...to...... 2... మూరలు.............or *cubits.*
do....మూర...............do.........to.......1½...అడుగు.................or *feet.*
do....మూర...............do.........to........2... జేనలు.................or *spans.*
do....అడుగు............ .do.........to......12...అంగుళములు..........or *inches.*
do....జేన...................do.........to.......9....అంగుళములు..........or *inches.*
do....అంగుళము...........do.........to...*one inch.*

One కుచ్చెల has eight గొఱ్ఱులు each of which consists of fifty కుంటలు.

OF THE DIVISION OF TIME.

The people of Telingana, following the astronomical system of the Bramins, divide what they term the infinity of time into four great ages, which they suppose to be in constant revolution; these they denominate యుగములు, or conjunctions; periods, which seem to have been calculated, by the Bramins, as the probable dates of some remote conjunctions of the heavenly bodies, which they assumed merely to assist astronomical computations, but which have been implicitly adopted by the vulgar as real eras.

The first of these four ages is named కృతయుగము referring, apparently, to some conjunction which is supposed to have taken place at the కృత *creation;* for, according to the Hindoos, the Supreme Being created the world in the first age of this name. It consists of 1,728,000 years. The second is denominated త్రేతాయుగము, the conjunction of the త్రేతా or *three sacrificial fires,* so called, because the great sacrifice in which these * fires are used is supposed to have been introduced during this period, which contains 1,296,000 years. The third is named ద్వాపరయుగము a compound of ద్వి *two* and అపర *the next,*

---

* These three fires are severally named గార్హపత్యము - దక్షిణాగ్ని and ఆహవనీయము The first is lighted, with particular ceremonies, in the west. The person who celebrates the sacrifice is considered particularly to preside over this fire, which being kept alive during his life, serves to light his funeral pile. From this fire, also, the other two are lighted; one of them is placed in the south, and offerings are made in it to the deity of Fire, to the manes of the Pitris, or certain progenitors of mankind, and to a few other deities; the other is placed in the east, and offerings are made in it to the principal deities presiding over the sacrifice, and to all the other gods.

that which followed the two first, viz. *the third*; this comprises 8,64,000 years. The fourth or present age is known by the name of కలియుగము, properly signifying *vicious* or *sinful*; to this age they assign a period of 4,32,000 years, of which 4,916 are already elapsed. If the years in the fourth age be doubled, the number of those in the third is given; if multiplied by three, the length of the second is found; and if multiplied by four, the product is the length of the first age.

Besides this grand division of time, common to all Hindoos, the people of the Peninsula have another epoch which takes it's name from an ancient prince named శాలివాహనుడు *Shalivahana*, and commences about the year of Christ 78; the present year 1816 is therefore the 1737-8 of this epoch. It is said that Shalivahana subdued Vikramarka (Bikramajeet) whose era is still used in the north of Hindoostan, and substituted his own era for that of his conquered enemy. The vulgar derive the name of Shalivahana from శాలి *a heap of straw* or సాల *a certain kind of tree*, and వాహన *a car*; viz. he whose car was a heap of straw or the సాల tree. In some encounter with Vikramarka, say they, Shalivahana was obliged to mount this tree, or heap of straw; but all traditions respecting this prince, are obscured in the most extravagant fables.

The people of Telingana class the years of the two epochs above mentioned in cycles of sixty, giving to each of the sixty an appropriate name, as shewn below.

ప్రభవ	is the	1st year of each cycle	ధాతు	is the	10th year of each cycle.
విభవ	do.	2d do.	ఈశ్వర	do.	11th do.
శుక్ల	do.	3d do.	బహుధాన్య	do.	12th do.
ప్రమోదూత	do.	4th do.	ప్రమాది	do.	13th do.
ప్రజోత్పత్తి	do.	5th do.	విక్రమ	do.	14th do.
ఆంగిరస	do.	6th do.	విషు	do.	15th do.
శ్రీముఖ	do.	7th do.	చిత్ర భాను	do.	16th do.
భావ	do.	8th do.	స్వభాను	do.	17th do.
యువ	do.	9th do.	తారణ	do.	18th do.

పార్థివ............is the...19th year of each cycle పరాభవ............is the 40th year of each cycle
వ్యయ.................do......20th do......ప్లవంగ.................do......41st do.
సర్వజితు.............do......21st do...... కీలక.................do......42d do.
సర్వధారి............do.......22d do.......సౌమ్య................do......43d do.
విరోధి...............do.......23d do.......సాధారణ.............do......44th do.
వికృతి...............do.......24th do.......విరోధికృతు.........do......45th do.
ఖర....................do.......25th do.......పరిధావి..............do......46th do.
నందన...............do.......26th do.......ప్రమాదీచ...........do......47th do.
విజయ.................do.......27th do.......ఆనంద..................do......48th do.
జయ....................do......28th do......రాక్షస.................do......49th do.
మన్మథ...............do......29th do.......నల......................do......50th do.
దుర్ముఖి.............do......30th do......పింగళ..................do......51st do.
హేవళంబి...........do.......31st do.......కాళయుక్తి..............do...... 52d do.
విళంబి...............do.......32d do.......సిద్ధార్థి..............do......53d do.
వికారి.................do......33d do......రౌద్రి.....................do......54th do.
శార్వరి...............do......34th do......దుర్మతి..................do......55th do.
ప్లవ.....................do......35th do......దుందుభి.................do......56th do.
శుభకృతు.............do......36th do......రుధిరోద్గారి............do......57th do.
శోభకృతు.............do......37th do......రక్తాక్షి..................do......58th do.
క్రోధి...................do......38th do......క్రోధన...................do......59th do.
విశ్వావసు............do......39th do......క్షయ.....................do......60th do.

In Teloogoo, the whole of these years, whether of the cycle of sixty, of Shalivabana, or of the Caleeyoogum, are calculated according to the lunar system, which appears to have been the most ancient method of computing time in India; and each year consists of twelve lunar months, reckoned from new moon to new moon, not from full moon to full moon, as is the practice at Benares.

The ecliptic is divided into twenty seven Nutchatras or constellations, each containing 13° 20', and every lunar month takes it's name from the particular Nutchatra near which the moon is observed to be *generally* at the full.

The following are the names of the lunar months, and their corresponding Nutchatras.

Months.	*Nutchatras.*
చైత్రము	చిత్ర - స్వాతి
వైశాఖము	విశాఖ - అనూరాధ
జ్యేష్ఠము	జ్యేష్ఠ - మూల
ఆషాఢము	పూర్వాషాఢ - ఉత్తరాషాఢ
శ్రావణము	శ్రవణము - ధనిష్ఠ
భాద్రపదము	శతభిష-పూర్వాభాద్ర - ఉత్తరాభాద్ర
ఆశ్వయుజము	రేవతి - అశ్విని - భరణి
కార్తీకము	కృత్తిక - రోహిణి
మార్గశిరము	మృగశిర - ఆర్ద్ర
పుష్యము	పునర్వసు - పుష్యమి
మాఘము	ఆశ్లేష - మఘ
ఫాల్గునము	పుబ్బ - ఉత్తర - హస్త

The moon is not *always* full in the particular Nutchatra from which the month derives it's name; but either in that Nutchatra, or in the one which follows or precedes it. This is the utmost extent of the variation; nevertheless, in whichever of the three the moon is full, the name of the month remains unaltered. The moon of the month చైత్ర may be full in the Nutchatra named హస్త, or in చిత్ర, or in స్వాతి, but the name of the month is always చైత్రము.

Each lunar month is divided into two portions termed పక్షము, of which one is named శుక్ల or శుద్ధ *the bright half*, the other కృష్ణ or బహుళ *the dark half*; and each of these two portions contains fifteen తిథులు which may be termed *lunar days.*

The bright fortnight commences with the new moon, of which the తిథి or *lunar day* is called పాడ్యమి or the 1st, and continues until పున్నమ or the full moon : the dark fortnight then begins, in the same manner, with a తిథి or *lunar day* named పాడ్యమి or the 1st, and ends with అమావాస్య or the change, when the moon, by it's conjunction with the sun, concludes the lunar month ; thus,

The bright half or increase of the moon, named శుక్లపక్షము	*The dark half or decrease of the moon,* termed కృష్ణపక్షము
పాడ్యమి.......... *new moon.*	పాడ్యమి *first lunar day of the dark fortnight.*
విదియ.................*second lunar day.*	విదియ.....................*second.*
తదియ............*third.*	తదియ.....................*third.*
చవుతి.................*fourth.*	చవుతి.....................*fourth.*
పంచమి............*fifth.*	పంచమి.....................*fifth.*
షష్ఠి....................*sixth.*	షష్ఠి.........................*sixth.*
సప్తమి................*seventh.*	సప్తమి.............. *seventh.*
అష్టమి............. *eighth.*	అష్టమి....................*eighth.*
నవమి............... *ninth.*	నవమి.....................*ninth.*
దశమి.............*tenth.*	దశమి.......................*tenth.*
ఏకాదశి.............*eleventh.*	ఏకాదశి...................*eleventh.*
ద్వాదశి...............*twelfth.*	ద్వాదశి.................*twelfth.*
త్రయోదశి.........*thirteenth.*	త్రయోదశి...........*thirteenth.*
చతుర్దశి............*fourteenth.*	చతుర్దశి...............*fourteenth.*
పున్నమ..............*full moon.*	అమావాస్య..........*lunar day of the moon's change.*

A తిథి or lunar day by no means corresponds with the solar day ; according to the Hindoos it is that period during which the moon travels through twelve degrees of her path, it may commence in the morning, at noon, in the evening, or at midnight, and contains a number of గడియలు, or Teloogoo hours of 24 English minutes each, varying from 54 to 66 according to the length of the తిథి.

Although the lunar day is of variable length, it's subdivision, the Teloogoo hour, does not vary, but consists precisely of 24 English minutes. The people measure this space of time by an empty vessel of a certain size placed in water; there is a small hole at the bottom of the vessel, through which the water is allowed to enter; and the size both of the hole and of the vessel is so proportioned, that, if care be taken, the vessel sinks at the termination of every 24 English minutes.

The orb of the moon is divided into sixteen phases, named కళలు; but as one of these is considered constant, and the other fifteen are supposed to revolve round it, like a garland of flowers on a string, each revolving కళ corresponds to a తిథి or lunar day.

Twelve lunations form a lunar year, but it requires only about 354 solar days to complete this period; so that the lunar falls behind the solar year (of 365 solar days) more than 11 solar days every lunar year. To adjust the lunar time to the solar computation intercalary months are inserted, and this is regulated by assigning to each of the lunar months a particular corresponding sign of the zodiac as explained below.

Lunar months.	*Corresponding sign of the zodiac.*	
చైత్రము	మేషము	*Aries.*
వైశాఖము	వృషభము	*Taurus.*
జ్యేష్ఠము	మిథునము	*Gemini.*
ఆషాఢము	కర్కాటకము	*Cancer.*
శ్రావణము	సింహము	*Leo.*
భాద్రపదము	కన్య	*Virgo.*
ఆశ్వయుజము	తుల	*Libra.*
కార్తికము	వృశ్చికము	*Scorpio.*
మార్గశిరము	ధనుస్సు	*Sagittarius.*
పుష్యము	మకరము	*Capricornus.*
మాఘము	కుంభము	*Aquarius.*
ఫాల్గునము	మీనము	*Pisces.*

So often as the sun remains in the same sign of the zodiac during *two* అమావాస్యలు or days of the moon's change, the month to which the last అమా

వాస్య belongs is named twice over; it is first considered అధిక or *intercalary*, and after being completed is reckoned over again, under it's proper name; for example, supposing the sun to have entered the sign *Aries* on అమావాస్య the last lunar day of the lunar month చైత్రము, and to continue in the same sign during అమావాస్య the last lunar day of the next lunar month వైశాఖము, the lunar month intervening between the first and the last అమావాస్య would be termed అధికవైశాఖము or *intercalated* వైశాఖము, and so soon as it expired, వైశాఖము *proper* would commece anew.

In the course of a certain number of years, two intercalary months occur within the space of one year; in other words, two months are reckoned over twice. In this case, the proper month intervening between the two is called క్షయమాసము *the wasted month*, and is entirely omitted from account. In every intercalary lunar month the sun does not enter into a new sign of the zodiac; in the course of the wasted month, he enters into two signs.

The new moon or పాడ్యమి in the bright fortnight of the lunar month చైత్రము is the first తిథి or commencement of the lunar year.

Besides the lunar years, months, and days, the people of Telingana use that subdivision of solar time which we term the week, the days of which they reckon from sun rise to sun rise, and name after the Sun, † Moon, Mars, Mercury, Jupiter, Venus and Saturn, in the following manner.

---

† I subjoin for the information of the reader a list of the Planets, as enumerated in Teloogoo Books.

సూర్యుడు............*the Sun.*
చంద్రుడు............*the Moon.*
అంగారకుడు..........*Mars, the son of the earth.*
బుధుడు...............*Mercury, the son of the moon by the Hyades.*
బృహస్పతి.............*Jupiter, son of Angerasa one of the seven great sages, and the preceptor of the gods.*
శుక్రుడు...........*Venus, the son of Bhrigu, and the preceptor of the giants.*
శని.....................*Saturn, the offspring of the sun by Ch'háyú* shade.
రాహు.................*Son of Sinhika, the moon's ascending node, reckoned the 8th planet.*
కేతు...................*The moon's descending node, reckoned the 9th planet.*

ఆదివారము...or...భానువారము...or...రవివారము............... *Sunday.*
సోమవారము......ఇందువారము.........చంద్రవారము.........*Monday.*
మంగళవారము...కుజవారము............అంగారకవారము......*Tuesday.*
బుధవారము.......సౌమ్యవారము..................................*Wednesday.*
గురువారము......బృహస్పతివారము.....లక్ష్మివారము............*Thursday.*
శుక్రవారము.....భృగువారము...........భార్గవవారము.........*Friday.*
శనివారము.......స్థిరవారము..............మందవారము..........*Saturday.*

In a few of the most southern districts, the people of Telingana, from their intercourse with the inhabitants of the Tamil Country, have adopted their solar computation of the year, of which, therefore, some brief notice seems to be necessary.

Every Tamil solar year has twelve నెలలు or months, which are named as follows:

చిత్రి.........................*April.*
వయ్యాశి.....................*May.*
ఆని............................*June.*
ఆడి............................*July.*
ఆవణి.........................*August.*
పెరటాశి......................*September.*
అల్పిశి.......................*October.*
కార్తికె.......................*November.*
మార్గళి......................*December.*
తైయి..........................*January.*
మాశి...........................*February.*
పంగుణి.......................*March.*

The Tamil calendar is not adjusted by intercalary days according to the European method; these months, therefore, do not correspond entirely with the English months by which they are represented. The Tamil year commences on the sun's entrance into *Aries*, and each month properly contains as many days, and fractional parts of a day, as the sun remains in each sign. The civil solar month, however, always commences at sun rise, and continues until the first sun rise in the following month; and to dispose of the fractional parts of a day, the

---

A star is termed..నక్షత్రము
A planet..గ్రహము
An eclipse..గ్రహణము

following computation is adopted. If the sun should enter a new sign of the Zodiac between sun rise and midnight, the day of his entrance is the first of the month; but if he enters a new sign between midnight and sun rise, the month commences at the following sun rise.

A దినము or solar day of 24 English hours is divided into sixty గడియలు each of which is equivalent to twenty four minutes: seven గడియలు and a half, or three English hours, make one జాము the corruption of the Sanscrit word యామము.

The solar year is also divided into two అయనములు, each of which consists of six solar months; it has also six ఋతువులు or seasons, each of which consists of two months; viz. వసంతఋతువు *the spring* comprehending చిత్రి and వయ్యాశి, గ్రీష్మఋతువు *the hot season* comprizing ఆని and ఆడి, వర్షఋతువు *the rainy season* including ఆవణి and పెరటాశి, శరదృతువు *the sultry season* comprehending అల్పిశి and కార్తికి, హేమంతఋతువు *the winter season* containing మార్గళి and తైయి, and శిశిరఋతువు *the cold season* comprehending మాశి and పంగుణి.

When *day* is used in contradistinction to *night* it is expressed in Teloogoo by పగులు; thus రాత్రిపగులుచదివినాడు *he read day and night*. A day of four and twenty hours is expressed by the words దినము or వారము, but these terms are not synonymous; దినము implies simply a day, without reference either to the date or the day of the week; thus, పదిదినములవెనకవస్తున్నాను *I will come after ten days*; వారము is applicable to the day of the week only; for instance, were I to ask, on what day of the week you intend to set out for Combaconum, I should say in Teloogoo మీరుయేవారముకుంభకోణానికిపోతారు, and if instead of వారము, I were to use దినము, in this instance, the person addressed would not understand that the day of the week was meant to be expressed.

ఉషఃకాలము or తెల్లవారి means *the dawn, the morning*, మధ్యాహ్నము *midday, noon*, సాయంకాలము *the evening*, రాత్రి *the night*, and అర్ధరాత్రి *midnight*.

I shall conclude the appendix with a list of the principal points of the compass, over each of which a particular genius is understood to preside.

POINTS OF THE COMPASS.		GUARDIANS.	
దిగ్వాచకములు		దిక్పాలకులు	
ఉత్తరము	*North*	కుబేరుఁడు	*The god of riches.*
దక్షిణము	*South*	యముఁడు	*Regent of death, and judge of departed souls.*
తూర్పు	*East*	ఇంద్రుఁడు	*Regent of the sky.*
పడమర	*West*	వరుణుఁడు	*Regent of water.*
వాయవ్యమూల	*N. West.*	వాయువు	*The ruler of the wind.*
ఈశాన్యమూల	*N. East*	ఈశానుఁడు	*The destroyer and reproducer.*
నైరృతిమూల	*S. West*	నైరృతి	*Prince of demons.*
ఆగ్నేయమూల	*S. East*	అగ్ని	*The genius of fire.*

FINIS.